Every Tiger has a Tale

Every Tiger has a Tale

Generations of grads from a Cleveland area high school
share their amazing life stories

By Gary Stromberg

iUniverse, Inc.
New York Bloomington

Every Tiger has a Tale
Generations of grads from a Cleveland area high school share their amazing life stories

iUniverse books may be ordered through booksellers or by contacting:

iUniverse
1663 Liberty Drive
Bloomington, IN 47403
www.iuniverse.com
1-800-Authors (1-800-288-4677)

ISBN: 978-1-4401-2748-9 (pbk)
ISBN: 978-1-4401-2749-6 (ebk)

Printed in the United States of America

iUniverse rev. date: 3/23/2009

Three quotes in Michael Krasny chapter:
    From *Off Mike, A Memoir of Talk Radio and Literary Life* by Michael Krasny, (c) 2008 by the Board of Trustees of the Leland Stanford Jr. University. All rights reserved. By permission of the publisher, www.sup.org.

Dedication

This book is dedicated to the teachers at Cleveland Heights High who served us so well over the decades. This salute is not intended for the teachers who chose to be on power trips, but for those who wanted to empower us with the desire to explore and learn. The teachers who thought of us as equals and as trusted friends. You gave us a shove as we set out on our life journeys. We would go on to find our own way, but your encouragement has lasted a lifetime.

Introduction

Steven LaTourette, Darrell Issa and Ron Klein have at least two things in common. They are all members of Congress, and they are all graduates of Cleveland Heights High. Their success is no real surprise. Heights High has provided a tremendous foundation for students for a century now.

But here is a sign of the times. The three congressmen do not represent adjoining districts. In fact, LaTourette is the only one in Ohio. Issa represents a district in California. Klein is a congressman in Florida.

Yes, graduates of Cleveland Heights High have gone on to success across the nation. When people ask me who might be interested in a book about Heights High students, I am quick to point out that Heights High alumni would certainly be drawn to it. So that should make it a best seller across the entire nation. We have spread out.

Heights High grads have indeed been on a path to success and happiness. Their journey has taken them to every corner of America. It all began with that first step into that massive building at the corner of Cedar and Lee. Heights High the home of the Tigers.

You are fifteen years old. You have finished your junior high days, and have taken that big step to the high school. You wander through the halls on that first day. You figure this has to be the biggest high school in the world. In the '60s, enrollment surpassed 3,200, and there were just three grade levels.

Which one is the up staircase? Which is the down staircase? What hallway has the even-numbered classrooms? Where are the odd-numbered classrooms?

Who are all these kids? How many of them will I get to know? That girl looks familiar. Did she go to the theater program at Cain Park with me when I was in second grade? Was that guy over there in my Boy Scout troop? Gosh, that was five years ago.

You keep walking. The incoming seniors look so much older than us. How many students have made their way through these hallways over all these decades?

This is the place where Sam Sheppard was a star athlete. Class president. A kid everyone looked up to. A dozen years out of Heights, he would be standing trial for the murder of his wife Marilyn. Sam and Marilyn had become an item back in their days at Roosevelt Junior High. Did Dr. Sam really bludgeon her to death? He would gain national notoriety during what was then thought of as the trial of the century.

That guy opening up the assembly in the auditorium is the student council president. He seems outgoing. He has a sincere smile on his face, but is there more going on in his life than we would suspect? What tragedy has changed his life forever? His life at home is a train wreck. How can he keep it a secret?

Just who is that guy sitting down next to you in history class? His parents were in Europe during the war. Did they survive the death camps? No, they were among the few who fled to the woods and took part in the resistance movement. Living on the run for years. Part of the underground fighters struggling to survive.

And in the mid-'40s, some of the students wondered who that Japanese American kid was. Where did he come from? He suddenly just appeared. Turns out, after the bombing of Pearl Harbor, more than 100,000 Japanese Americans were uprooted and sent to detention camps. His father, desperate to get his son an education, found out he could ship him to a Jewish orphanage in University Heights. His son could attend Cleveland Heights High, a couple of thousand miles away from home.

The journey of a teenaged boy from Cleveland is far shorter. Just five or six miles. He winds up at Heights High after his mother dies from drug abuse. She was only twenty-eight. The boy is sent to live with relatives. He is determined not to make the mistakes his mother made. He becomes a judge.

A Heights student knows his father runs a gambling business in Geauga County. It was legal back in the '40s. But a new governor starts clamping down. The boy's dad pulls up stakes and becomes one of the founding fathers of the entertainment capital of the world, Las Vegas.

A young man travels to Israel with his father for a gathering of

Holocaust survivors. He winds up at a hotel registration desk at the same moment a young woman arrives. A chance meeting. He proposes the next day.

A university president encourages a waitress to follow her dreams. She puts her children in day care, enrolls in college, and eventually becomes a doctor.

The fellow who randomly finds an apartment to rent. His neighbor suggests a job for him. A successful sales career is followed by an opportunity to become one of the highest regarded sales trainers in the nation.

Oh, the twists and turns we make on life's journey. A photographer for the school newspaper winds up face to face with Elvis. Another photographer lands a job with *The Cleveland Press,* and goes on to shoot more than thirty covers for *Sports Illustrated.*

The Heights grad who wants to be a reporter, but everyone seems to discourage her. She refuses to take no for an answer, and becomes an anchorwoman on a national news program.

A scientist who realizes that even those blessed with engineering brilliance can still develop a warm heart. He reaches out to help those in need of medical care around the world.

Unexpected detours. A parent suddenly vanishes. Was he murdered? Lives going along smoothly until the unexpected passing of a beloved spouse. A successful career right on track until a diagnosis of cancer during the prime of life.

Children raised in poverty during the Depression who attain success and devote their lives to helping others.

A man who makes a fortune and builds his family a palace on a hillside. A mudslide begins. He slips into bankruptcy.

Unlikely career changes. A young woman who had been making custom jewelry, winds up yodeling and belting out cowboy songs in Wisconsin.

Several of the Heights graduates featured here, did not abandon Cleveland and try to strike it rich elsewhere. They stayed behind and took over the businesses that were started by their parents. The challenges they face are often more complex than the one's faced by their parents. What can they do to keep those businesses alive?

Sure, everybody has a story, but as you read the profiles in this book, you will see that the graduates of Cleveland Heights High just happen to have some world-class stories. They are tales that begin in Cleveland Heights or University Heights, but these are stories of universal interest. Every generation has its own set of challenges, but what was it that made these Heights grads keep pressing ahead? A strong work ethic? Solid Midwestern values?

This is a collection of amazing stories. Triumphs, with some setbacks along the way. The book shines a spotlight on some lessons we learn not just in our classrooms, but in our life journeys as well. This is really a book for people who grew up on both sides of the river. East of the Mississippi, and west of the Mississippi.

How can one high school contribute so much, both to a city, and to a nation?

Every Tiger has a Tale. I know you will enjoy the tales that follow.

Bruce Davis, class of '67

"Don't look back. It's over. Look forward. That's all you can do. If you look back, you get aggravated."

Thankfully, Bruce Davis follows that advice. If he dwelled on the past, he would be swallowed up by it. His life has been blessed in many ways, yet he has been plagued by bad luck and misfortune.

"Life's full of bumps. As bad as it was, and it was bad, at least my children learned a lesson real fast. They found out what a dollar means."

Bruce's three children spent their early years surrounded by dollars, plenty of dollars.

"I was makin' money like the U.S. government was printin' it."

Bruce was one of the one of the founding partners of Waterbed Emporium. The company took off like a rocket. At its peak, there were twenty-three stores. Most were in northeast Ohio, but there were also stores in Pennsylvania and North Carolina. It became the second largest waterbed company in America.

1

"We were rockin' and rollin'. Makin' money."

Bruce grew up on Coventry. His house was nine away from Mayfield. His father ran the produce department at H&W Bi-Rite at Cedar and Green.

Bruce was in his mid-thirties. He was cashing in on the waterbed craze. He made more money in a couple of years than his father did in his lifetime.

"We had a blast. Money was flowin' in. I was earning over two hundred grand a year. It was great, I took nine vacations a year. My wife didn't have to work. She raised our kids. I had a Corvette, an SUV, a TR3. I had more money in my checking account than I could spend. That's when I built that house."

You could say Bruce's world started unraveling the moment he decided to build his dream house on that mountain top. It seemed so perfect. A wonderful setting in Moreland Hills. A spectacular lot on River Mountain Drive. It would be here that Bruce could provide his family with a luxurious home. It would sit above all others. He had reached the summit.

The house would be six thousand square feet, and that didn't include the basement. The basement was completely finished with two bedrooms, a pool table and a workout room. The great room upstairs featured a thirty-one foot high ceiling. Bruce says it was so big you could hold a church service in there.

"I wanted to build a bigger house. I figured the best thing you could do is build a big house that's going to appreciate, only go up in value."

Construction got underway in 1989. The contractor started running into problems. Building on that mountain top wasn't easy. The builder said he had to put in extra footers. He said he had to hire an engineer to help.

"Nobody in the city of Moreland Hills told me don't buy this property. It's un-buildable. They let me buy it."

Bruce says after he provided the builder with additional funding, the builder suddenly stopped work and said he was filing for bankruptcy. Bruce said he was saddled with a three hundred thousand dollar construction lien. He found a contractor to finish the project.

"The house is all built. I put in a swimming pool. The Moreland

Hills inspector gave me a permit for the swimming pool. I called the inspector to come over and give me an occupancy permit. He says I can't. I said why? He said you have a mudslide problem. I said why didn't you tell me that when I put the shovel in the ground?"

Bruce's dream had turned into a nightmare. He was outraged. He spent seven hundred twenty-five thousand dollars to build the house. In 1991, Bruce moved his family in.

"It took me three or four years to get an occupancy permit with a contingency that if I ever do sell, I have to let people know there's a mudslide problem. A problem Moreland Hills didn't tell me when I started building."

One of Bruce's partners in Waterbed Emporium decided to sell his interest in the company. Bruce and the remaining partner took control, but then that partner wanted out. He sensed the waterbed craze was fizzling out. Bruce still had faith. He took out a five hundred thousand dollar loan to continue the business. That turned out to be a mistake.

"The whole waterbed business dried up."

His company was failing. He was deep in debt. His house was a growing worry.

"Had it been on any other piece of land, it would be worth a million and a half dollars. Instead, it's worth nothing. I had to file bankruptcy cause I couldn't sell the house."

The bank foreclosed on the house. It went on the auction block. Marc Glassman, the owner of Marc's Deeper Discount stores, purchased the house for six hundred sixty-six thousand dollars.

"It's the devil's number. He didn't do his due diligence. He bought the house. He thought it was a good investment. He then sold the house to Coach Robiskie. He never told him about the mudslide problem, thinking he didn't have to since it came out of foreclosure."

Browns assistant coach Terry Robiskie was living in the house when some of the hillside started giving way. Because of his prominent position, the house on the hill started getting plenty of media attention. Robiskie filed suit against Glassman and the realty company.

"He won two million dollars. Got all of his money back from Glassman and won one-point-six million from the realtor, four hundred thousand in legal fees, and I got nothing."

Bruce testified in the trial. Why did he get involved?

"I got screwed and Robiskie got screwed. I wanted to make it known."

Waterbed Emporium closed in 1992.

"Then the banks came after me and the credit card companies came after me. I used to have credit. I'd walk into the bank. Want a twenty-five thousand dollar loan? Sign here Mr. Davis."

Bruce now runs Bellastanza Wholesale Furniture across from Southgate.

"We struggle. We know how to work it. We work it and we work it. It's pure guts and hustle."

It's a far cry from the cash cow days of Waterbed Emporium.

"I predicted in 1999 when I had to go bankrupt, I said this country was like the Roman Empire and it's going to collapse. It's in financial ruins. You look at all the guys who worked in America buying product, living a good life, having the American dream. Owning a car, owning a house. You took their jobs, sent 'em to China. You are making your furniture in China. You are making your tires. You are making everything in China."

Bruce Davis says greedy corporate businessmen have sold out America.

"They are all crooks. They are thieves and crooks. They are worried about lining their own pockets. They don't care nothin' about tomorrow. Where the Japanese care five hundred years from today, we care about five minutes from now. They plan. They plan. They look out for future generations and they plan. We just live for today, not for tomorrow."

Bruce says the terrorists who attacked America on 9/11 were sending a message about what is going on in our country.

"9/11 showed America, you are greedy. We don't like your lifestyle. We don't like the way you live. We don't like the way you do everything. We are showing you change the way you live."

Bruce says for a short time we did change the way we live.

"As you recall, after 9/11, when you went to pull a car out onto the street, the other car would stop to let you in, maybe. They were a little bit nicer for about three weeks. Then they forgot about it. We don't even know how to be nice to each other in this country."

Bruce survived the loss of the house on the hill. He survived the collapse of his business and bankruptcy. He calls himself a "cockroach."

He says it's impossible to kill him. But in 2002, the real test would come.

"They found renal cell carcinoma in my right kidney. The doctor removed fifteen to twenty percent of my right kidney. He told me I was cancer free."

Four years later Bruce was getting a lot of pain on his side. He thought it was something like pancreatitis. Tests were conducted and he was told the cancer from his kidney had metastasized to his pancreas.

"The doctor went in to remove part of my pancreas and in so doing, had to remove my spleen, too. When he pulled it out, he punctured my stomach and didn't realize it. He sewed me back up. The next day I started blowing up like a balloon and started getting sepsis. He had to cut me back open, emergency surgery to find the hole in my stomach, and patch it up. I was in the hospital for thirty-five days. I couldn't eat or drink. I nearly died twice during that episode."

The next year, the cancer metastasized to Bruce's liver. The doctor told Bruce he had six months to a year to live unless he took dramatic action.

"He said I should do the Interleukin-2 injections. It's available in Columbus, Pittsburgh or Bethesda, Maryland. I said sign me up."

Bruce began treatments at the James Cancer Center in Columbus. He would go into the hospital for one week, return home for a week, and then go back in for another week. He would then take seven weeks off before the next series of treatments.

"Once the Interleukin kicks in, about an hour and a half after the injection, every fifteen minutes you go into these shakes, like fever shakes. It causes your immune system to boost you up and make you sick, so your body eats the cancer."

The regimen calls for three daily injections of the Interleukin, along with numerous injections of two other drugs.

"It puts you in nowhere land. I'm talkin' to dead people. I'm thinkin' I'm in other places. I think I'm at my store, waiting on customers. I try to walk out of my room. My wife has to get in front of me. There must be a family member or friend with me at all times, 24/7 cause I'm so delusional and crazy."

Bruce doesn't regret signing up for the treatments.

"It's called staying alive. It's insanity, insanity. I just said I can't believe it. I'm living in a fantasy world. Why is this happening to me? What did I do wrong? I have been through hell and back three times. I am going through hell again. Every time I go to Columbus, it is pure hell. It's rough. A lot of crying. A lot of bullshit."

Bruce says he is going through this living hell for his family.

"I got a wife, three kids, a grandchild. I've got a lot of good family. What would you do if somebody told you, you were going to die? I put up with the pain. I refuse to not do the most that I can to make the cancer go away. I'm going to beat it. That's the mindset you have to have."

Throughout all of the turmoil, one of the constants in Bruce life has been his close friends from his days at Cleveland Heights High. He graduated in 1967.

"How many people do you know that can tell you they have six friends who have been great friends for forty-five years, that are still great friends today."

Bruce says his buddies have been a source of strength during his battle with cancer.

"I love seeing them. I talk to them all the time. High school was the best days of my life. I had respect, played football was a member of BAT (a social club). I got away with just about anything. I was rowdy, but we didn't murder anybody. We had a good time. It was just a blast. We goofed around."

His friend Fred Elsner moved back to Cleveland and gets together with Bruce about once a week. How does Bruce relate to guys like Fred all these years later?

"Just like I did fifty years ago. Nothing has changed. They are my buddies. They are my friends. The guys I grew up with. My high school friends, I go deeper with them."

Bruce admits he did some crazy things at Heights, but appreciates the law and order atmosphere that prevailed back then.

" You couldn't wear jeans to school. Today at schools kids walk around with their pants falling down and their underwear showing. You learned their rules at Heights. These kids now don't know from rules because the lawyers got involved. They are suing them."

Bruce says he has a couple of signs on the wall in his office. One reads, "Tact is the art of telling someone to go to hell in such a manner that he anticipates the trip." The other reads, "If you aren't the lead dog, the scenery never changes."

Bruce's house on River Mountain Drive never slid down the hillside, but the ground nearby has shifted several times.

"The ground is silty. It hardens up in the summertime. When it's not wet, it's like concrete. When it gets wet, it's like Jell-O."

After Butch Davis was fired as Browns head coach in 2004, Terry Robiskie was named interim head coach. He was able to win just one out five games.

Chuck Wien was one of Bruce's classmates at Heights and also was one of his roommates at Ohio State. After one of the Browns losses, Chuck said he was thinking of calling into Robiskie's TV show to say that on game day, Robiskie's house actually gained more yardage than the Browns offense.

Despite all he has been through, Bruce Davis would have laughed at a line like that. Bruce has learned many lessons the hard way. He has never lost his drive.

"You gotta bust your balls to make it in this world. You gotta hustle."

Michael Ryan, Class of '89

Walk into Judge Michael Ryan's courtroom, and the first thing you notice is that it's rather small. Defendants are anxiously waiting their turn as the judge makes his way through the docket. On this day, he will hear the usual lineup of cases. Driving on a suspended license, domestic violence, and a dispute concerning a traffic accident.

The judge is just shy of forty years old, but looks younger. He runs his courtroom with a firm hand, yet you can tell he has compassion for the people who stand before him. Some twenty years ago, it would have been more likely that Michael Ryan would wind up standing in front of a judge, instead of serving as one.

He had the odds stacked against him. An upbringing full of tragedy. One setback after another. Somehow he managed to stay one step ahead of the chaos and make sure he would make something of his life.

Michael's biological father was named Richard Solomon. He was convicted of robbing a bank and was sent to a federal prison before

Michael was born. For most of his childhood, Michael never knew about his real father. He thought his stepfather Allen Douglas was his father. It's not like Douglas was a better influence. He was in and out of prison and was addicted to drugs and alcohol.

"My mother died when I was in eighth grade. She was addicted to heroin. She contracted a disease, I think from using dirty needles. It completely shutdown all of her organs."

Marguerite Ryan was just twenty-eight years old. Family members have told Michael that in her early years, his mother appeared to have a bright future. She was intelligent. She was taking honors classes in high school.

"She just excelled, and that old adage you can have all the book sense in the world, but common sense, well she was just naïve. The drugs overtook everything else and it superceded everything else. All that promise she had, it was gone."

Marguerite became pregnant at fourteen and gave birth to Michael when she was fifteen. Little more than a year later, Michael's sister Sharese was born. As time went on, his mother couldn't care for them.

"As a child, I was mad. I was angry. I was angry especially when we had to go move in with my grandmother. Now all of my mother's responsibility is out the window. We periodically saw my mom on weekends during that last year and a half before she died. It was troubling, really troubling."

Years after his mother's death, Michael confronted his stepfather about drugs.

"I sat him down and asked him how long he had been using drugs. I said to him why is this so hard for you to break this habit, seeing what happened to mom, and he said he had been using since he was fifteen."

Their drug use is a haunting memory for Michael. His horrors go back to when he was four or five.

"I know they were smoking marijuana because I remember that. I never told anyone this, but they actually smoked marijuana one time, and they blew it in our noses to try to get my sister and me to go to sleep. I don't know if they did it more than that time, but I do remember that."

It was Easter Sunday 1985 when Michael's mother died. His stepfather had just been released from prison again.

"He came home. He had been drinking and he was addicted to drugs and alcohol. I don't know where he was going to take us, but he put us in the car with him and he couldn't even make it out of the driveway. He ran into some bushes in the back. Then he stopped and turned the car off and he told my sister and me our mother had died."

Michael and Sharese wound up living with their stepfather's mother. She would die a year later. They were taken in by another aunt. That was a bad environment. Sharese was so upset, she ran away.

"My other aunt who lived in Cleveland Heights, she said 'I'll take Michael and Sharese.' She already had six kids. Four of them were still in school, two of them were grown."

Michael's stepfather, was addicted to drugs and he could be blamed for Michael's mother's addiction. In a twist of fate, he wound up dying because of the actions of another addict.

"He was the victim of an aggravated vehicular homicide. The driver, there was sufficient evidence the driver has high on wet. He had been smoking marijuana that was dipped in formaldehyde, so he was just out of his mind.

"My stepfather and his fiancée were sitting at E. 79th and Kinsman at the light where the hill is there. This kid just came barreling down Kinsman Hill and my father, there was another vehicle in front of him. He was going no less that 75 miles per hour down the hill and he ran into the back of them.

"The force of the impact caused my stepfather's fiancée to propel through the front windshield and into the back window of the car in front of them, so she died on the scene. My dad, even though he was strapped in his seatbelt, the impact was so severe, that it caused him to hit the front portion of the vehicle. It caused a severe hematoma. He was on life-support for three or four days before he died."

By that point, Michael had already transferred to Cleveland Heights High and graduated. He said his teachers there were inspirational. His teammates on the football team called him "the professor." There was good reason Michael was so focused on his schoolwork.

"I felt I was losing every other aspect of life in terms of having good parents, living in a safe environment, being able to have a good healthy diet. All of those things, I said there's got to be something I could be successful in that I can control. I couldn't control any of those other things. School turned out to be the one thing I could control. I put every effort that I had towards school."

Michael was placed in honors classes when he enrolled in Heights High in eleventh grade. Most of the other students had been classmates in the honors program all the way through school.

"I was blessed to be gifted like my mom in terms of being able to grasp different concepts. I understood a lot of stuff and I was getting really high marks in school, so that encouraged me and I took it to another level.

"Mr. Quail was my physics teacher. I loved Mr. Quail, but I thought he was the craziest guy. He just looked weird. He was all over the place. He had these big glasses. He was very motivational. He wouldn't let you slide. The projects we did, they opened our minds up as students.

"I know that Heights helped me. Cleveland Heights High education refined me. I really appreciated the effort the teachers showed to me. Just the name Cleveland Heights High School on your transcript, sent to a college, has a lot more pull and a lot more behind it than my first school, John Adams.

"I appreciated the opportunity I was given to take advantage of that education. I knew I would be academically challenged at Heights."

Michael Ryan wasn't a sensation on the social scene at Heights.

"I didn't look like most of the kids at Heights. Generally the kids at Heights, they had both parents at home, the parents were both working. They had the latest styles. I didn't have that."

Michael Ryan had his sights set on college. He went to Allegheny College in Meadville, Pennsylvania.

"I knew at some point in my life, I was going to have a family. I said no way do I want to put my kids through all the trials and turmoils I had to go through as a kid. The best way to establish myself is get the education I need so I can have a good job and they won't ever have to experience the things that I did."

In fact, Michael's career goal was to become a teacher and inspire youngsters in his own classroom, but in his freshman year at Allegheny, he decided he wanted to go to law school. That was a major turnaround for him. Becoming a judge had been the furthest thing from his mind.

"I wanted to avoid the criminal justice system completely. I didn't want to have any involvement because of what I was exposed to as a child. Besides my father and stepfather going to jail, my uncle went to jail and my cousins were sent to detention homes. The only lawyers I saw were the ones puttin' my relatives in jail, so I had this disdain for the legal system."

Michael Ryan thinks he has a mission as a municipal judge.

"I hope people will still see me as a humble person who is considerate of other people's feelings. I'm trying to convey to people what the justice system is all about, so they don't leave the courtroom confused. I don't think serving as a judge has changed me at all. I'm still the same person I was before I got on the bench."

The judge says domestic violence cases can be difficult, but he knows the court system is a needed refuge for victims.

"The person feels protected. They feel vindicated. They feel justice has been served because they were injured and now that person is being punished."

So many times in his life, Michael Ryan felt like he didn't fit in. Even on the Heights High football team. He was a wide receiver. The team relied on a wishbone offense, so it was rare when a pass was thrown.

"I remember one game we were playing Euclid. It was fourth down and twenty yards to go. We ran the ball and I would think this is NOT a good offense. They changed the entire offense the year after we left."

He was bewildered as a child. His mother's life just spiraled out of control. He used to be angry.

"Not anymore. I used to be when I was younger. I couldn't understand the hold the drugs had on her. Before she went on drugs, she was a beautiful young lady. She wasn't one who was hostile, evil, or nasty to people. She wasn't like that toward Sharese and myself. She was trying to do everything she possibly could. She tried to make sure we ate, but that addiction just took over, so she couldn't. She was neglectful most of the time. She was high most of the time. She couldn't work."

Michael Ryan has fulfilled his dream. He and his wife Robin have two children, Lauren and Michael. He has survived a long journey to get on the bench in that small courtroom. Michael isn't running from his past. His past is his constant motivation.

"My wife always says, 'Why do you work so hard?' I say I don't want Lauren and Michael to go through what I did."

They won't.

Lindbergh Kawahara, class of '45

"In those days, minorities used to pick names of famous people. I was named after Lindbergh, the flyer. My brother Herbert was named for Herbert Hoover."

The Kawahara brothers were given all-American names, but they would learn early on in their lives that freedoms are not always guaranteed. Two young boys growing up in Los Angeles would be uprooted after the bombing attack on Pearl Harbor. They would first go to a relocation camp and eventually wind up in a Jewish orphanage in Cleveland. They were in a sense, foreign exchange students at Cleveland Heights High. Except for the fact they weren't foreign, and they didn't sign up the way traditional A.F.S. students did.

Lindy Kawahara's grandfather, Masao, left Japan in 1879 and settled in Honolulu, Hawaii. He was a businessman there. Lindy's father, George, was born in Hawaii, as was his mother, Edith. His family moved to California in 1925. Lindy was born in San Jose in 1927.

When Pearl Harbor was attacked by Japan in 1941, Japanese Americans were looked upon with suspicion. The government was convinced their loyalties would be with Japan. Perhaps those here would engage in espionage or sabotage.

"Suddenly what I thought were my friends, were antagonistic to us. Everything changed. I felt we were people without a country. Japan was never fond of us because we left their country and never looked at us as Japanese citizens. The U.S. government started taking away our rights. I felt I was a person without citizenship.

"We had to evacuate from Los Angeles. If we moved to the interior, they said we wouldn't have to leave the state. We had a distant cousin near Fresno, in a city called Parlier. We voluntarily left in May of 1942 and lived in central California. The government decided to change their mind and we still had to leave California. We were shipped out to Arizona, where they built a camp on an Indian reservation. We were able to take only fifty pounds of belongings when we entered the camp."

People left homes and most of their possessions behind. Many of their belongings were stolen while they were in custody. Farm owners had little notice they were being shipped away. Many sold their farmland for pennies on the dollar. It was land they had toiled on for many years. Lives were just put on hold.

"It was the Gila River camp near Gila, Arizona. We lived in barracks. They had quickly built these structures for us as living quarters. The barracks were divided into these four units, so there were four families in each barracks. They had sub-floors, so all of the dust and the insects could enter through the floor. It was very hot in the summertime and cold in the winter. They provided us with an oil stove. That was the only heat we had."

The older generation in the camps tried to provide for the children there. Lindy remembers the adults fashioned a basketball court for the youngsters. They built a school, but under the circumstances, the quality of education was lacking. Many of the people in the camp had extensive agricultural backgrounds. They developed the nearby fields. Detainees at the Gila River camp provided vegetables to all ten of the relocation camps.

"I didn't think it was very fair. We were citizens and we were denied our rights. We were shipped off. We didn't have very kind thoughts about President Roosevelt or General John DeWitt. We couldn't take any radio or camera or any sort of communications into the camp because they thought there were threats of spying."

George Kawahara wasn't happy about many things, but one of his biggest concerns was the fact his sons were getting a poor education.

"He saw we could get a better education. In 1944, he saw an ad where people could come to the Jewish orphanage in Cleveland. If we had a sponsor, we would be able to leave the camp. The Jewish orphanage named Bellefaire sponsored my brother and me, so we ended up at Bellefaire."

The accommodations were by no means plush. Lindy and Herbert lived in a laundry room on a concrete floor. The room as very bare.

"We were working twenty hours a week for our room and board. I did all kinds of work there. Shoveling coal, and I worked in the kitchen. I learned a lot."

Lindy and his brother enrolled in Cleveland Heights High. There were about a dozen students there from a number of relocation camps. Lindy says most of the Heights High students were unaware of his circumstances.

"My experience in Cleveland was very positive. I have fond memories of Cleveland Heights High. It was an eye-opening experience because it was the first time I went to the Midwest. There were many experiences like the snow and working. We had no one to depend on except ourselves. It's interesting how you survive. Even if you weren't feeling well, you went to school, because there was no one to take care of you anyway. We did a lot of public transportation and a lot of walking. We had no money to speak of. We made the best of it.

"Most of the people we met were very nice. I did my senior year at Heights. Herbert was a year and half younger. He did very well on his own. There were an awful lot of smart students. We didn't get to socialize very much. We really weren't a threat to anyone. On the West Coast, they saw you as Japs, we don't want you here, and they treated us like enemies, although there was no basis for that. It was like war hysteria."

"It was an experience that changed my life. We try to look at it in a positive way. For us, we were younger, so there wasn't so much for us to lose. The older people they lost a lot. They lost their homes. They lost their businesses. Their careers were altered. They may have lost someone in their family because of a lack of medical care in the camps.

"I feel sorry for the guys older than myself cause they had the brains and skills and didn't get a chance at a career. Even after the war, they couldn't get jobs because of the anti-Japanese feelings. Even if they had graduated college, all they could do was work at a fruit stand cause no one would give them a job. Many of them never got to do what they were trained for."

"Most Americans don't know what transpired at that time. It violated everything in the Constitution, but Roosevelt got away with it."

Lindy graduated from Heights right at the time the war was ending. He headed back to Arizona and reunited with his family. They then moved back to central California. He remembers his family moved into an abandoned store. At one time nineteen people were living there. Lindy attended community college for a year.

"We didn't have much money. I had to quit college to help in the farm fields. My dad suggested if I joined the service, I could get the GI Bill. I wound up in the Army at Ft. Lewis in Washington. I went to Tokyo and worked with the military intelligence corps."

After a couple of years in the military, the family decided since Lindy liked to work with hands, he ought to study dentistry. He enrolled in UCLA, and eventually went to dental school at the University of California, San Francisco. He started work as a dentist in 1955 and still works part-time at age eighty-one.

Besides his contributions as a dentist, Lindy Kawahara's three sons have been productive as well. His oldest son earned a Ph.D. at the Rochester Institute of Technology and works in the bio-tech field. His second son went to Harvard Medical School and is a surgeon and a dentist. His third son earned a law degree from the University of Chicago and works for an American law firm in Japan. A family deprived of many fundamental rights has indeed pursued the American dream.

"When you suffer, you usually come out ahead because of it. It offered me more opportunity, because the way sentiment was, we couldn't stray too much from our own community. No one was friendly outside our circle. We weren't accepted. We suddenly got a chance to live in other parts of the country and fend for ourselves. I couldn't have imagined going out of state. In a way it opened doors.

"Even before the war, we were seen as a threat economically, and people tried to suppress us because we were smart, willing to work, and willing to put up with adversity. There is still discrimination. You can't get rid of that.

"The only regret I have is, during those years, I missed out on life. What occurred in life. When you look back at your teens, what are the things you enjoyed in your life, and for me it's a blank. When they have programs on TV of what happened in those years, you don't recognize some of the people. You don't remember events. You didn't get to participate. You talk about the war effort, well we couldn't do it.

"When it comes to my grandchildren, or children, I encourage them to enjoy their lives at the time, cause it's a journey. I feel like part of my journey was interrupted. Enjoy your life now, because it won't come back again."

Susie Gharib, class of '69

"Now you tune into CNBC, all these babes are covering business news in sexy clothes. But it took a long time for women to go on Wall Street to cover business news or to cover business news in general."

It is a bit difficult to think of Susie Gharib as a pioneer, but there's no question she is. If you tune into the *Nightly Business Report* on PBS, you would be surprised to learn she is in her late fifties. She looks much younger. In fact, in news stories she has been called Wall Street's original Money Honey.

Her good looks have not hindered her TV career by any means, but Susie's intelligence and determination are what have really paid dividends for her over the decades.

She was one of four daughters raised in a home near Berkshire and Euclid Heights. Her parents were both born in Iran. Ali Gharib and his wife Noma both came to this country when they were in their twenties. He became an anesthesiologist and wound up on the faculty of the Case Western Reserve Medical School.

Initially, Ali Gharib was thinking of returning to Iran, but after the revolution there, Susie says things got "bumpy." With the political unrest, he determined it would be best to raise his family in the United States.

"I wouldn't be doing what I'm doing today, and all of my sisters are very accomplished career-wise. It wouldn't have been possible if they returned to Iran because of the revolution."

Though out-numbered five to one, Ali Gharib was a large presence in that household.

"He was a visionary. He thought in big ways. He was a leader. He had strong opinions and he passed that quality on to his daughters. He was always telling us to be a leader, not a follower. He stressed the importance of our education. It was still a very male-dominated society. He came from an old-world culture, and yet he felt very strongly that we pursue our dreams, pursue goals, and pursue a career."

Susie says her father was a big believer in having a good family life. He wanted his daughters to get married and have children, but he wanted them to do something intellectual as well. The Gharib girls were brought up in a conservative traditional household. Ali Gharib was their moral compass.

"He kept us all in a very healthy, focused kind of life. While I resisted much of that, growing up as a teenager, now that I am raising my own children, a lot of his views and values, I have incorporated in parenting my own children."

Susie's mother was a strong influence as well.

"She came from an amazing family. Her father, Hussein Razzaghmanash, was like the Rockefeller of Iran. A big industrialist. At a time when no one was traveling out of the country, he was doing business all over Europe, Western Europe, with Russia and bringing all sorts of Western goods into Iran. He was the first person to bring a car into Iran in the 1930s. It was a Packard. The Shah of Iran still didn't have a car, so he didn't drive his car until the Shah got one. He was a very influential, very, very wealthy man."

Susie says her mother grew up in a large family. She was part of high society in Iran.

"My mother had the style, the creativity and a sense of glamour. My father being the hard-nosed academic, professional physician type. He grew up in a family that was hundreds of years of professors and academics."

So this Moslem family settled in Cleveland Heights. The youngest three daughters were students at Cleveland Heights High.

"I felt totally isolated, especially in such a Jewish high school. When I was at Heights, people would say, 'Gharib. What kind of name is that?' I said Iranian. They had no clue where Iran was. It was such an oddity. They just didn't understand. I remember some of my friends coming to my home and we would have Middle Eastern food. Rice and lamb, things my mother would make. My friends were used to hot dogs or hamburgers or spaghetti."

Providing religious training for the Gharib daughters was a challenge.

"It was difficult to teach us that here, growing up. My parents were observant, but not in an orthodox way at all. They were very modern-minded, especially my mother. We did everything other American kids did. They told us about the basics of the Moslem religion but a lot of it, I don't even know. There was no vehicle, or no way to really learn it here, growing up in the Midwest.

"When people today talk about globalization, and the world is flat, yes it is now. People are going to Dubai. They are traveling to India and China, and the world has gotten so much smaller and friendlier. Everybody is so much more aware. It wasn't like that in the '50s and '60s in Cleveland, Ohio.

"Everybody loves to go to Middle Eastern restaurants, shish kabob places. There are ethnic sections in grocery stores. Now when my friends come over, they say please make Persian food."

Susie looks back on her years at Heights as an amazing academic experience.

"It was so competitive. Great teachers. It turned out students who went to the best colleges, pursued careers they were well prepared for. I would compare Heights High with the finest private schools in New York. Some of my teachers were real standouts. I remember Dr. Hutchings, who was my biology teacher in tenth grade, was a Ph.D. I always thought it was really amazing a Ph.D. would be teaching in high school. I had bright teachers. I got a great education.

"You were friends with everybody. You knew everybody. I liked the tradition of raising the flag. The color guard. Everyone would stand wherever they were in the courtyard."

She worked on the *Caldron* her senior year, but she always had one major regret about her years at Heights.

"I wanted to be a swim cadet. I never made it to swim cadets, but I was in the swim club. My dream was to be swimming in a black and gold bathing suit and be in those swim shows they would have every year."

When Susie graduated from Heights High, she didn't travel very far. She went down the hill a couple of miles to Case Western Reserve. With her father on the faculty there, he insisted all his girls get their undergraduate degrees there. They could go anywhere they wanted after Case.

"When I went to Reserve, I signed up to work on the student newspaper, *The Observer*. What a great time to be working on the school newspaper in college. The student body was very anti-war. It was during the Kent State shootings. Jane Fonda came and spoke at the school. Hanoi Jane. I covered that. Gloria Steinem came. I interviewed her. Julie Eisenhower came and I was on the press bus with all of the national press corps. The White House press corps, and I thought this was the coolest thing. This is what I want to do with my life."

Susie had her career goal, she wanted to write for *Time* magazine. She was not enrolled in a journalism program at Northwestern, Missouri or Ohio University. She was concerned that might hurt her chances.

"Case Western Reserve did not offer a journalism degree. I went to the English department and I said, how do I do this, and they kind of laughed me off and said yea, yea, yea. Dream on, little girl. One professor said study whatever you like, and learn as much as you can, because being a good reporter is having interest in a lot of topics, and learn to write.

"So I majored in English literature and French literature and minored in art history. On the side, I worked for *The Sun Press,* covered all of their little local stories. I went over to *The Plain Dealer* because I was interested in writing for them and they said no, no, no.

"They had a summer internship program and they said 'We don't take anybody unless you have a journalism degree.' But I hounded them, and I pestered them, and I kept calling them. I kept sending them clips of stories I did with *The Observer,* and they finally hired me for the summer internship program. I was the only person they ever hired from Case Western Reserve. The only one who didn't come from a journalism school."

Susie not only landed that internship, but her hard work convinced the editors there to hire her full-time at the end of the summer. Romance then intervened. Sue's cousin introduced her to a friend of his. Foreydun Nazem. He was born in Iran, but educated here in the United States. After a year courtship, they married and moved to New York to attend graduate programs at Columbia University.

After a series of internships, Sue landed a job at *Fortune* magazine and worked there for nine years until a new opportunity came her way. She had no television experience, yet was recruited to work on a program called *Business Times.* It was set to air on ESPN on weekday mornings from six until eight. It's hard to imagine these days that ESPN would cough up two hours of its sports programming for a syndicated business program, but in the early day of cable, it did.

"TV always thought business was boring. They would just have a little story, the Dow Jones went up, or consumer prices were, whatever. They would show video of a grocery store. They thought nobody liked business stories."

The producer of the show pledged to make the topic interesting. He was determined to hire people who knew business. Sue says she knew absolutely nothing about television, and like most print reporters, she had a lot of disdain for TV reporters. She always thought they barged into press conferences and they often copied stories from print people.

"All of those people who came on that program were from print. From *The Economist, U.S. News & World Report, Business Week* and

Fortune. The show earned lots of awards and then it ran out of money. We went off the air."

Sue says she has tapes in her attic of her early days in television. She says she is afraid to look at them because her performance is probably so bad. She actually worked with a TV coach when she broke into the business.

"How long is it going to take me before I look really natural on TV?" she asked.

"Four or five years," he replied.

"Four or five years! I've got to be good right now. I can't wait four or five years."

He said, "Okay, three or four years."

"Three or four years? Oh my God."

The coach reassured Susie that she was steadily getting better.

"But you know, he was right. It took about four years. Four years for me to feel totally myself on TV."

Susie had turned the corner. There was no turning back to print journalism. She free-lanced for CNN, worked as a business reporter for WABC in New York City, anchored for CNBC and then was hired to be on the *Nightly Business Report.* It's broadcast on three hundred PBS stations across the country.

"We reach 800,000 people every night, sometimes a million, depending on what is going on. It's all age groups, but primarily thirty years old and up."

In March of 2008, Susie traveled to the White House for a one-on-one interview with President George Bush.

"He was very personable, both before and after. He answered all of my questions. He didn't know what they were going to be. He's not the brightest President we have had. But afterwards, he was very kind. He spent a lot of time talking to me. He's eager to get on with the rest of his life. He was talking about the book he wants to write.

"He is self-effacing about himself. His daughter, Barbara, was in the same class as my son at Yale. Graduated the same year. We were comparing notes. He was saying he had his Yale class reunion. He invited the whole class to the White House. I asked what it was like and he said it was a lot of standing around, shaking everybody's hand. Everybody was in such awe to come to the White House. But he says,

'I'm just a regular guy. It's not a big deal being President.' I couldn't believe he said that.

"He's a nice person. As a President, that's another story. But how history will judge what he did and what he didn't do? As a human being, he's a nice person. If you are going on vacation, he'd be a nice person to go on vacation with."

In 1999, Susie Gharib had interviewed President Bill Clinton at the White House. It was towards the end of the Monica Lewinsky scandal. She was told the scandal was off limits for their conversation.

"We talked about the economy. He has such an incisive mind. He had so much to say. They said I would have a ten-minute interview. He was having such a good time, he shoo-ed away his handlers and said, 'Let's keep talking.' After the interview was over, he stayed with me another twenty minutes, talking some more.

"He loves to talk. So articulate. No matter how many follow-up questions I asked, he had more to contribute. With President Bush, every time I asked a follow-up, he would repeat what he said in the first answer. He just had this superficial knowledge, a superficial briefing of what he wanted to say about the economy, the stock market, oil prices or inflation.

"President Clinton was far more engaging. A great mind. Oozing of charisma. Very personable, very warm. He posed for pictures with the camera crew. He brought in his dog Buddy. A very relaxed setting. Afterwards, I got hundreds of e-mails. People were upset, wondering why we would waste air time on him."

Susie says there is no routine to her daily routine. The only constant is she has to be in the anchor chair at six-thirty every evening.

"I start every morning at nine o'clock. There's a morning conference call. Some mornings, I am already out the door on assignment, interviewing somebody, gathering the news, talking to people. I'm either doing interviews or preparing for a live interview. Planning for the next day, planning for the next week, or planning for the next month. It's very hands-on. I write my own copy on the stories I read. The stories written for me, I rewrite those so it's in my own voice.

"I do research for all of my interviews. I book my own interviews, although the assignment desk occasionally comes up with high-profile guests.

"Because it's public television, we don't have a whole lot of people or resources like the commercial networks do. I like doing my own stuff. I like to own it. My specialty is doing the interview. I have interviewed many of the big-name CEOs, as well as the newsmakers in Washington."

Susie gets to rub elbows with the power players in the business world. She says she is never nervous or intimidated.

"I like have no nerves. I'm very comfortable. I feel at ease. My nervousness is in the preparation. I hope I ask the right questions. I hope I haven't missed anything. I hope the people watching at home, they won't say, 'Why didn't she ask this?'

"I just hope I can tune into the mentality of my audience. What do they want to know? I am going to be their intermediary to ask those questions to the President of the United States, the CEO of Exxon or the CEO of General Electric. But once I am sitting there, I feel completely at ease."

Susie gives a lot of credit to her mother. She says people were constantly coming and going in their home. People from all over the world would visit. Her father was always bringing home residents from the hospital. It was like the Iranian Embassy. Susie got used to carrying on conversations. It became very natural for her to be in a social situations. She has transferred that into her work life.

With the volatile nature of the stock market, some magazine articles have urged people to just tune out the business programs and not stay plugged into the daily setbacks.

"That doesn't make any sense to me. It's like saying if you have a medical problem, you shouldn't go to the doctor. I think at times like this, you want to know more, so you can make the right decisions.

"There are things you can do to ride out the storm. I know people are tuning in, because our ratings are way up. I know they are watching us and they are watching our competitors. Knowledge is power. The more you know, the better decisions you can make. This is not a time to hide under the covers. Your financial assets are at stake, and that goes for your decisions about your kids going to college, your retirement savings, or if you are in retirement, how to preserve your capital. Wouldn't you want to know the best ways to do that instead of running away and saying I just don't want to hear about it.

"If people say I'm too scared to look at my 401K statement, I can understand that. I'm scared to look at mine, too. But at some point, you should look in the envelope, and say, now what am I going to do and what's the smartest thing I can do?

"I don't think our program, or any program has the answers. All we can provide are guideposts. We guide you to other places to look, to know what the issues are, and you can make informed decisions. You can ask informed questions of the experts, your financial planner, your banker, or your stockbroker."

The CEOs of the Big Three automakers flew to Washington on private jets to ask Congress for loans to bail out their slumping companies.

"How out of touch they are with the pain everyone is feeling. For AIG, the company came hat in hand to Washington for money and then after they got the money, we find out that they are having some sales conference at some resort. It's upsetting, and they are clueless. They are not all like that. I have interviewed a lot of CEOs. Many are very in touch, in good times and bad times, with their customer base."

Susie Gharib has come a long way from those days on the yearbook staff at Heights High. She has been a trailblazer. Things have changed dramatically.

"When I started at *The Plain Dealer,* there was a whole issue about women working on the police beat. They didn't want women doing that. They started them on the society page. They were worried about their safety. But the police beat was the only way you could get into the high-paying jobs. From the police beat, you would go to the city beat and you would cover city hall, and ultimately the Washington Bureau.

"But if you didn't start on the police beat, there was no way you were going to go to Washington from the society page. Just when I was starting there, women were breaking through to cover the police beat.

"In the early '70s, the TV stations had no women reporters. They were all behind the scenes. When a few were hired, the headline of *The New York Times* was 'Nylons in the Newsroom.'

"When I was at *Fortune,* they felt boardrooms were dominated by men and they didn't have many women reporters. They thought it was a man's profession. Out of sixty reporters, five of us were women.

"Now you have women working as foreign correspondents in war zones like Christiane Amanpour. When I was starting in the profession, they didn't want you to cover a fire or a crime. When I tell this to my kids, they kind of stare at me. We lived through all of that. We lived through a very pioneering change in society. Whether it was about race, gender or religion, there were a lot of barriers.

"There were two or three years of people ahead of me who broke down a lot of those barriers. I guess I was one of the pioneers of business journalism."

Michael Hennenberg, Class of '66

Michael Hennenberg was nearly thirty-three years old. Single, a successful lawyer who had purchased a sprawling home in Pepper Pike.

Susan Spitz was twenty-seven. She worked for a marketing firm in Phoenix.

The chances were slim that these two would meet randomly, halfway around the world, fall in love instantly, and get married.

Their chance meeting in Jerusalem that summer day in 1981, came during the World Gathering of Holocaust Survivors. Michael's father, Jacob Hennenberg was a survivor.

Susan's parents Harry and Anna Spitz were also survivors.

Jacob Hennenberg devoted his life to documenting the story of the Holocaust. He talked about it openly at home.

Michael said, "It was part of my life. I knew all about it. I heard all about it. I was surrounded by adults who had survived, and other children my age who were the children of survivors. It was constantly around me. Dad was talking about it. I was hearing stories of heroism. Stories of righteous gentiles who saved Jews. I was hearing the good side of this horrible event."

Stories of the Holocaust would haunt Susan as a child. She said, "I thought about it probably every day when I was growing up. I used to think somebody was going to come and get me, that the Nazis were going to come.

"My mother's mother went to the gas chamber with her young children. She had the chance to go to another line, but the children were in line for the gas chamber. She didn't want to leave her children. I don't know when I heard this story. I had to be very little. I would always, always think about it. I thought, why did she do that?

"I remember when I turned ten, I said, I can't believe I'm ten years old and I haven't done anything with my life before the Nazis come."

Michael heard his father tell stories of struggling to survive in forced labor camps in Poland.

"Everyone who survived was in the middle of death. They were constantly surrounded by death and brutality. As my dad said, if a guard was in a bad mood, he would kill you. They would take you out of the barracks at four in the morning, workers were always naked, it was freezing, and they would make you stand there for a couple of hours. People just froze to death, fell over and died."

Susan said her father, at age nineteen, was forced to work at a factory in Czechoslovakia.

"There were Christian people coming into the camp working in the factory, alongside the Jews. They could leave at night. The Jews had to stay. They slept on the concrete floors. My father befriended a gentile boy. He brought him a change of clothes so he would look like he was Christian. He wound up escaping in the middle of the night."

Harry Spitz made his way to Budapest, Hungary and he worked for diplomat Raoul Wallenberg at the Swedish Embassy.

"He would go to the trains and he would have papers. He dressed like the SS. He would go onto the trains and he would call names of Jews and he would take them off. They wouldn't know he was one of them. They assumed he was with the Nazis. He did this for a number of months."

Michael marvels at Harry's courage.

"This guy is in a train station loaded with soldiers and murderers, and he is wearing one of their uniforms. Wallenberg is handing out Swedish passports and identification cards. These people on the trains were getting these Swedish passports and then they were taking them off the trains and to safe houses.

"This guy had incredible guts. He's got to be smart and savvy. It's like walking right into the fire."

Susan says this plan to save Jews from the death camps began to unravel.

"The Nazis got wind of this. They figured it out. After he had taken some families off, they surrounded all of them. A couple of dozen, maybe. They lined them all up in front of the river and they just shot everybody.

"Everyone died except for my father. He was shot in the leg and fell into the water and just pretended he was dead. He was in the water for hours and hours until sunset. When he was sure they were gone, he could get out."

Back to how Susan would meet Michael.

Michael said, "The conference was being held because of the Holocaust deniers. The idea was to bring ten thousand survivors and their children to Israel to have this mass showing of survivors."

Susan had traveled to Israel with her father and her younger brother. The first three days of the event took place in Tel Aviv. The next six days were to be in Jerusalem.

"We moved from Tel Aviv to Jerusalem. I was supposed to be in a hotel with my father and brother. It was already prepaid and set up, but there were so many people and there was so much commotion, the hotel didn't have a room for me. So they offered to put me in another hotel. I wasn't thrilled about that because my father and brother were in this hotel. I didn't have a choice. There were no rooms whatsoever."

Michael was standing at the front desk of the second hotel when Susan walked up to check in.

"I said, I'm Susan Spitz. Is my room ready?"

The room wasn't ready, the desk clerk said it wouldn't be ready for two or three hours.

31

"I let out a sigh. Michael was just a few feet away. He said to me, 'Oh, come now. It can't be all that bad?'

"I said, How do you know how bad it could be?"

The lobby was completely full of people. It was chaos. People were sitting on couches. Others were sitting on their suitcases.

Michael said, "I'll put your luggage in my room and that way you can go out for a few hours and do whatever you want to do."

Susan took him up on his offer.

"For one thing, I knew he was a child of survivors. We were all there for the same thing. He looked very credible. I wasn't very worried. I didn't want to be sitting in the lobby. I wanted to go around and do things.

"I said I'll walk up to see where your room is. We wound up talking for the next four hours. We just talked and talked and talked. It went by in just an instant."

Michael was so taken with Susan that he had completely forgotten that he had left his suitcase and his father's suitcase in the lobby.

"Our passports were in there, our money was there. I ran downstairs and there was our luggage just sitting there in the middle of the lobby. I had left it there four or five hours earlier."

But a romance was definitely brewing. What were the odds of a guy from Cleveland and gal from Phoenix winding up at a hotel front desk in Israel at the same split second? They would embark on what has to be one of the more unusual first dates.

"We went with Michael's father to Yad Vashem, the Holocaust Memorial, for a ceremony that night. That was our first date. That was our first evening together."

The next day, Michael found a jewelry store and bought Susan a ring. He proposed. He had known her little more than twenty-four hours. She accepted.

"It was a magical story, but my friends and family in Phoenix still looked at me like I was out of my mind. I'm leaving my job, leaving Phoenix. I'm going to Cleveland, after knowing someone just a few days."

Michael and Susan are the parents of two daughters, Julia and Debbie.

Susan said, "I was always worried they were going to elope or find someone and marry them after a week."

Michael said, "They think it's a nice story. They think it's great."

So a couple of children of survivors married. Susan says survivors and their children have many perspectives on the Holocaust.

"My mother was only fourteen. She was barely a teenager. She was very young and she survived. She came from a different background than someone who may have gone in while in their twenties and who lost their own children. Everybody had different experiences. Some parents talked about it, other parents didn't talk about it."

Michael Hennenberg knew that his father had five sisters. Only one survived and she died a couple of years after the war ended. His father was already in a forced labor camp when the Nazis came to round up the rest of the Hennenberg family. The Nazis were not interested in the infants.

"Several of the Hennenberg sisters had been ordered to throw their babies on the street and get on the truck. They refused, and they were shot with machine guns right on the spot."

Michael says when the SS took over the work camps, things went from bad to being really bad.

"They would have people line up and count off by two's. Put them in two different groups and they would murder all the one's. Machine gun them down. They would tell the two's, you better work hard tomorrow. Next day they would count off again and murder all of the two's. There were all these dogs, screaming, and machine guns. If you looked somebody in the eye, they would kill you, that was it."

Jacob Hennenberg would play a major role with the Kol Israel group in Cleveland. He did all he could to share the history of the Holocaust with all who would listen. At one meeting, Michael was called upon to share his feelings.

He told the survivors gathered there, "Their eyes had seen such horror, and the worst of the worst. And those same eyes came to a new land and could see a future and could see children and normal lives. People can't put these things out of their minds, or put it behind them. But they proceeded in spite of what they had seen, the smells, what they felt inside. The degradation, the suffering, the loss of loved ones, and went on to make new lives and have children and raise those children. They were special people to me."

Michael and Susan Hennenberg. A special romance. A love that has intensified over the years. A common family background. Two daughters with a wonderful future ahead. Two of life's blessings.

Joy Marshall, class of '66

The year was 2000. My father Sanford Stromberg died in March. Just five short months later, my mother Helen died as well. A letter arrived a few days later. It was written by a former Heights High classmate, Joy Marshall. Here is what she wrote.

I heard last week or so, that your mother had died. I wanted to tell you I have been thinking about you. Knowing nothing about your family, I felt compelled to write to you anyway.

My father died at the age of eighty. He had been sick for a few years, literally a shadow of his former self. I don't know how many people came up to me and said things like, "well that's a blessing," or "such a nice long life." I can remember looking at these people not knowing how to respond. He wasn't old, he wasn't sick. He was my dad and he was gone.

It took a dinner conversation ten years later to give me an understanding of how I had felt back then - indeed how I feel today, twenty years after daddy's death. The dinner was at Nighttown. A friend of ours who was in his early seventies had just lost his ninety-eight year old mother. As we toasted her memory, he looked at me and said, "Well, so now I am an orphan."

And so it is.

No matter how old we are, no matter how old our parent was, even if they had a "good" life, even if the manner of their death was "good," or "right," or "fortunate," the loss is still poignant and deep. And as "grown up" as we are, as mature, as objective as we may be, there will always be a part of us which is left bereft - as if we were still children.

There's something comforting in that child, long dormant, resurfacing, I think. Maybe the loss of those we love, keeps us mindful of our own vulnerability, our fragility. Maybe in the "big picture," it reminds us of how dependent upon each other we are - just because we are human beings. And, I guess, this is a good thing - the death of someone we love, their memory, becomes the glue which reaffirms our humanity.

Those words touched my heart at that time of sorrow. I have passed them on to others when they have suffered a loss.

Joy Marshall's road through life has not been traditional. She started dating Peter Wood in tenth grade. Nine months after graduating from Heights, they were married. Unlike other graduates, they didn't head to college, but made their way to Mexico.

They wound up in Oaxaca. Joy said they didn't do drugs. They weren't hippies. They just thought they could get by on their own, far away from home.

"We had no money. We started working as tour guides for visiting Americans. If you got busted, then they would ship you off, because you weren't allowed to work in Mexico without papers. We had a little house. It cost twelve dollars a month. It was in San Felipe in the foothills of the Juarez Mountains."

Joy started working as a waitress on the beach. Money was so tight, Peter took on a job working as a turtle fisherman.

"You go out and you hunt these poor, pathetic thirty-five or forty year old turtles. You get up at four in the morning. You see these little islands in the middle of the ocean. You come up behind them. You turn your little launch motor off. You jump on them. You grab them. They start swimming, diving down. You just force them up. They come up to the top. You smash them over the head, totally illegal, throw them into the boat. There are rich doctors from Mexico City who would take the skin from their arms, legs and tail and turn them into bags, women's shoes and wallets. It was really grotesque. It was disgusting. They were making thirty-five dollars a turtle."

Life in paradise had its challenges. Joy got hepatitis. She fell off a ladder and broke a bone in her foot. In 1968, while in Mexico City, they got caught up in the rioting. The decided to come back home.

Peter landed a job at Republic Steel and Joy got a job at Genesis, a vegetarian restaurant on Euclid Avenue. That was followed by a job as a waitress at the Last Moving Picture Company night club in downtown Cleveland.

Joy then got involved with a new restaurant on Coventry. She ran the kitchen at Toutlemond.

"I totally didn't know what I was doing. I made all the bread from scratch. The only thing that wasn't from scratch was the tomatoes."

Joy and Peter both worked at a restaurant in an old coach house in University Circle. That place was called Fantomas. Their goal was to provide affordable food for the working class at lunch, and elegant dinners for the rich at night.

"We could have great stews and soups during the days and sandwiches on whole wheat bread. At night, we could have really excellent food for those whose had had the money to spend. There was no head lettuce, no creamy salad dressings. We were making three-dollars-and-fifty cents an hour."

It was during this era, that Joy gave birth to the first two of her four daughters.

"Peter ended up taking off for California. I ended up being here on welfare, with the kids. I started working at Nighttown as a server."

While working there, Joy got to know one of the customers, Louis Toepfer, who was the president of Case Western Reserve University.

"He was just a lovely, lovely man. He asked me what I was doing with my life, and I said, I know it sounds kind of silly, but I always wanted to go to medical school."

At this point, Joy was twenty-eight, flat broke and a single mom. She had never taken a college course. She told Toepfer she was thinking about going to Cleveland State University. Toepfer told her he ran a "fine little university down the hill." Joy was intrigued, but told Toepfer that her grade point average at Heights High had been a measly one-point-seven-five.

"He said that was ten years ago. He said you have been to Mexico. You speak Spanish. You have run restaurants, you have children. I said yea, but I don't have any money."

Joy sent a hand-written letter to the admissions office, explaining why they should take her in. Welfare would provide some of the funding for her education. Four years later, Joy was named outstanding non-traditional student at CWRU.

Joy went on to graduate school for two years, earning a degree in Medical Anthropology. Her father Edward had been a gastroenterologist, and she still had the dream of becoming a doctor. She spent another two years taking pre-med courses in order to qualify for medical school. She was thirty-six years old when she was accepted to the med school at CWRU.

Joy remarried, and she gave birth to her fourth daughter during her first year at med school. Raising four children while going through the rigors of medical school was a daunting task. Joy relished being a mom and a homemaker.

"I wouldn't give that up. I always made my own thread, my own pastas, my own jams and jellies. I insisted I wasn't going to sacrifice one for the other. People in my class hated me."

Joy got through the first year of med school. The second year was more of a challenge. Joy said her fellow students made life difficult for her. One of her professors admitted she had the deck stacked against her.

"Classes seem to take on personalities and you had a mean class."

The pressures mounted. Joy said she was always insecure. She questioned whether she belonged in medical school.

"I was always expecting someone to come and say there was a mistake made, we didn't mean you. I couldn't believe I was actually accepted to medical school. I was the odd-man out. It was ugly."

Joy completed her second year of med school. She took the board exams and flunked them. She had a choice. She could throw in the towel, or she could repeat the entire year of med school.

"The fear and embarrassment. The humiliation of being a failure."

Joy didn't give up. She decided to return and repeat that second year.

"I was taken into a nice class. They liked me, they were nice to me."

Joy was also able to find a mentor. Cuyahoga County Coroner Lester Adelson.

"He was like my other father. I loved him. He called himself a family practitioner for the bereaved. My experiences with him were just stellar. He was such a great, wonderful man. He said death doesn't harden you, it makes you softer. He said there are only two ways to come into this world, Caesarian or vaginal birth. There's myriad ways to go out."

For her residency, she was medical director at the Cleveland Free Clinic. Joy's early years in medicine were at Mount Sinai Hospital. She said it was a wonderful experience. She zeroed in on a career in family practice, and provided medical care to people in low-income families. Later, she was affiliated with a number of area hospitals. Her experiences were not as fulfilling as she would have hoped.

"We live in a horrible, horrible system. It's vicious, cruel. No one gives a damn about anybody. They don't care. I'm talking about the patient, but I'm also talking about the social workers and psychologists. I'm talking about all the myriad counselors and people in a position to be able to help people get going."

Joy said the system helped her become a doctor, but now the system is broken.

"I was able to go to school because of welfare. If I hadn't been on welfare, I couldn't have gone to college. Welfare considered me going to college, a job. I got food stamps. I got my rent paid. I got utilities. I got health care and I got day care. Clinton came in, not Reagan, and destroyed welfare as we knew it."

Joy says the programs allowed her to make something of her self.

"Women can't go to college on welfare any more. They can get a temporary job at McDonald's. They can get trained to work at McDonald's, or they can be a nursing assistant, which pays eight dollars an hour. Women are absolutely saddled by poverty and it's just getting worse. It's a nightmare. It's a disaster."

Joy now has a medical practice at West 55th and Franklin. She is part of the Lutheran Hospital system. She commutes from her home in Cleveland Heights on her bicycle almost every day. She travels down Cedar Hill and across town on Carnegie.

"Euclid Avenue has that nice bike lane now, but I don't like to take it because there's no pressure. I kind of lolly-gag when I go down Euclid. When I go on Carnegie, you gotta move. It's only scary half the time because the herd passes me by, and then I have a nice clear, clean shot until the herd comes up on me again. There's about three herds that go by me on the way to work."

The ride back home provides the biggest challenge. At the end of a long work day, Joy has to pedal up Cedar Hill.

"You get used to it. It's only hard when you don't do something, right? Once you start doin' it, it's not hard. You know that, right? If I don't do it, when am I going to work out? Then I have to figure out a way to get a workout in, and if I get home late, I'm tired, I don't want to do it."

Joy didn't finish medical school until she was forty. She raised four daughters. She chose to provide medical care to the underprivileged. People who needed help the most. Yet few people had ever heard of Joy Marshall or her achievements. That all changed one night in Cleveland Heights in 2000. Joy had a particularly rough day at work. She had just told a teenaged girl that she had a serious medical problem. That night she had to unwind. She slipped into her roller blades, took care of some errands, and then was blading down Cedar Road toward Nighttown.

"I open the door to Nighttown, and I hear someone say 'hey you.' I had my earphones in. It was a cop I had just passed.

I'm like, huh? I said why are you screaming at me?

I told you to stop.

No you didn't.

Yes I did.

What's your name?

Doctor Marshall. I usually never say doctor. Never, but to this guy, I'm saying doctor.

I didn't ask you what you did

Well, I'm doctor to you."

Another police officer is called to scene. They conferred for twenty minutes trying to figure out what charge should be leveled against Joy.

They finally came up with a 1941 ordinance, no roller skates or scooter in the street.

"It ended up on the front page of the paper. What the heck is that all about. The hate mail. Letters to the editor. 'Who the heck does she think she is? She's a doctor. Why didn't she have a helmet on. She deserves what she got.' I got to hang by myself. There was no support from anyone."

She went to court. Joy was found guilty. She says she had to pay fines and court costs of 500 dollars. She says Cleveland Heights police started driving by her house all the time. She says the police once cited her for not having her dog tied tightly enough to a parking meter. The roller blade incident changed her.

"It definitely cut me back. I have been intimidated. Chief (Marty) Lenz won that one. In a way, he intimidated me. I don't want to get arrested again. No one supports you. No one gives a damn."

Some people may have moved from Cleveland Heights after that episode, but not Joy Marshall.

"I love it here."

Joy has remained committed to the high school she attended. All four of her daughters graduated from Cleveland Heights. The school's enrollment was predominantly African American.

"A great education. They all got a great education."

In regards to many white parents moving out of the district, or sending their children to private schools.

"It's called racism. Everyone is afraid. What do they say about crime? Do you want to keep crime down? Walk the streets. You want to keep your school good? Keep your kids going to the school. We have got to be a part of the process."

Joy has been a big supporter of the schools and she has stood by the teachers in the district.

"I walked the picket lines for the teachers, because I am putting my kids in the school basically eight hours, and I shouldn't think they should get more money? I can never understand how you can pay a teacher too much money. That is something that has always escaped me."

So what type of foundation did Joy's daughters get at Cleveland Heights High. Lor graduated from the University of Michigan and the

University of Chicago. Clementine graduated from St. John's and the University of Albuquerque. Calin is in medical school at St. Martinus in the Carribean. Liza graduated from the University of Michigan. Not a bad track record.

"They had fabulous teachers at Heights. Some parents are denying the fact they are uncomfortable with their kid going to a school that is predominantly black."

Joy said there was only one painful incident for one or her daughters at Heights.

"One of my daughter's very best friend joined a gang, and didn't want to associate with her any more. She had her heart broken. Her best friend abandoned her. She blew her off. They were friends since they were three. You lose your best friend and it was a blow, and it was about race. She decided you are white, and I don't like you any more."

Joy's younger sister Gay was in my class at Heights. I knew Gay better than I knew Joy. Yet when my mother died, Joy still took the time to write that letter to me. Joy explained to me I made an impression on her through the years. Memories endure.

"Without memories, we lose the best stories. There is no life. The saddest thing you can do is lose your memory, because that's what keeps you alive. Stories keep you alive."

And Dr. Joy Marshall is quite a story.

Howie Chizek, class of '65

"She said my voice rang in the ears of children playing in their driveways for a decade."

The writer for *The Plain Dealer* spoke of the legendary voice of Howie Chizek. Most people would not recognize him as he walked down the street, but his voice is unmistakable. He sat behind the microphone at Cleveland Cavaliers games and his trademark was the refrain, "Craig Ehloooooo, for Thareeeee."

"When children were taking that last-second shot in their driveways, they were using my voice."

The Chizek family has a deep connection to sports at Cleveland Heights High. On Washington Boulevard, not far from the box office at the football stadium, there is a plaque honoring Howie's uncle Dave Chizek.

"In 1928 my uncle was considered the best high school quarterback in Cleveland. He was rated tops in the first fifty years of the twentieth century."

Eighty years later, Howie is revealing for the first time, how his uncle wound up playing at Cleveland Heights.

"If my dad went to Glenville, how did my uncle go to Heights High? My uncle went to Heights High illegally. He lived in a boardinghouse on Lee Road. My uncle told my grandfather that he was not going to go to Glenville, he was going to go to the new school up on the Heights. I would imagine he paid for the boardinghouse himself. I can't imagine my grandfather giving him a nickel."

Howie doesn't think his football-hero uncle divorced himself from his family down the hill.

"I assume he used to go home on the weekends. He was the first person not to pay tuition at Heights High, and we are not paying it back now."

Howie says Dave Chizek was only fourteen or fifteen years old when he struck out on his own to further his football career.

"The lady who owned the boardinghouse contacted us in the mid-'50s. She said she was in love in with him, and had all of these clippings in boxes. We came to her house in 1956 or 1957. She was very ill and gave us all the clippings, and said she loved him as a son."

No doubt some of those clippings dealt with Dave's football career at Ohio State. Sadly, tragedy would limit the number of articles about Dave's college years.

"He was second-string quarterback in 1930, he had just come in, hit five passes in a row against Michigan. They called it blood poisoning back then. They didn't have penicillin. He later made a recovery, but fell ill that spring and died."

It started out as a skin infection of some sort. It entered his bloodstream.

"He was a sophomore. He was getting better and then something happened. He settled back and just passed on. His weight went down to a hundred pounds at the very end. All for want of a vial of penicillin. In 1930 they didn't have it."

When he was a student at Heights, Howie remembers seeing a display with a game ball marked with the final score of a Heights-

Lakewood football game. Dave Chizek led the Tigers to a 10-7 victory.

"They said he was the best. There were huge memorials and the Heights High field was called Chizek Field for many years."

Howie was a member of the Heights High Choir. He said it was considered one of the top high school choirs in the nation. He said the experience was magical.

" I used to go to choir practice at seven in the morning. We would have breakfast at Mawby's at six-thirty Wednesday mornings. I think ham and eggs was a buck and a quarter."

Howie was probably the only member of the choir to drive to school in a Corvette. His father Joe was a used car dealer. He specialized in Corvettes. The lot on Pearl Road closed down to make way for I-480.

"You could buy a great used Corvette for about three thousand dollars. I should have bought ten of 'em and put 'em in the garage. Be better than having a 401K."

Joe Chizek sold used cars for thirty-five years. The Vietnam War era was not good for business.

"We had fifty-five to sixty Corvettes on the lot at one time, until Lyndon Johnson sent all of the customers off to Vietnam. That killed business."

Howie Chizek may have tooled around in a Corvette, but that didn't earn him a spot in any of the social clubs at Heights like BAT.

"I don't think I was cool enough, even though I had my moments."

Howie was cool enough to put together a rock band called the Runaways. He points out that he had the name the Runaways several years before an all-girl band by that name came on the scene. Howie is still proud of the fact that his band actually released a record. Appropriately enough, it was called *I'm a Runaway*.

The band played at local dances.

"We also did an opening of an Arnold Palmer Putt-Putt in Parma. He was supposed to be there, but they said he had intestinal problems and wasn't coming. We also did a live Higbee's Auditorium gig with WHK disc jockey Ron Britain and the Tulu Babies. That was my first example of lip-synching. I said, my gosh, you can make a living doing this thing. They don't know if you are making mistakes, they are just playing the record back stage. We never made it like Sonny Geraci or anything like that. We were just a local band."

That high school era?

"It was wonderful. It was right out of *Father Knows Best*."

Howie went to Ohio University and landed his own program on the campus radio station.

"Joe Tait became the announcer for Ohio University sports teams in my sophomore year. He came from Monmouth College and besides the games, he was hired to work with young people and help them shape their careers. He was there for two years before he sent out the memo that was heard 'round the world. It basically told everyone to jump off a cliff, but not in such nice terms. Joe had a tough time dealing with all the committees at OU."

Howie became the public address announcer for Cleveland Barons hockey games at the Cleveland Arena. Joe Tait helped Howie get that job. Somebody else was doing the PA work for the Cavaliers. Howie said he had trouble with the hockey gig.

"My eyelids were like flickering. I'd be driving down the street, then it dawned on me. They had chicken wire netting. They didn't have Plexiglass. They had chicken netting. It went all around. Well, when you are looking through the net, your eyes are still picking up the fact there is something in the way, and it was causing my eyelids to flicker."

Howie said he earned ten dollars a game from those American Hockey League games. He wound up doing the Cleveland Crusaders games. That was the World Hockey Association and Howie was paid fifteen dollars a game. He even got a shot to do play-by-play at a Cavs game.

"That was when the floorboards were connected by little metal pieces, and it was a warm day, and there was ice underneath for the hockey, and it made the floor slippery with condensation. Bob Neal is doing the broadcast on Warner Cable to about twenty people in Akron and he just ups and quits. They went, 'Oh my God, oh my God, who can we get to do the cable broadcast?' So I did the Cavs on TV on Warner Cable back to Akron in 1973 and I got the fabulous sum of forty-five dollars per game."

The next year the Cavs moved to the Richfield Coliseum. Howie wasn't so sure that was the best idea.

"They put a ski resort right next to it, so somebody must have known it snows there, and that bridge over the Cuyahoga River, before we had front-wheel drive, was a real exciting moment home."

In 1975, Howie was given the job as public address announcer for the Cavaliers. He would handle that assignment for twenty years.

"The players were as nice as they could be. Craig Ehlo was very pleasant. Mark Price was a nice person. A little to himself. Larry Nance has remained a friend. Larry and his wife are very generous. They help us with feeding children at Christmas time."

Howie retired from the Cavs in 1995. His workload was too much for him. He had some health issues back then. He misses the old days with the Cavs, but thinks the NBA has become too glitzy.

"The most wonderful halftime entertainment in the NBA used to be when the Boston Celtics would roll out a rack of balls and they would say it's halftime, go to the bathroom. You don't need any dancing girls. Just buy a beer and go to the bathroom."

As many people in northeastern Ohio can tell you, Howie's day job has been hosting a call-in radio talk show on WNIR in Akron. His booming voice and colorful personality fill the airwaves from ten o'clock until three o'clock on weekdays, and just for good measure, another three hours every Saturday. He has hosted the show for thirty-five years.

"I have America's longest-running radio talk show, and according to *Insider Radio* magazine, WNIR is America's number one FM talk station. A higher percentage of people in Akron, Ohio listen to radio for entertainment than any other city in the United States."

Howie is radio's marathon man.

"I've done, I believe, eighty thousand hours. I've been on radio for more hours than anyone in history. I'm too stupid to get off. Who else wants to work twenty-eight hours on the air a week? You gotta be crazy."

Howie claims to be a registered Democrat, but while listening to him on the radio, you get a clear picture that he tends to be conservative in much of his thinking.

"I invented the phrase, 'truth on the radio.' I invented the phrase, 'crime is down, it's right down the street.' And, 'it's so easy to succeed in a world full of failures.' I have 312,000 listeners a week according to Arbitron."

Howie's formative years in talk radio took place in Youngstown. He was a producer for host Dan Ryan at WBBW. Howie says he recalls there was still concern about the influence of the Mob back then.

"We learned about Youngstown politics. When to have the paperboy start your car for you. If it blew up, you could always get another paperboy."

Howie said Dan Ryan would be tough on the air, until he was convinced to back down.

"Occasionally, a deep-throated voice, anonymous, would call and say we know exactly where your car is turning, at what moment of the morning. Don't talk about so and so. And as Dan and I used to say, I just forgot all about it."

Howie maintains that he has the youngest audience in talk-radio. He says the demographics show he attracts a surprising number of young women in the 25-34 age bracket. He says he is number one in every male category.

"If you listen to the show, you'll think my listeners are older. The callers tend to be older, the listeners are not."

He says once people start listening to his program, they are hooked.

"A lady collapsed on her kitchen floor. The paramedics came in and she said, 'I'm not going anywhere until this show is over.'"

Howie has been a pitchman on radio and television for the Klaben auto dealerships in Kent. He says that income has gone to support his various charitable campaigns.

"I have an organization called New Adventures. We have spent over $400,000 of my money, taking five adults and ten children down to Walt Disney World. We do that every June. We don't stay at the Days Inn. We stay at the Hyatt Regency Grand Cypress. We don't go on the cheap."

Howie's organization selects the boys who attend from several communities. They range in age from twelve to fourteen. The spend eight days and eight nights in Florida.

"Everything is chaperoned. It's on the up and up. The kids don't have to be rich, they don't have to be poor. We take kids who need it. There's something missing in his life. We specialize in taking boys who have four sisters. They wind up in a room with another boy who has four sisters, and they bond really well."

Howie was one of the early selections for the Cleveland Heights High Hall of Fame. He points out that he was inducted well before developer Bart Wolstein was. Howie says that probably happened because he served as a football coach in the Northeast Football program.

"The Hall of Fame selection committee played Northeast Football for me when they were younger. So it was easy get in. The selection committee was made up of the offensive backfield from the team I coached."

For the last seventeen years, Howie has been on the coaching staff at St. Ann's Church in Cleveland Heights. He grew up on Silsby in University Heights and used to spend most of his time on that part of town.

"I didn't know there was this side of Cleveland Heights. I thought if it wasn't at Geraci's, it wasn't anywhere."

Howie has been known to reach into his wallet for kid's sport teams. He bought a new gym floor at St. Ann's and recently purchased a new blocking sled for the football team.

"I'm referred to as the assistant head coach. You cut yourself during the game, I'm the trainer. If you are crying, you can come to me, because I won't yell at you."

Howie is deeply involved with his Heights area community and is a supporter of many causes in his work community, Akron. He's generous and civic minded. He cares about upcoming generations. Surprisingly, he steers clear of Heights High reunions and old classmates from the sixties.

"I don't cross paths with anybody from back then. I would tend to say most of my friends are younger, and it's okay with me. They don't die as often."

As far as his successful run at WNIR.

"You have to be at the right place at the right time. It's been wonderful."

But Howie is quick to tell young people now, a career in broadcasting is not as promising as it used to be.

Gary Stromberg

"Nowadays, everyone wants to be in broadcasting, slash journalism, slash sports announcing. I've got news for you, the broadcast world is changing and I would recommend getting into sports medicine before getting into a field that is laying off lots of people."

Lew Allen, Class of '58

It was November 23, 1956. The Elvis Presley freight train was well out of the station, and was gaining speed. He was about to revolutionize American popular music. On this evening, fourteen thousand Elvis fans would pack the Cleveland Arena. Lew Allen, at age seventeen, was among the small number of men in the crowd for the Elvis concert.

One would assume reporters and photographers from *The Cleveland Press, The Cleveland Plain Dealer* and *Cleveland News* would flock to the Arena to catch a glimpse of this budding rock 'n' roll superstar. They were nowhere to be found.

"There was a newspaper strike. A press conference was called. No press. So they invited me and a reporter from *The Black and Gold,* the Heights High student newspaper. We got on a bus to go to the Arena, lugging a huge camera and two cases full of 4x5 film holders."

Lew was a junior at Heights. He was not only the photo editor for the school newspaper, but for the yearbook, the *Caldron,* as well. He had skills far more advanced than a typical high school kid. A couple of years earlier, he spent a summer working for a professional photographer. He wasn't paid in cash.

"At the end of the summer, he gave me a High Speed Graphic camera, film holders, film hangers, an enlarger, a complete darkroom. He bought himself new stuff. So I came out well ahead."

Lew worked out a deal with the company that published the *Caldron.*

"I would take all of the pictures I wanted to take, and they would supply me with film, chemicals, and paper that I required. They didn't pay me any money for doing it, but they supplied everything I needed to do it. It was no cost to me. I already owned the camera."

After that bus ride down Cedar Hill and along Euclid Avenue, Lew found himself in the Arena. The crowd was 90% teenaged girls. While they took their seats, Lew made his way backstage.

"All of the RCA/Victor executives were there. They had a couple of models hired. We posed the models for some pictures with Elvis. A bunch of people that brought their kids, important people, had their kids sit on Elvis' lap and say hello."

Lew had professional equipment. He didn't necessarily look like a seventeen-year-old. He was skilled at his craft. Lew didn't cave under the pressure of this big assignment.

"He treated me like I was a regular press photographer. He had no idea I was a high school student. He was very friendly and very nice. If I followed the rules of what I had been taught, I could easily take beautiful pictures."

At twenty-one, Elvis was just four years older than Lew. The young photographer got a good early impression of the singer.

"The things he did that night made me think well of him. He made a telephone call to a girl who was in the hospital. She had tickets for the concert and she was sick, so she couldn't come. He called her in the hospital, and talked to her before he went on for the show. It held up the show for fifteen minutes, something like that. He was that kind of guy. He was not the Elvis you would see in Las Vegas."

Lew had unprecedented access to Elvis that night.

"Whatever I wanted. Wherever I wanted. He was talking on the phone, I was there taking his picture. I got on the stage for one of the shots. I was standing on the stage in the corner and shot across the audience. I was on the stage, I was below the stage. Wherever I wanted to go. Nobody said boo. I was right up his nose. I liked him. He was fun. He was a nice guy. He was polite. He was great."

More than fifty years later, there is one visual image Lew can't seem to shake.

"A girl was at the back of the Arena. All the way at the very furthest distance from the stage. In front of the stage were three policemen. Big, fat, heavy guys with bellies on them. Elvis was above them on stage. The girl starts running down the aisle, screaming, running the whole length of the aisle, looking at Elvis the entire time. She smacked into the cops, bounced off of them, landed on her keister, still looking up at Elvis. I wasn't ready to take a picture. I could have had a classic."

Some of Elvis's fans snapped pictures with their Brownie cameras that night, but Lew Allen was the only professional photographer in the house. What were his thoughts at night's end, when he got back home?

"I didn't think much about anything. I was just tired and glad to be home, and anxious to develop the film to see whether I got anything at all."

Gary Stromberg

Lew snapped dozens of pictures that fateful night. His work was dazzling.

"One picture was used in the high school newspaper. I sold, God knows how many in the high school cafeteria at lunchtime. I set up a table and sold prints for five dollars each. Five bucks. It was a lot of money back then. They were glossies, 8x10.

"My dad loved the Elvis pictures. He never saw any commercial value in them other than the money I made selling prints in the cafeteria. At that time, there was no market for them."

Lew had captured a piece of music history that night.

"At the time, I had no full appreciation of what it was. Number one, Elvis wasn't Elvis yet. It was kind of frowned upon, the whole thing. You gotta understand Elvis Presley represented a threat to every female in existence. Mothers were hiding their daughters. It was crazy. They were afraid their daughters would come home with that kind of guy."

The Elvis pictures were a feather in his cap, but Lew says his work didn't change his social standing at Heights High much.

"Sure, everybody started asking me for copies of them, but I wasn't a real social person. I was very much into my photography. I was literally running an entire business at the age of seventeen while still going to school. It's not like I made so much money, but the sense of responsibility was great. Think about going to every football game, every basketball game, every wrestling match, every swim meet, and then to cover all of the clubs, take the pictures of club activities as well as the group pictures. Go to school and take high school newspaper pictures. It was a full plate."

Lew advanced his skills by studying photography at the Rochester Institute of Technology. In 1958, he shot a couple of rock 'n' roll concerts there.

"These weren't concerts where thousands came to see one entertainer. It was a couple of buses that loaded up with maybe six, or eight, or even ten acts and they went on a tour and made a show. I took shots of Frankie Avalon, Bobby Darin, Buddy Holly and the Crickets."

Lew didn't go around bragging on his college campus about the pictures he had snapped of Elvis a couple of years earlier at the Cleveland Arena.

"I didn't tell anybody. I was kind of embarrassed because they didn't come up to the standards of what the current rock 'n' roll photographers were taking. They were doing color, they were doing available light, in a room or on a train, things like that. They were more exciting at that time to me."

Lew was overly critical of his work. He says that mid-'50s style became outdated rapidly.

"I acquired a distaste for those pictures because they weren't technically what was en vogue at the time. When I took them they were fine, but when I went to the Rochester Institute of Technology, I learned 35 millimeter, available light, all kinds of other things to put in a picture besides a guy standing on stage. As I became more creative in my photography, I didn't appreciate my Elvis pictures because they were straight-on, flash, black backgrounds. They were really good, but I couldn't see that because I was looking at it from a standpoint of a freshman in photography at R.I.T."

Lew stayed in Rochester after finishing college. He and his brother-in-law launched a photography business. They specialized in wedding pictures. So what happened to those priceless Elvis pictures?

"The negatives sat in my basement. My nephew discovered the box of negatives and immediately wanted me to do something with them. He was excited about them. So the first thing he did was take and copyright them all."

Word got out about the pictures and Lew was contacted by a publisher in England. The photos were featured in a high-end coffee table book. A very limited edition.

"My pictures were very, very, rare. That's why they ended up going in that book. Those books were eight hundred dollars each. There were only 1,725 printed."

Lew has now hosted exhibits of his Elvis photos across Europe. In Liverpool, London, Amsterdam, and Helsinki. He hopes to exhibit them in the Far East as well.

That night at the Cleveland Arena in 1956 has become a big part of Lew Allen's life again. Back when he took those pictures, did he think Elvis was going to dominate show business like he did?

"I didn't give it much thought. I gotta really admit, I really wasn't an Elvis fan before, and after that show, I became somewhat more of one, but it was mostly because I was so involved with the pictures."

So if you pick up a copy of the 1957 *Caldron,* and see your picture with the A Cappella Choir, or with the Orchestra, keep in mind, it was probably snapped by the same fellow who hung out with Elvis back then.

Lew was impressed with the young Elvis at the beginning of his career, but not impressed by the way he ended up.

"I so disliked him for what he did to himself. Here I had these pictures of this gorgeous guy, and here's this fat slob, with all the money in the world, and not enjoying it. He's dead, and his estate made $56 million this year."

Tommy Fello, class of '70

"There's no way I should still be here. I made so many mistakes. I always tried to do the right thing. The honest thing. Have good food, but the knowledge wasn't there. I didn't know what I was doing. The neighborhood, no matter what I did, they seemed to want to support me."

Tommy's restaurant on Coventy is an institution on that colorful street. Owner Tommy Fello is humble when he talks about his success there, but he has overcome the odds in a challenging business, and he has survived one firestorm after the next.

Tommy grew up on Wilton near Somerton. He started out at St. Ann's. That's where his first business venture began.

"We would sneak down and buy candy from Mitchell's and Ace's Drug Store and bring it back and sell it on the schoolyard."

There were five children in his family. His parents couldn't afford

57

to send them to a Catholic high school, so in ninth grade, Tommy entered Roosevelt, and would go on to Heights High.

"I'm going from St. Ann's to Roosevelt. Most of my friends went on to Latin and Ignatius. I didn't have a lot of friends, so I just got a job."

Since the owner of Ace's was familiar with Tommy, they hired him to come in after school and sort-out pop bottles that were returned by customers.

Ace had taken over the location that was Merit Drug for many years.

"It had a little lunch counter with seven seats. They had those little ovens with two light bulbs, heat lamps. We warmed up sandwiches in them. We didn't have very good food, but we had great milkshakes. People would come in for the shakes, but they really didn't like the food."

When he was in tenth grade, Tommy's older brother Bob was a star receiver for the Heights High football team.

"It was really exciting for me. I was real proud of him. I'd say, 'That's my brother Bob.' I was pretty much a wallflower at Heights. I couldn't swim. Mr. Fellers, the swimming teacher, would hold this hook over me as I tried to swim a lap. He'd say, 'Come on Fello.' It wasn't that I wasn't athletic. I just didn't know how to swim."

While Tommy struggled to keep his head above water in the Heights High pool, he continued working at the drugstore. Fawze Sadie and his wife Helen took over as owners. They were Lebanese, and decided to expand the limited menu at the lunch counter. It took on a Middle Eastern flavor.

"I remember tasting my first piece of pita bread and eating the whole bag cause I loved it."

When Tommy graduated from Heights, he enrolled in the Institute of Computer Management at E. 19th and Euclid. There was no food available there for lunch, so Tommy started bringing sandwiches to class from the drugstore. He would sell them to the other students. It was the first time they had tasted things like baba and hummus.

"I just started feedin' off that real positive feedback from the students."

Customers in the store also started taking notice. Fawze and Helen decided to move back to Lebanon. Tommy was only eighteen, but he decided to buy the store. He paid Fawze six thousand dollars. That was mainly to buy the recipe for the hummus, baba and falafel. He borrowed much of the money from his mother.

"Early in the morning, I would go down to the market to buy my produce. Then I would rush to get back to the store before the kids would come in before school. They would come in at seven-thirty or eight. I would hope to get some sales for candy. Then I would stay all day at the store by myself until midnight, six days a week."

Tommy was becoming more interested in the lunch counter side of the business, yet he still had to keep the drug store end of the business going.

"When I took over, I would go to Revco and buy three of each thing I wanted, mark over their price, and I would write my price on it. It was still cheaper for me than buying from a wholesaler. The customers could see the prices had been increased, but I think they liked that kind of honesty. They sort of adopted me as the stupid little guy who runs the store on the corner."

Ace evolved into a restaurant surrounded by a makeshift convenience store.

"I would go to Seaway Foods and I would try to get deals on cat food. A lot of people in the neighborhood had cats. They would come in for the cat food and while they were there, they would have a sandwich or a milkshake."

The menu at the lunch counter was evolving. Customers would special order. They would request hummus or baba with tomatoes and alfalfa sprouts on pita bread.

"The same person would order the same thing, so I would just the name the sandwich after them. Instead of taking time to write down their order, that's how the names for the menu were created. If people wanted to get their name on the menu, they would come in and create things."

In the early days, things were still primitive at Tommy Fello's place.

"I was using a little piano-wire thing to slice the cheese to make the sandwiches. Back then, it didn't matter cause we went through a five-pound block in like six days. Now we use over six hundred pounds of cheese a week."

Tommy's parents were both Italian, but somehow they found themselves supporting their son's efforts in his Middle Eastern style restaurant.

"My mom would make the stuff at home cause we didn't have a kitchen there. She would burn the eggplant on her four-burner stove in the basement at home because you make baba by burning the eggplant and peeling the skin off. So it would smell up the whole neighborhood. We used to make a bag of falafel in my little Fry-Daddy fryer, and bring it down to the store."

In the mid-'70s, the neighborhood was starting to undergo a renaissance. A developer created Coventry Yard. New shops and restaurants sparked new interest in the area. Sadly, a failure to upgrade the electrical system led to a fire in the building. Tommy's drugstore suffered extensive damage. Customers volunteered to help him clean up the mess.

"That's when we started throwing away the shelves for the school supplies. We put a few tables in and bought some booths from a pizza place on Mayfield that was remodeling."

Tommy's rent had been just two hundred fifty dollars a month, but he lost his lease and had a decision to make. Should he find a new location? Should he specialize in food only?

"We moved down the street, and right after we opened Tommy's, the waterbed store caught on fire. It damaged the dining room we had just finished building. So we were left with just a little balcony area that had four tables. People would come in to eat when we first opened up, and let's say you came in by yourself, and there were a couple of ladies who came in, my dad who helped me seat people, he would just seat you with the two ladies."

That cozy arrangement added to the charm of this fledgling restaurant. Some people didn't like their assigned seats, but others did. Tommy says at least three couples wound up getting married after being told to share a table.

The year was 1978. The restaurant mogul was only twenty-six years old. It took him four months to repair the fire damage and open the full seating area for the first time. The opening came just in time. Tommy said he was down to his last penny.

Tommy's was gaining a reputation as a place to go for good, healthy food. You could go Middle Eastern, vegetarian, or order a hamburger if you wanted.

"Back in the early days, when the kids were the vegetarians and the parents were the meat-eaters, they could still all come in and get something to eat together, because it's really important to be a family.

"We have both kinds of blue-hairs. We have the spikey blue-haired people coming in, as well as the grandmas who have the blue hair, so we get both blue-hairs.

"We have people pullin' up in their Rolls-Royces. You have people who can push their Volkswagens up here."

Life was good for the Catholic kid who had no friends at Heights, who couldn't swim a stroke. It was too good, and like clockwork, Tommy's was due for yet another fire.

"It was November of 1988. The apartments upstairs still had knob and tube wiring. We were on three different floors in the building. I would have to cook the soup in the basement and we had a prep kitchen downstairs and the dish room was down there.

"I had a worker, his name was Dayenu. He was like a self-ordained, some sort of rabbi. A black guy, probably about five-foot-six, two hundred eighty pounds. A big, round guy. He was always like 'The Boy Who Cried Wolf.' 'Oh Tommy, this is broken, the sink doesn't work right, oh the slicer doesn't work.'

"Well this day he comes up and says, 'Tommy, I think I'm smelling smoke.' I said, Dayenu, I'm very busy. I was short a cook. I said just go down there and I'll come down and check it. He had to come up like two or three times that morning to tell me. Finally he comes up to me and goes, 'Tommy, you can fire me, but I'm not going back down to that basement.' I go down the basement and there's black smoke pouring through the wall.

"Right at that time, the guy from next door was running in asking me if I had a fire extinguisher. The fire was seeping through the masonry. They didn't have fire stops in the walls.

"Here this poor guy, Dayenu, had come up to me. At the time it wasn't funny, he was trying to tell me this the whole time. I think back on it, he was trying to save the building. We could have saved the whole building if I had just listened to him."

Once again, Tommy Fello had to pick himself up and start all over. He says his loyal customers supported him all the way.

"It's like an extended family where they really watched out for me and made sure I stayed in business. There was a couple of times I was down to my last pennies to get things done. They just supported me. I'll never forget that."

Tommy has been around forever. He looks many years younger than a man of fifty-six. He is often called the mayor of Coventry.

"It was a real honor for people to refer to me as the mayor of Coventry. There's a bunch of times I could have moved off the street. People wanted me to move somewhere else, but I didn't want to go because I felt comfortable here. Plus I felt, not that I owed it to the neighborhood, but I wanted to be here.

"When you do things from your heart, it's easy to follow your heart. If it's dollar driven, sometimes you make mistakes. My heart was comfortable here, and I felt comfortable having that interaction with the customer."

Tommy is thrilled that some of his current employees are the children of his workers from the old days. He often shares stories about the times when their parents were on the staff. Plenty of former workers have gone on to big success. *Saturday Night Live* star Molly Shannon was one of his employees.

"She was like a wallflower She never said much at all. That shows you what you can do if you put your mind to it. Who knew when she sat in the corner doing her homework, when she was supposed to be working, that she was going to go on to be this flamboyant, whole different person."

Tommy likes to think he has had a small hand in the successes of his former employees. He says that is a nice feeling to have.

Tommy's got some national exposure when Rachel Ray brought a crew in to tape a segment for the *Food Channel.*

"Someone who used to work here was sitting in a bar next to one of her producers and they said they were coming to Cleveland. They said if you are coming to Cleveland, you better go to Tommy's. They have been around for a while and have this really neat menu.

"They ate a lot of food and they were so nice. It was really a lot of fun and they still play it every once in a while on the TV now. People come in and say. 'I saw you on TV.' I say you are kidding me cause that was back in 2003. That was really a treat."

Tommy says the shops and restaurants of Coventry have played an important role in the vitality of Cleveland Heights.

"Right now you have these lifestyle centers like Legacy Village and Crocker Park. Well Coventry was the original lifestyle center. You had housing. You had everything you needed there. You had the library. Everything was right here. This street has always been a strong anchor for the city of Cleveland Heights."

Tommy's has always been a place ahead of the times.

"The oils we use, we filter all of our water, don't use MSG. We use seaweed to flavor the soups. We have an onion soup that doesn't have any meat in it."

Tommy has maintained that you have to treat customers the way you would like to be treated yourself.

"When a customer asks you where the restrooms are, you might have answered that question a thousand times, but it has to be like the first time. 'It's right down there.' You have to be pleasant. It's a reflection on the place. The workers affect our reputation in the first seconds they are working here."

Tommy never wants the menu to overwhelm anyone.

"If someone comes in and doesn't like something they ordered, they can try something else. They don't have to pay for the first thing, cause if they try something else, and like it, then they are going to come back. So try something new. Try something different. Don't be afraid if you don't like it. It's not the end of the world."

Tommy admits he can sometimes get angry when a cook or a waitress messes something up, but moments later, when a regular customer walks in and asks how things are going, Tommy switches back to his pleasant outlook.

"They don't need to hear about that stuff. They don't need to know about it. They are out to have a good time and nothing happening at the restaurant is the end of the world."

Marissa Nance, class of '87

"These women were home alone most of the day. Mom stayed home. Kids went to school. Dad went to work. They wanted a fun distraction to occupy their time while they were cooking, cleaning the house, ironing, or doing the laundry. So every day, we brought 'em a story, and at the end of the day, we didn't solve it. We just kept it going day after day. It was serialized like the *Lone Ranger* was on radio."

To hear Marissa Nance talk about the beginning of soap operas on television, you might presume she graduated from Cleveland Heights High in 1947.

"Instead of the *Lone Ranger*, or *Dick Tracy*, let's make it romantic.

Let's make it something where these homemakers really want to tune in. That's how soap operas were born. They were created by the soap companies."

Marissa is actually a 1987 graduate. She knows television. She knows advertising. As an executive with a company called OMD, her job is to be a liaison between television producers and the people who pay the freight, the advertisers.

"To do what I do, you have to be a bridge between our clients and the creative producers of the actual shows. So you have to be able to speak both of their languages. I have spent a lot of time honing my skills to speak to the needs of our clients. Understand what the advertisers are looking for, and why. I have to align those effectively with the needs of the creators and producers."

Marissa's parents, Bruce and Carol, were childhood sweethearts at Cleveland's Glenville High. Bruce found the family a home on Powell Road in Cleveland Heights. He worked for State Farm and she worked for the Regional Transit Authority.

Success is not a stranger in the Nance family. Former Cavs basketball star Larry Nance is a cousin. Mark Nance is also related. Before the days of Tiger Woods, he made a name for himself as one of the more accomplished African American golfers. Fred Nance is a cousin. He is a well-known Cleveland lawyer who was talked about as a candidate for the job of NFL commissioner. He played a major role in bringing the Cleveland Browns back to town, and is a front-man on numerous pivotal projects.

Marissa says she was fortunate enough to attend Cleveland Heights High at an exciting time.

"My experience in my generation at Heights was such a beautifully woven tapestry. There was not just one segment of the population. You saw a multitude of people from all walks of life, from all backgrounds, and everyone got along. There were no huge issues. There were no big fights. It was very Midwest, middle class and upper middle class. It was kind of a perfect storm. The previous generation was very homogeneous. I feel I got there at the right time to experience what it was like to have a wonderful blend of people. Instead of just one, or the other."

Marissa was involved in student government at Heights. She played field hockey, and devoted a lot of her time to her high school sorority.

After graduating from Howard University, she went to New York City and was hired by an advertising agency. She worked as a media buyer. She purchased advertising time for the clients she represented.

That agency and OMD are among the agencies owned by a much larger company called Omnicom. Marissa says she has really worked for one entity ever since she finished college.

"It's like my father's life. My Midwestern stability. A bi-weekly check and benefits."

Marissa says sponsors played a vital role in shaping television programming from its earliest days.

"*The Texaco Star Theater, The General Electric Theater*, the soap operas sponsored by Procter and Gamble. They were at the forefront of creating content using advertising dollars. This was more than just placing advertising on shows, they actually created shows."

Advertisers can bankroll a show, and they can also request product placement in programs. Products can be offered as prizes or they can be showcased in the program as subtle reminders to viewers.

"With Mark Burnett, we did a show called *Survivor*. We've done a show called *The Apprentice*. We integrated our client's products into the show. On *Survivor*, not only is there a popular vote by the people living on the island, but there are also challenges and different activities people have to participate in. We put some of our products in some of the challenges people had.

"Eight weeks in, I might have handed a woman a phone with cellular service, so she could call her five-year-old. If you had been away from your child for two months, and you are a mom, you get to speak to your four, or five-year-old. That's a pretty good reward."

Marissa was in on the ground floor of the reality TV explosion. She traveled to Borneo to work on that first season of *Survivor*.

"The inaugural year, Mark Burnett came into the agency and said, 'I'm gonna do this show. People are going to go on an island, and have to work hard to survive.' I said what if somebody dies, or something bad happens? He said, 'It's going to be great. It's going to be in Borneo.' He was so passionate, so enthusiastic, and so smart. CBS said come on, let's do it."

The rest is history. *Survivor* changed the landscape of TV. Reality shows were the latest craze. But Marissa points out, reality shows were part of TV way back when.

"I like to remind people where it really all started. Television was *Queen for a Day,* and *To Tell the Truth.* It really took some time to get into scripted formats because it cost more money. It was much less expensive to find something people wanted to watch with real people you didn't have to pay. So reality shows are nothing new. It's how television was founded."

Marissa doesn't think all reality shows on television should be lumped together and thought of as mindless fare.

"A lot of it is done well. A lot of it is done in ways, perhaps I wouldn't do. Everything in life goes around, so I am sure in the next few years, we are going to go from the reality craze to something that is more scripted."

Marissa says she serves as the bridge between advertisers and TV executives. She can assist in the task of actually creating specials or TV shows for advertisers, or she can direct advertisers to the existing shows that would meet their specific needs. She is there to shepherd advertisers through the entire process.

Besides Borneo, her assignments have taken her to Australia, Mexico, Puerto Rico. She shuttles between New York and Los Angeles. She says the television world is constantly changing.

"If you look at what's going on in the marketplace, NBC is giving ten o'clock to Jay Leno, which could be a really brilliant move, and really I don't know how much worse things could be for them. *American Idol* runs three nights a week on FOX. *Dancing with the Stars* runs three nights a week on ABC. You are looking at a time when lineups are polka-dotted. Programming is scarce. The programming you are getting, is the programming you are getting. You gotta like it. A whole generation is being trained to like what they get, not get what they like. In my opinion, I think as a whole, the viewing public may be getting shortchanged."

There are growing concerns about the way minorities are being served by the networks. Advertisers are eager to reach them, but have trouble finding programs on which to place their commercials.

"The NAACP is thinking of boycotting the networks next season simply because the networks haven't had any multi-cultural, particularly

African American themed programming on. They have taken all of that off. We know our advertising clients want to reach that audience. Our clients are finding it harder and harder to find content that reaches that audience. We think there is a lot more that can be done, and that will be done. We are looking to find partners we can do that with."

Marissa offers guidance that can pay off for everyone involved.

"Let's say my product is Depends, and I'm insisting, if I spend this media money to put these ads in you program, that you can do product placement. Let's say the show is *The Bachelor*. I don't think anyone on *The Bachelor* is going to want to put Depends on, or use Depends as a placement. Someone has to communicate effectively to the client what works.

"Depends is not going to work there. Maybe we could something if there is a show called the *Golden Girls*. It should be a really funny show, and one of them is an older woman. That is what you do for a client. On the flipside, you work with the creative team on the show to make sure that your client's need works for them, so they can effectively make it a success story for everyone."

Marissa says advertisers are becoming more savvy. It is more critical than ever that they spend their media dollars wisely. They have to reach their target audience.

"Advertisers are saying just because this is a program you have on your schedule, doesn't mean I need to buy it. I think it it's a very powerful thing that a show can succeed or fail based on the advertising support it got. More and more, we say we don't like what you are airing, so we have come up with this idea ourselves, and we'd like to co-produce it with you."

Marissa says over the years, she has blossomed. She has learned and sharpened her skills. Her husband Sean Montgomery says his wife's job is somewhat like herding cats.

"What he means is, cats notoriously do what they want to do, when they want to do it, how they want to do it. Dogs sit and stay. With cats, it doesn't work. So trying to herd an entire group of them is near impossible.

"Many times I am dealing with a group of people, each of them so passionate about their position, that they want to do what they want to do, the way they want to do it. That makes it a little more difficult to be that bridge, to connect those parties. But you have to, and we do."

Marissa says her mother's parents divorced. Divorce wasn't common back in those days. Her grandparents both moved on to second marriages.

"So I had three sets of grandparents. Including my parents, I had eight people shaping my life. I had a large extended family. A lot of what I know, and what I took away, came through multiple generations of people.

"My mother taught me perseverance and flexibility. My mother would always say don't move so quickly. If you run too fast, you are going to run right past the door you were looking for to get out. You'll be runnin' around and around and around, and you'll never get through.

"She taught me, if you are looking for an answer, stop and let the answer find you. Don't just go round, looking, looking, looking for it. Sometimes you won't find it. Let it find you."

Marissa maintains a hectic work schedule, but she has found time to be an advocate for groups pushing for a cure for autism. She is committed to promoting the humane treatment of animals. She has served on the board of directors for the Harlem YMCA, the Apollo Theater and the Gay & Lesbian Alliance Against Defamation.

Marissa Nance remains confident and self-assured. She believes if she finds a good balance in life, everything will work out just fine. She tries not to worry if the economic conditions will have an impact on her work.

"All I can do is be me. Stay in my lane. Work hard at continuing to make as many people happy with what I do, as I can. Please the people who have influence on my ability to put a roof over my head."

Hal Becker, class of '72

"In my entire life, let's say I have trained forty thousand people a year, I've never in my life had a salesman say, 'Yea it's me. It's not my product. It's not my competition. It's not my price. It's not my boss. It's not my territory. It's me!' They are always going to blame someone else. Of course it's them."

Hal Becker crisscrosses the country teaching salesman how to sell. He admits it's always an uphill battle.

"You'll never see a sales book reviewed in any newspaper. Sales people don't buy books. They are too lazy and stupid. They don't want to better themselves. They'd rather play golf or take part in their hobbies. The term professional salesperson is an oxymoron."

Hal Becker has completed his fifth book about the world of selling. His first book, *Can I Have 5 Minutes of Your Time?*, sold 200,000 copies.

"Companies buy books for salespeople. If you are in sales, you won't go to a course or a seminar on your own. Only two to three percent will. The rest won't. A great doctor or a great pilot will always go in for more training. Even a pro golfer will continue to train. Outside the United States, people really want to learn. In the United States, it's like, 'Yea, we know it all.'"

Hal Becker makes 170 sales presentations a year. He is on the road constantly. He says the pace is brutal.

"To me, the best speakers on the planet are comedians and preachers. They don't use PowerPoint. It's all about substance. For me, the sales information has not changed in one hundred years. The most published book in sales was *How to Win Friends and Influence People*. It was written by Dale Carnegie in 1936. So, once you get the substance down, and it really becomes part of you, then the rest is timing. It's like a golf swing. Once you get the golf swing down, the rest is perfecting it.

"My perfection is timing. Energy. When to pause. When to put the humor in. The audience wants three things. Number one, is to learn things they forgot. To be entertained and hear jokes. And they want to walk out feeling good. You gotta hit 'em between the eyes. If after an hour or two speech, they are feeling differently, I did a great job."

Tim Russert was one of one Hal's fraternity brothers at John Carroll University. Tim spearheaded the move to bring Bruce Springsteen to campus for a concert. It was early in Springsteen's career.

"We paid $2,250 for him. Tickets were $2.50. My job was to set up the stage, get the lights, do all the stuff to make sure the concert went off. Instead of going into the audience, I stood behind a speaker for three and a half hours mesmerized.

"I realized what made Bruce Springsteen the greatest rock superstar of his generation. His voice sucks. His music is good, his lyrics are good. But his energy and his performance made him a legend.

"I decided that if every seminar I did was going to be my last one, how would I give it? If there was one person or two thousand, just be genuine. Give it the best shot you can. Your goal is to have them talk about you, remember you, and if they do that, you have done great. It's hard work. At the beginning of your career, you are starving. You've got to stick to your goals and your beliefs."

Hal says Tim Russert was one of the most intense people he ever met. But intense in a positive way. He says he was always true to himself. The "flash" in life was not important to him. When he learned of Tim's death, Hal was reminded that you take one day at a time. You never know what tomorrow will hold.

"Don't save a sweater for the day you will never wear it."

Hal Becker certainly knows life can be full of setbacks. In the early '50s, his mother was taking a drug called DES. It was supposed to prevent miscarriages and morning sickness. Hal believes it was the reason he eventually developed testicular cancer. He was only twenty-eight years old.

"By the time I was diagnosed, it had spread to my abdomen and my chest. It was stage three. I was down to eighty-three pounds. I took pictures of myself when I was that sick to remind me that you can't ruin my day. What are you going to do to piss me off.

"My treatment was experimental. They did a couple of surgeries, then intense chemotherapy. It was the most toxic kind of chemotherapy. I would become violently ill, so they kept me sedated most of the time. I never saw my father cry in my entire life until then. I am an only child and my poor parents are watching me die."

Hal had just launched a new business three weeks before his diagnosis. He had put all of his savings into the venture. He was completely wiped out financially.

"Every day I wake up, I realize I've got one more day. My poor mother, until she died, she felt guilty for giving the cancer to me. I don't think it was her fault. By taking that drug, she thought she was doing the right thing."

Joe and Eudice Becker lived in half of a duplex, a few steps away from the University Heights police station. Hal had fond memories of growing up there.

"University Heights was a level playing field. Nobody was super rich. Nobody was super poor. It was really a cool, stable place to grow up. Your parents went to Scott's Five and Dime, and they left you in the car with the engine running when they went in. They would be put in jail for doing that now."

Hal says his father had a successful run as a bookie, but when the penalties for taking bets were increased, Joe Becker decided to try his hand at something else. He started Oxford Motor Sales at E.81st and Euclid. His used-car lot was in the middle of a string of auto dealers, but Hal says his dad was different than the others.

"They used to call him Honest Joe. People would come back and they would say, 'I don't like this car.' He would say, 'Do you want a new car? Do you want a better car? Do you want your money back?' Believe it or not, that was from a used-car guy. People would always tell him he was honest."

Shortly after Hal was born, his father suffered a heart attack. It wasn't until Hal was in third or fourth grade that his mother told him that his dad once had a heart attack. It haunted Hal. It made him worry about his dad.

"I remember standing at the front of the house, looking out the big window onto Warrensville Center. It was a December night. It was dark outside. I was waiting for my father to not come home. I was afraid of him dying."

Honest Joe would be at the car lot six days a week. He was away twelve to fourteen hours a day. He died shortly after Hal's battle with cancer. Hal learned a lot from his dad.

"My father taught me street smarts. Values. Honesty. Integrity. Don't ever be greedy. He taught me common sense, to balance yourself and your life. Don't work too hard. Don't party too hard. Work, work, work. Study, study, study. Hang out with good people and use prophylactics."

Eudice Becker smoked cigarettes until she was diagnosed with emphysema. She quit, but it was too late. She was sixty-three when she died.

"My mother was a sweet woman. I'm not saying this because she was my mom, but if you talk to anyone who was friends with me, they all remember her as being the most empathetic person they ever met. I was really lucky. I really had good parents. There was no dysfunction. I had a great childhood growing up.

"If I could see my parents. I'd just say thank you. I'd just want five minutes to say thanks for all the guidance and morals you gave me."

Can Hal's presentation get salespeople motivated? Can they improve their salesmanship by spending a couple of hours listening to him?

"What makes a surgeon better? What makes a pilot better? Flying more, going to seminars and practicing. What makes Tiger Woods better? Practicing. If I am better than my competitors, it's because I'm really into what I do. I'm obsessed with every book I can read on sales. I read everything I can find to make myself better. I think my presentation skills are more fun than other trainers. I'm a little bit off the wall. A little left of center."

Hal thinks many people are one way with their friends, and another way around their business associates. He says he always remains the same person. He doesn't think you have to pretend to be someone else when you are at work. Is he a better trainer than when he started out?

"I'm better than I was three weeks ago. I go through my materials and I realize I have forgotten about this or that. I am constantly gaining more information. What I have forgotten could probably be a whole seminar.

"It's just going back to what you do best. Staying focused. There are people who really take pride in their work. Whatever you do, if you are good at it, it's impressive. It's great to see someone who is a master at what they do."

Hal Becker shares simple lessons with people who will listen.

"If you don't like what you are doing, you should quit. I don't want to go to a doctor and say, 'Doc, my left side, my back hurts. My left leg is driving me nuts.' And the doctor says, 'I hate the left side. I hate the sciatic nerve. It's so boring.' Well I hear that, and I'm going to another doctor. You have to like what you are doing.

"You have to make a number of sales calls consistently every day. Make sure you are seeing the right decision-maker, not some secretary or office manager. And you have to ask questions. Find out what they are looking for, not what you want to sell them."

Hal not only leads sales seminars, but he writes a weekly column syndicated in fifty-six newspapers across the country. Writing books is also a passion that keeps him busy. So was it clear during his days at Cleveland Heights High that Hal would evolve into a nationally-known sales guru?

"I was a total screw-up at Heights. I had a 1.8 grade point. I asked myself what I was going to do with my life and I didn't know. If you know what you are going to do with your life while your in your twenties, you either have a rich father, or you got lucky."

When Hal graduated from John Carroll, he couldn't find a job.

"I kept getting rejected. A guy who lived across the hall, his name was Art Shibley. He was a salesman for Xerox and he said, 'Why don't you come and work for Xerox?' I went to their training facility. It was so intense and so well thought-out, I go, wow! I was money motivated and I did whatever I had to in order to make money."

Hal says he got on the fast track at Xerox. His second year there, he was the number one salesman in the nation. At the time, Xerox had 11,000 salespeople.

"I became a student of my profession. I decided I wanted to be an instructor and write books. I started teaching adult education courses in University Heights for twenty-five bucks or fifty bucks. I worked my way up."

The idea that a salesman first has to sell himself to customers is nothing new. Hal knows it's fundamentally important.

"Customers have to know what I say, they can take it to the bank. They know they can count on me and know everything I said, will come true. That's the mark of a great salesperson. Personality is secondary. Just don't be a jerk. You don't have to be high energy. High energy can sometimes work against you. You can be low-key and still effective.

"Sometimes I'd tell a customer they don't need a new copier. If they wanted one, that's different, but I would tell them if they needed one or not. My job was to find out what they are doing, what they like, what they don't like. Provide them quality products at a competitive price."

Hal regrets he waited until he was forty-four to settle down and get married, but career-wise he thinks he has been right on track.

"I didn't get greedy. I made a great living. I could retire and enjoy my life."

Hal does his best to wipe negatives from his life. He looks for life's silver linings.

"The economy will improve. I can't tell you when, but it will. Great employees will always be employed. If you are great in sales, any company will take you. Not average, not below average, but great.

"Now you just have to work harder. Now you have to stay in touch with your customers more. You gotta make two more sales calls a day. Whatever it takes."

Bob Malkin, class of '80

"I met my wife when the Cleveland Heights High Orchestra went on tour to Toronto. She was the principal violinist. She was one of the best players in the orchestra. I was one of the worst players, in the worst section of the orchestra, all the way in the back."

Bob Malkin and Alexandra Gruber have been making beautiful music together for nearly three decades now. A versatile talent, she went on to be an opera singer for fifteen years. After dabbling in music at the University of Michigan, Bob turned his attention to electrical engineering. His decision has helped to make the world a better place.

Bob looks back fondly on those orchestra days. He gives credit to the teachers in the music program at Heights.

"They were much better than we deserved at a high school. There were a fair number of kids who were the children of members of the Cleveland Orchestra. They were really good players. You look at high school programs in some communities today. Some high schools barely have a music program at all, some have none."

Bob's prowess on the French horn did not land him a spot in the orchestra hall of fame. His skills as an electrical engineer, turned out to be world class. Early on, he was hired to design pacemakers and defibrillators for a company in Florida.

He then took a job in Switzerland designing defibrillators for European companies. He also designed the electrical circuits for numerous watchmakers in Europe.

But even in his twenties, with tremendous success already achieved, Bob Malkin knew he wanted more out of life.

"After seven years as a engineer, I decided working for a living really sucks, so I decided to move away to Thailand and teach English as a second language. There were villages in the jungle. Eight hundred people. They had huts made of sticks and some corrugated steel.

"They were selling their daughters into what amounted to sexual slavery in the sex industry in Thailand. We were trying to train them to do something else."

The villagers were taught to make shirts, rugs and throw-blankets on a loom. Products to sell to the tourists in northern Thailand.

"My job was to teach them English. Some of these things had English words on them. If they made more money for their products they could go to markets for themselves, and communicate with the tourists directly. They needed some amount of English to be able to do that.

"As it turns out, I don't really know English that well. I never realized how little English I knew until I had to teach someone English. I didn't know when you say which and when you say that. I was not a particularly good teacher."

Bob says the Thai woman who ran the program was surprised a guy like him applied for it. She wondered why an engineer would want to do something like that. She was eager to take a chance on a guy like Bob.

In 1989, Bob left Thailand to latch on to an opportunity at Duke University. He was now twenty-seven years old and he was wanted to do research on how defibrillators could be made smaller and lighter. If they were more compact, they could be placed in police cars, in airports and on airplanes.

Bob's task would be refining the particular way of delivering the energy used in those devices. He knew this would be a great opportunity to do interesting research. He left Thailand, but he never forgot the poverty and the daily struggles the villagers faced just to stay alive.

Bob eventually moved on to teach at the State College of New York, the University of Memphis, and in 2004, he made it back to Duke.

Through all of those stops, Bob always knew engineers could make a difference in the world. The deep poverty he encountered in Thailand remained a motivating force in his life. He was surprised to find there were no organizations matching up medical engineers with medical needs in developing countries. His colleague, Mohammad Kiani at the University of Memphis would often dwell on the need to fill this gap.

"We had students who really wanted to get involved. We knew our students had enough talent to make a difference. Had knowledge and skills. It was very frustrating."

Bob and Mohammad first approached professional engineering societies to get things going. They tried that for several years and got nowhere. They just couldn't get the leaders of the societies to make a commitment. In 1999, they decided they were going to have to do everything on their own.

They got guidance from Dr. Bill Novick. He was a pediatric cardio-thoracic surgeon and director of the International Children's Heart Foundation. Novick had been assembling teams of ten to fifteen medical professionals. They would travel to a country like Nicaragua, and perform heart operations on children. Invariably, once they arrived, a key piece of medical equipment would break. The members of the team would just sit there helplessly for two weeks, unable to perform the needed surgeries.

In 2000, Bob and Mohammad formed an organization called Engineering World Health. Volunteers would go to developing countries and make repairs to medical equipment. They would do routine maintenance on other devices.

"We soon realized the problem was much, much larger. There was all of this broken equipment, and places were still very desperate for help."

Many of the engineering grads who travel to foreign lands with EWH are women. Some go for one trip. Others have made as many as five trips. In 2009, sixty-five trips are scheduled to places like Kenya, Nicaragua, Honduras, Guatemala, Tanzania, Liberia, and Sierra Leone.

The volunteers will devote their time and talents to repairing X-ray machines, ultrasound machines, incubators, and blood pressure machines. They will also go into medical labs and repair things like microscopes.

"We work on everything you have ever seen in a hospital and some things you have never seen. From the most sophisticated pieces to really, the most basic, including thermometers."

Bob Malkin says the volunteers who sign up to help, are stunned at what they encounter in these impoverished lands. It's an eye-opening experience.

"They really have no idea what the depth of poverty is like. Basic things, like almost none of our hospitals have electricity 24/7. In the United States, if you have ever been in an operating room, you will notice they are closed. No windows at all to the outside. That is to prevent dust and also contamination.

"In the developing world, every operating room has a big window in it, because that is the only way you can get light during the operation in the daytime, when the electricity is off.

"They do not provide food or medicine or equipment. So if a person needs an IV, the family is expected to buy the IV at a pharmacy, or some local store, bring the IV to the nurse. The nurse will install it. Most of the engineers say it's a life-changing experience. It's absolutely shocking to them."

Engineering World Health is on a roll. The number of participating volunteers has doubled every year, as has the number of pieces of medical equipment put back into service. More than two thousand pieces of equipment have been restored. Those pieces are worth more than five million dollars. EWH has become the largest provider of working medical equipment in the world.

Several hundred volunteers have taken part, yet Bob Malkin says the hospitals are still desperate and need extensive help. EWH is adding more hospitals to its roster and is even trying to assist smaller clinics that are in need of help now.

Bob is bolstered by all of the success of Engineering World Health, yet the organization has to contend with an ongoing problem. It relies on hospitals to donate its older medical equipment for facilities in developing countries. Yet the quality of the equipment leaves a lot to be desired.

"The majority of the work we do is fixing equipment that other people have donated. More than eighty percent of the donations don't work. So we spend most of our time fixing other people's donations. Year after year, you see another container-load of equipment delivered that is just not working. It's very frustrating and disappointing."

The hospital that donates equipment usually get some sort of tax write-off. Bob Malkin hopes they don't look at their program as some sort of dumping ground.

"It's actually quite expensive to throw away medical equipment. In many cases, hospitals find it cheaper to give away medical equipment than to throw it away."

But Bob says if a hospital donates one hundred pieces of equipment and thirty pieces work, that's thirty the organization didn't have before. Things have gotten a little better. The hope is to eventually repair most of the remaining pieces.

Bob Malkin wants his students from Duke and the other EWH volunteers to understand they can make a real difference in the world. They can do it using their skills as an engineer. He says the program is an educator's dream. He often hears students tell him it was a life-changing experience.

"We make five-year commitments to the hospitals. And at the end of five years, we hope they graduate and can take care of their own medical equipment. They don't need us coming all the time. We have hospitals graduate, and it's incredibly satisfying. A children's hospital in Managua, Nicaragua, they maintain their own equipment now and do a pretty good job. Things can get better."

Bob Malkin has come a long way from the orchestra at Cleveland Heights High. His decision to abandon music was a wise one. He became a scientist, but not one who just buries his head in scientific journals and pays little attention to the woes of the underprivileged.

He has not only helped the needy, but he has encouraged others to get involved as well. Our health system in the United States may not be perfect, but compared to what Bob Malkin has seen, it is pretty impressive.

"You are so much more thankful for everything we have here. My wife just went through gallbladder surgery. I told her this would be so much more challenging to get this done in the developing world. Most of the people I see in the developing world who have gallbladder problems, said they didn't have it removed because it is so dangerous.

"My daughter had a problem at birth. She would be dead, if we lived in the developing world. I'm totally certain. But here, it was a relatively minor procedure. We are more than thankful for what we have."

Sherry Conant Tanno, class of '67

"I went too far, and I lost my way. I ended up with this Indian chief. He wanted to marry me, because I was this skinny, little, flat-chested person. He didn't know what the hell I was, a boy or a girl. He thought he had something no other chief has."

Sherry Conant Tanno was in her early twenties. An attempt at marriage to a high school sweetheart had failed miserably. She was running away from everything, and wound up in Guatemala with her friend Sharon.

"I wanted to get away from my husband. I didn't care where. I went far to the other end of the world. To me, that wasn't far enough. We lived with the Mayan Indians for three months. I ended up loving the simplicity of everything they did."

But that one day, Sherry split off from her friend and wandered into the jungle. That's where she encountered the chief.

"I couldn't speak his language, and he was making these gestures, and I was running as fast as I could, but I was running further from wherever I was supposed to go."

Sherry and her pursuer eventually reached a clearing where she approached other Mayan Indians.

"I told these people, this guy was chasing me, tell him to leave me alone. Thank God someone there could understand me, and said, 'That Indian chief wants to buy you.'

"No, get away from me. You tell that Indian chief, I am not for sale. I was scared out of my wits."

Fear had not been part of Sherry's life until that point.

"I wasn't afraid when I grew up in the '70s, and hitchhiked across the country three times. Never once afraid then. But this scared the hell out of me. I didn't know if he had a gun or a knife. You didn't know."

Sherry got a new perspective on life by staying with the Indians.

"Everything is so different the way the Indians lived. It's a beautiful life. The family is their whole life. Everything they eat, they make or grow. Nothing is showy. It's a different life, so I was confused by our life. But I never want to go back. It's such a poor country. I'll always appreciate the experience, but once is enough."

Sherry remembers sitting by a lake in Guatemala. It was near the end of her stay.

"I just looked up and asked how did I get here. It was like a revelation, like, hey you can go through anything, but you have to believe in your heart, that really, you don't have anyone in your life, but yourself. Anything else is a plus. Any friends you have. A wife or husband. A child you have, is a plus. I learned you can do anything you want. No one is stopping you."

There was one aspect of Sherry's visit to Guatemala that turned out to be positive. In fact, it helped shape the rest of her life.

"When I was living with the Mayans, I baked with them, and I learned how they bake from scratch. I'm talking soybean scratch, corn. I got so into working with the natives and the kids, and that got me so interested in going further with it. Not just baking and selling, but teaching it."

Sherry returned to Cleveland. She first had to deal with some health issues.

"I was sick. I was down to eighty-six pounds. Eighty-seven on a good day. I couldn't get my ex-husband out of my mind. I couldn't get the life I had, out of my mind. I was going through so much with my husband. Was it me? What did I do? I just thought if I can't be whatever he wanted me to be the best at, I can be the skinniest that I can be.

"Anorexia is a mental disorder, not a physical disorder. I got that skinny for me, so I could be the best at something. Obviously, I failed in some way. So I could still be the best skinny girl. I was a size two, and even if my clothes were zipped, I could slip out of them. I thought it was me. I didn't believe in myself."

After Sherry settled in Cleveland Heights again, she started putting things back together. She got a job as a secretary with a physical therapist. Her health improved. After her divorce was final, she met Rick Tanno and married him.

Now she was ready to develop that seed of an idea that started growing in Guatemala. She developed a persona called Betty Buns. She would organize classes for young people. Teach them about food and how to bake. She set up shop at Hathaway-Brown school for girls. It was an after-school class.

"When I first started at Hathaway-Brown, they shipped in boys from University School. That was chaos. The boys loved it, but they threw knives. That was it. No more University School kids."

Betty Buns also started a business at the Heinen's store at Lander Circle in Pepper Pike. She would have baking classes there for boys and girls. She also has been putting on birthday parties there.

"Every child makes a little cake. I give them paper chef hats and they decorate their own paper chef hat. Then I bring out a Heinen's quarter sheet cake and they decorate the whole border. Then they write their name in chocolate. I give them snacks, like carrots and dip, pretzels, popcorn, and grapes. Once the little cakes come out of the oven, they decorate the cakes they make. During the party, the parents are in the store shopping."

Betty Buns is always thinking. She has an idea to hold similar birthday parties at Heinen's for grownups.

"There aren't any, anywhere. If you don't have it at your house, where are you going to go and have a blast and decorate your own birthday cake? The store has a wine license. So the people could buy some wine and bring it in to the party."

Working with kids has been Betty Buns bread and butter. She doesn't think kids are exposed to baking in their own kitchens like they should be.

"Parents don't take this kind of time with their kids because it's messy. They don't want to. It's a hassle. It's a hassle to get out the pots and pans and watch 'em. They want to push 'em out of the way and put 'em in a class where someone else is doing the work. They don't want to do it.

"Kids are constantly scheduled. They have the ballet. They have the swimming. Then they have the Betty Buns, and then they have something else. The parents don't want to be put upon. There's a lack of having fun with their kids."

Sherry realizes there are a lot of moms who work, and are pressed for time. Her dream is to have a Betty Buns show on television.

"The kids could stand in front of the TV, and I could do what the parents should be doing. All they have to do is turn the oven on and make sure the kids are safe. The kids can have Betty Buns time. Hey, the Betty Buns Show. Let's bake with her. Even if the moms are working, they would know their kids will at least get it from me."

Betty Buns has made a good number of appearances on local TV programs. She has dropped letters to Oprah and Ellen DeGeneres.

"Hey. Hello. Here I am. I want somebody to believe I can do this."

Sherry says her Betty Buns character has developed into somewhat of a celebrity in kid circles.

"Kids make me feel like a movie star. I give autographs to kids. I've been doing this so long, I love it. Kids love it. They love to bake. They love to cook. They love to get dirty. They love to be allowed to do what they want to do."

Being Betty Buns is no piece of cake. Sherry has to constantly worry if enough children will be signed up for her classes or birthday parties.

"Sometimes I think I would like to have just one job that I can go to, do it, and come home. Being Betty Buns, I'm responsible for everything. The thought of it, the set up, the clean up. The works. It would be really hard to walk away after all these years. With the world the way it is, can people afford this? Will I have an income? I am not secure in what I do, and it's getting on my nerves. But I'm so Betty Buns. I'm more Betty Buns than Sherry."

Sherry's parents divorced in 1960. She doesn't recall hearing about any other marriages in her neighborhood that fell apart. Divorce was uncommon back then. Sherry was eleven years old.

"I only recall my father sleeping on the couch. From that point on, I knew something was up."

Sherry's sister Robin was only five years old at the time. Sherry remembers the day when she and her sister got in the car with their dad. There was a decorative Easter egg in the car.

"Don't touch that! That's for another little girl."

Those words from Sherry's father shattered her little sister. That egg was to be a gift for the daughter of the woman her father would eventually marry.

"I don't know what was wrong with me, but I was always happy. I don't know why I didn't take it on like my sisters did."

Sherry's older sister Carol was a little more than a year older than her. Their mother Elayne, worked in a factory to help make ends meet. Her mother married Dave Conant. Sherry looks upon him as her father. He was like an angel. Sherry's birth father just walked out on his family.

"That bastard gave us up. But I won. I got my Daddy Dave. He was the best thing in the whole wide world. As far as my birth father, I don't have a memory of him. Not a memory of him taking me anywhere. No memory of him going to my school, anything."

Sherry says she regularly travels to the Cleveland Clinic and holds baking classes for children there. Some are in-patients there. Others come in for occupational therapy. Some of the children are missing limbs. Others are burn victims. Some are autistic.

"Working with them is fantastic. It's something I can give back. When they are in my class, they are kids again. Like you and I were. Without ailments. When they are cooking and baking, they can go back to being kids again. For some, I take their arms or take their hand and help them mix. They forget they don't have an arm or a leg. A lot of the kids have gone through brain surgeries.

"I love these kids. I can see a transformation. Most have a real burden. There was one who was in therapy after being severely burned while horsing around with some buddies. He has to be thinking, 'I was normal and now, I'm not. I never will be again.'

"When you first walk into the class and see what these children are dealing with, your heart jumps out immediately. But you have to forget about that and bring to them something they can do to make them feel like they are a kid again, if only for that one hour."

Michael Krasny, class of '62

"I also thought, as I spoke with (Ted) Koppel, of my old pipe dream of filling in for him on "Nightline." But I had changed, ambition tempered by time. I didn't daydream about that kind of perch now - any more now than I did of writing the great American novel that would do to the largely Jewish suburbs of Cleveland what Thomas Wolfe's Look Homeward Angel did for Asheville, North Carolina, or Roth's Goodbye, Columbus did for Newark and East Orange, New Jersey. I knew now, at last, that that was not what my life had been about. I realized, too, that honors and recognition lose even their fleeting pleasures as years pile on, and both have felt embarrassing and ill-deserved to me: like the bickbats and nastiness any public figure also gets, all of it comes and goes, often as mysteriously as rain."

Michael Krasny's powerful words in his book *Off Mike, A Memoir of Talk Radio and Literary Life.* Many of us would be thrown off a bit during a chance meeting with Ted Koppel in a San Francisco restaurant. But for Michael Krasny, Ted Koppel was just another famous person. He is probably the only Heights High graduate to have come face to face with just about all of the leading novelists, poets, playwrights and journalists of our time. He has interviewed Joyce Carol Oates, E.L. Doctorow, Amy Tan, David Mamet, Gay Talese, Joan Didion, Michael Chabon, Maya Angelou, Edward Albee, Tony Kushner, Salman Rushdie, Philip Roth and Michael Crichton.

Michael is an English professor at San Francisco State University. He took on a part-time job hosting a talk show at a small radio station in Marin County. That led to a late-night talk show at KGO radio in San Francisco. Some listeners thought Michael brought an intellectual sensibility to the medium. He was perhaps better suited for the NPR set, and that is indeed where he has wound up. He is on the air at KQED in San Francisco from nine to eleven every morning.

"Larry King brags he never reads the book of a writer or an author. I do it because I am somewhat anal retentive, but I also do it because it's much more respectful. People come in and they seem kind of shocked, sometimes in awe that I have actually read their book. If I am going to talk to one of these major writers I admire, I want to know their work and I want to know it as thoroughly as I can. I think people like to listen to a more informed, more literate conversation."

The fact that a kid who grew up on Beachwood Avenue in Cleveland Heights would wind up in the intellectual fast lane would come as a shock to many of his teachers.

"A sixth-grade teacher, a British guy, used to drag me into the boy's room at Boulevard and beat the hell out of me. It was something I was silent about for many years, but I was a bad kid. I was searching for an identity. I was this bad boy, but also wanting to be a good kid, I wanted to be academic. I wanted to succeed, be popular and all of those kinds of things, so I really didn't know who I was.

"I was a handful. I was kind of a sloppy kid. My shoelaces were untied, and sometimes my shirt wasn't tucked into my pants. I don't know how my mom let me go out like that, but she did. That teacher would put me up on a chair in front of the class and dress me. That was humiliating."

Humiliation was already a part of Michael's vocabulary. He was nine years old when he went to Camp Wise. At night, he would wet his bed.

"The other kids discovered I wet my bed, and that's all young boys need to know to become relentless. So it was pretty awful. A lot of those things had an impact on me. I needed to work things through in an aggressive way. By the time I got to Heights High, I was running with wild guys, thought I could do whatever I want, and get into trouble."

His father's name was Hyman, but his friends called him Zaz. His mother's name was Betty. Michael's upbringing was basic. He would agree that he, like many of the other Roosevelt kids, he grew up with a bit of Wiley envy. The kids in University Heights lived in newer homes, brick homes. Their dads drove fancier cars. The Wiley kids dressed a little better and their school was modern, not weather-worn like Roosevelt.

"Especially when you got into the nicer areas. I used to look at the houses on Milton and Churchill as mansions. It seems funny now. There was definitely a sense of people in University Heights being, when I was growing up, much better-off."

Zaz Krasny always claimed he was denied admission to the medical school at Ohio State because, back then, they kept an eye on the number of Jews who were accepted. His undergraduate degree was impressive enough. He majored in bacteriology. His relatives owned the Eagle Dairy Ice Cream company. After finishing college, Michael's dad wound up working there. Perhaps he meant to stay for just a while. He would stay there all of his working years. Tinkering with the machines, making sure the production line ran like clockwork. Like many dads of that era, Zaz Krasny disappeared into that job. His three children would rarely see him. Long hours. Sometimes six or seven days a week.

"My dad was a man who wanted nothing more in life than to be a doctor. He was thwarted in his ambitions by quotas, by circumstance, by economics, by all kinds of things. He worked like a dog in this factory, despite the fact he was an educated man. A man of real wisdom, of real sensibility. Nevertheless, he didn't have the pride in himself. We were the poor relatives. He wasn't a man who had a career or a profession. He was a blue-collar worker. From the time I was a kid, he said, 'Be a white-collar worker, be a professional.'

"My parents were good, decent people and loving people, and yet didn't have a sense within their hearts that they are people that are truly worthwhile people. My parents, they certainly didn't despise themselves, but they certainly didn't see themselves as successful, as making worthy contributions, because they didn't make money. They were great people and gave a great deal to their children in terms of love and a legacy of ethics."

Michael Krasny settled in San Francisco in 1970. He calculates that he has now spent twice as long in that city as he did in Ohio, but he has never diminished the importance of his roots.

"Nothing has had as much influence on me. First of all, because these were the formative years. Your character and destiny are shaped. I learned a lot about life on Beachwood Avenue, Cedar-Center and hanging around Heights High. I was living in a world where I was a young Jewish guy, kind of mobile and realized I could, even though I wasn't a *mensch,* I could act like one, get approval from girl's parents, be invited into their homes. I could get girls from finer backgrounds interested in me."

Over the years, Michael developed a friendship with filmmaker Barry Levinson. Levinson's childhood reflections were featured in his movie *Diner.*

"Barry Levinson would ask me, 'Were you interested in anything in high school besides girls?' Not much. Then I began to discover I had a mind, and having a mind was somewhat a way of impressing girls. Reciting poetry and things like that.

"Lily Tomlin once said the '50s was a generation of foreplay. We weren't liberated by The Pill, or by promiscuous and free sexuality. Drugs weren't into full swing. It was a particular place and time unto its own, that we won't see the likes of again."

As an interviewer probing into the minds of the greatest writers of our times, has Michael Krasny found generally happy, contented artists?

"I know some of the more tortured ones, and some of the more brilliant and successful ones. Maybe I couldn't be the novelist I wanted to be, because although I was neurotic enough, and was driven enough, I wasn't tortured enough in the ways I needed to be tortured.

"Someone like Barbara Kingsolver comes to mind, because she seems to be relatively centered with herself. I think that is by and large true of some women writers. Isabel Allende is a dear friend of mine. She's wacky, full of frenetic energy, but she's pretty happy and she gives a lot, and that's the difference. Kingsolver, her and Amy Tan they haven't let the fame go to their heads and they do a lot."

Michael touched on the concept of happiness in his book *Off Mike*. His friend nicknamed Swat, had joined Michael and his wife for dinner.

"I ask myself the question all the time - Are you happy? - and it is a question that begs THE question, and THE question is can we ever really be...happy? Even now I say, "I want my wife and kids to be happy," or I tell them, "I'm happy if you're happy," and I mean it. But my more doleful, philosophical alter ego scoffs at the idea of happiness, thinks it is somehow ontologically at odds with the human condition, with suffering, with privation and morality. Can one be happy when the world, as Wordsworth said, is too much with us? Instead of happiness, I think of how life could always be worse. I told Swat that one of our more popular classmates lost his daughter to suicide. Now there was a real tragedy, a life of heartache. "It can always be worse" isn't necessarily a bad way to think when things get upset, smashed or go to hell, as they often do, in spite of our certainty that we are happy, or believe in the moment that we are, as I did over wine and pasta, with my wife and my old friend Swat."

"A lot of people who are driven, whether its toward fame or toward art, or toward creativity are driven by devils that are angels. People who knew me at Heights, knew there were a lot of devils driving me in those days. I think what I was able to do was harness them, or at least find an outlet for them."

Michael is thought of in the Bay Area as man who allows people to understand difficult intellectual topics. He brings intelligence to the masses. He is well-liked and recognizable, but has he found happiness?

"It depends on what day you ask me, and what's going on in my life. On some levels, I don't know if I believe in happiness. Isabel Allende said America is the only country guaranteeing you life, liberty as well as the pursuit of happiness. Pursuing happiness is one thing. Achieving it, and especially on some kind of level, really living it to the fullest extent, can be very difficult especially for certain souls.

"You know I have my moments, when I try to favor joy, and I have moments when I try to, when I'm with my family back in Cleveland, with my niece and nephews, my sister and niece's kids, when I'm with my own children, when I am experiencing something esthetic, sometimes when I'm on the air, or in front of a classroom, doing things that I know I do well, I can feel moments of joy and moments of real pleasure, a peek at that sort of feeling."

Many students at Heights High sought happiness by joining a social club. Those clubs were often affiliated with religious organizations like AZA, or BBG.

"There was a kind of social hierarchy depending on what club you were in. There were good AZAs and then there were these AZAs that were kind of off the radar. Nobody knew who they were. We wanted to start a club named after Cleveland Browns place kicker Lou Groza. Lou the Toe. We thought he was Jewish. Then we found out, to our dismay, he was Hungarian Catholic. It was a little of a disillusionment.

"You felt like you belonged to something. It was not quite like being in a gang. Some of the older guys who started our club were athletes and animals. One went to jail for selling drugs. Some members liked to fight. I liked to fight. Then there was a second tier of clubs. Guys were more *mensch*-like. Not as wild. They liked girls a lot. Liked cars, teenager things. Those guys weren't as popular as the club I belonged to. They weren't as reckless and wild. As I got into my junior year, I found myself drawn more to that group."

Michael also began to focus more on academics and his love of literature at that time. He knew Cleveland Heights offered great educational opportunities, but felt that some of the students had an inferiority complex.

"We were not from Beachwood, Shaker, or Pepper Pike. We were kids from Cleveland Heights, and we were, many of us, socially mobile. We wanted to move up in the world. We wanted to make a mark for ourselves. A lot of us with Jewish backgrounds particularly. We wanted to find someway to success."

Michael's radio program on KQED is called *Forum*. He hopes to advance his crusade for intelligence, culture, and literature every time he steps in front of his microphone. Most of the time, it all comes together.

"Sometimes it feels like I'm just doing a job. Putting something up in the air every day. Some days, it really feels like I am flying. I'm soaring. This is the way it should be. Everything is fluid and everything is lively and animated. I have to think on my feet. I'm really stimulated, my guest is stimulated, engaged. It's exciting. It's everything it ought to be. Sometimes it just drags. You gotta put life into it. Come in at a different angle. Try to be innovative."

Michael admits that his radio persona can be a somewhat souped-up version of his off-air persona.

"When I'm on the air, I'm more engaged. I'm surprised at how much more lasered my thinking is, because I'm performing, or I'm in that zone, or whatever it is. I tend to be a lot sharper than when I'm off the air."

How would Michael Krasny describe his interviewing style?

"There's a guy like Charlie Rose, who often puts himself right in the center of the interview. He becomes a part or a co-equal of the guest, giving his own opinion and all that. Then there's Jim Lehrer who dares to be dull, and puts himself out of it. He thinks all the focus should be on the person you are talking to. I think I am somewhat in between those two."

There are severe time restrictions on interviews on most TV and radio programs. Michael often devotes a full hour to his interview subjects. The guests feel this is a real luxury. He can go in-depth. Good radio, he says can be a theater of the mind.

"I like to be so well-prepared that I have something to offer. People often tell me I know more than my guests do. I take pride in that."

Michael isn't afraid to interview a physicist who has won the Nobel Prize. Even though the scholar's knowledge of science far surpasses his, he can approach that person from a lay level and carry on a conversation.

"The fact I can do it, strikes me as a real asset. I always come in with much curiosity, hoping to engage the guest in terms of controversy, in terms of disseminating information, illuminating things and that it doesn't matter what the topic is. It can be something political, something psychological, science, the arts. It's fun and it's a challenge for me."

In reading Michael Krasny's book, it is plain to see just about everyone in his Heights High days was given a nickname. Michael says that was just what went on back then, and he admits he is the one who handed out most of those nicknames. Nearly half a century after some of those nicknames were earned, they still endure.

"My friend Pissy grew up to be an MD. My mother would always ask me why I am still calling him that. I said what do you want me to call him? Dr. Pissy?"

Michael grew up not far from Heights Pharmacy at Lee and Euclid Heights. As a child, the store was the center of his universe.

"I still have dreams about it. You could buy so many things there. It was kind of an emporium. It was my first notion of conception. I would ask my mother where babies come from, and she would say, your father plants a seed, and then we prayed to God. So you would go to Heights Pharmacy and they would have seeds for sale there for amateur gardeners, and I'd say, Oh. These are baby seeds."

Michael says he had his first encounter with Santa Claus at Heights Pharmacy. He sat on Santa's lap and asked him if he was real, and if he should believe in him. Santa assured him that he was real.

Not as real as Michael's neighborhood.

"It was a real mix of humanity. A lot of human tragedy. It was like a human carnival. It was a neighborhood with a certain kind of coherence to it. The neighborhood had incredible characters."

His mother Betty never liked to see young boys throwing punches at one and other in the neighborhood. When she walked back from the butcher shop and spotted boys slugging each other, she would always intervene.

"One time, she started grabbing at the boys, and saying, 'You boys shouldn't be fighting,' and she says 'Michael, it's you.'

"I've never forgotten where I've come from. I know that's trite and a cliché, but I never have, and I never will while I'm breathing. My neighborhood had incredible characters. As I got older, I knew I wanted to prove something to those I grew up with in Cleveland Heights. That it mattered a whole lot to impress upon them that I had succeeded and made something of myself. It was a real engine behind a lot of the successes I've had.

"I thought my great unrequited love, Cheryl Sandler would realize she made a mistake by not falling in love with me. As you get older, you accept your limitations. You get a little longer in the tooth. You get a little taste of fame in northern California. You realize you want to not be addicted by it. You want to not be made to feel there's an emptiness inside that has to be filled with fame."

What does fame matter as we take in our final breaths? In his book *Off Mike*, Michael Krasny shares a story of a dying man's last request.

"A father is dying, with his daughter at his deathbed holding his hand. They both know the final curtain is about to come down. He tells her he smells kugel coming from the kitchen and he says he would like a last taste before he dies. She says, "Of course, Daddy," and jumps up and heads to the kitchen, but she is gone for quite a spell. By the time she returns, he is gasping his last breath. "Where's the kugel?" he manages to eke out as his death rattle begins. His daughter: "Mom says it's for after."

Fred Weisman, class of '44

Fred Weisman never met his grandfather. Jacob Weisman had died at age thirty-six in Boston. He was father of seven young children. Jacob's passing had an dramatic impact on the life of his oldest child, Max Weisman.

"My father Max said to his mother, 'I've got to help you some way. I'm going to quit school.' He grabbed a corner in Boston and started selling newspapers. He was in fifth grade. He was as tough as nails. He could handle himself."

That young boy hawking papers at the corner of Boylston Street and Massachusetts Avenue soon earned the nickname Lefty, and he befriended baseball legend Tris Speaker. Speaker was centerfielder for the Boston Red Sox.

"He said to my dad, 'If I become manager of another club, maybe

I'll take you as my trainer.' My father didn't know beans about doing that."

Sure enough, Tris Speaker was named manager of the Cleveland Indians. He lived up to his promise. He brought Lefty Weisman to Cleveland. Lefty was twenty-six years old.

"He went to night school at Cleveland College. He bought a bunch of books. He didn't know what the books meant. He bought a dictionary. He said he used the dictionary more than the books. He worked with physicians and surgeons at University Hospitals. He became known as one of the best, if not the best, trainers in organized baseball."

Lefty and his bride Sally Miller settled on Kensington Road in Cleveland Heights. Several years later, they moved into a house on Meadowbrook Boulevard. Lefty was not only popular with the Indians players, but got to know many of the players from opposing teams. Sally was always ready for the unexpected.

"I don't know how my mother did it. She was so amazing. The place was like an open house. She had a great personality. People were always welcomed. My dad would call her up at two o'clock and say, 'Sal, can I bring a few of the New York Giants over for dinner?'"

The Giants were in town for an exhibition game with the Indians.

"She said, 'Oh no problem.' Two or three hours later, she would have chopped liver, and brisket. It was never a problem."

It was 1933 when the Giants popped over. Fred was six years old. Seventy-five years later, Fred proudly shows his priceless autograph book. It features the signatures of Hall of Famers Mel Ott and Carl Hubbell. They were among Lefty and Sally's dinner guests that night.

It was 1936 when Fred would gain a place in Indians lore forever. The team was embarking on a twelve-game road trip to Boston, New York and Philadelphia. Lefty brought his son with him to experience life on the road.

"I was the batboy for that trip. I was the good luck charm for the Cleveland Indians. I wore Hal Trosky's uniform. My dad had to take a uniform and cut off the sleeves so I could wear it. I would go out before the games with Mr. Averill, Earl Averill, and shag flies. I was a pretty good ballplayer.

"Lloyd Brown, the left-handed pitcher for the Indians, would fungo balls to me. Averill would say, 'Move to the right, or move to the left.' Nobody else was on the field. They would have twenty or thirty thousand people in the stands, and I'm catchin' fly balls.

"We'd come in and Averill would say, 'Give 'em the cap.' So I would doff my cap and everyone was applauding. I thought I was Bob Feller. I'd do that while they were dragging the infield, cleaning it. The fans thought that was cute. Here's a midget catchin' fly balls out there."

It was no coincidence this nine-year-old boy was comparing himself to Bob Feller. Feller actually joined the Indians for the first time on that road trip. He was only seventeen. He had just completed his junior year of high school in Van Meter, Iowa.

"He pitched seven games for his high school that spring. Five of those victories that spring were no-hitters."

During that Eastern road trip, Fred and Bob became pals.

"I went out with Feller every morning at nine. The rest of the players got there at eleven. We would work out, throw and run."

Fred was indeed a good luck charm for the Indians on that road trip. They won ten of the twelve games. When they arrived back in town, Bob Feller lived with his family on Meadowbrook for a couple of weeks.

"It was great. To me it was no big deal. I had a lot of fun. I brought guys over. They got autographs. One night, we had seven or eight people around the dinner table. My mother served applesauce in a crock. She put it down and Bob ate the whole thing. We didn't want to embarrass him, so nobody asked for applesauce. He thought it was all for him.

"The ballplayers were sensational. There were very few creeps. They were wonderful guys. Joe Vosmik. The owner of the Indians, Alva Bradley actually came up with the name for my younger brother Jed. He said he should be named after the Million Dollar Outfield. J for Joe Vosmik, E for Earl Averill, D for Dick Porter."

Tris Speaker was a major influence on Fred.

"He was my Uncle Tris. I called him my uncle. He was a wonderful personality. Fabulous, fabulous guy. Absolutely delightful. Outstanding, outstanding guy."

Lefty Weisman traveled with the team on all road trips. When the team was home, he put in long hours. Fred wasn't able to spend a lot of time with him.

"He was rough. He was tough. Tough on me."

Milt Galatzer played for the Indians in the '30s. He was Jewish. It wasn't often that Lefty Weisman was around other Jews in the Tribe locker room. Many major league players at the time were from the South and were not open-minded.

"Probably the biggest anti-Semite on the team was Ben Chapman, the great leftfielder. He was a racist and a Jew-hater. He was no good. Some of the anti-Semitism was probably kept mute. My dad got very little of it. He was rough enough. I didn't think anyone was going to make a move on him, but there were isolated incidents."

Fred 's father Lefty was forced to grow up overnight when his father died because of that heart attack in Boston. Fred's mother Sally had her share of hardship as well. Her father had abandoned the family when Sally was thirteen years old. He took off for California and left three children behind.

"My mother never once complained about that, or said anything bad about her father, ever. She was the essence of appreciation. One of the definitions of happiness is, a hearty appreciation for one's lot. She was appreciative of everything."

Lefty Weisman's life came to an early end.

"He died in my arms of a heart attack at age fifty-four. We were in the house on Meadowbrook. It was about three o'clock in the morning."

Those who knew Fred Weisman at Cleveland Heights High might not have guessed that he would become a highly respected personal injury lawyer. He didn't seem that driven back then.

"Heights was a great social scene. My major, as far as I was concerned, was dancing and girls. I was a very average scholar. It bored the life out of me. Everything was memorization. I didn't cotton to that too well. I got into Western Reserve on academic probation. I knew if I didn't make C's, I'd be thrown out. I had grown up a lot when I was in the Navy. At Reserve, I was always on the Dean's List."

To make ends meet while he was in college, Fred "hustled" dry cleaning on campus. He would go to the fraternities, sororities and dormitories to pick up dry cleaning. His enterprise was quite lucrative. He pulled in as much as one hundred dollars a week back then.

When he finished law school at Western Reserve, Fred had a decision to make. Should he sign on with one of those huge law firms.

"I was interviewed by big shots. Fancy guys. They bugged me. I knew I wanted to represent the little guy. I knew right away. It was instinctive. I couldn't stand that snotty, big shot attitude."

Fred went to work for another lawyer and was earning one hundred fifty dollars a month.

He left for a bigger firm and then in 1963 launched his own law firm. He welcomed the opportunity to go before a jury and try a case.

"You could have a great office lawyer, who got diarrhea every time he has to walk into a courtroom. That represents 90% of the lawyers. That don't want to screw around with that kind of stuff. They don't have the gift, the constitution, the appetite, or whatever you want to call it."

Fred Weisman is convinced a law degree is the most valuable piece of paper you can have.

"I encourage every kid I ever talk to, to go to law school. Get law training, because the study of law is so beautiful. You are hittin' philosophy, morality, what is right, what is wrong. Who is the good guy? Who screwed screwed who? You have dealings with language. It's beautiful. You have phenomenal writing.

"Whatever you want to do, you can do it with law training and do it better. You get a leg up. They overrate the hell out of us. If you have ten people up there, and one of them is a law grad, chances are, the employer will say, 'Oh, that's great. He's a lawyer. Let's take him.' They won't take the other guy with a master's degree. They will give the nod to a lawyer. You should go to law school. If only to give yourself, a hell of an opportunity you are probably not entitled to."

Fred's skill as a lawyer led to one of his clients winning a $10.1 million judgment in a medical malpractice case. It was the largest such award ever in the state of Ohio. His advice to anyone who wants to be a trial lawyer.

"Talk straight to people. Try to avoid lawyer talk. Fancy words. Nobody is interested in that. If you start doing that, you're a loser. You're dead. You can't talk to 'em in those terms. You are already a loser.

"The first thing, they can't understand you, so what are they going to listen to? Something they don't understand?"

Has Fred been able to impress juries?

"I got through to them pretty well. By and large, I was straightforward with them. I have a natural empathy for people. A feeling about what is wrong and what is right. Most of the time, if you are that kind of person, you are going to get along with people. You are going to have a lot in common with a lot of people. They know what you are talking about.

"I like to concentrate on the truth of my case. You can't have all of the truths. The other side has something going too. But you know how to do it. You handle your truths and be able to look anybody straight in the eye. Talk to 'em and talk about that which is true. If there are too many things that are weak, you shouldn't have the case in the first place.

"Theatrics and personality play a role. But phony theatrics play a significant part. It will blow your case sky high. What they are looking for is sincerity. They want the truth. They want to do the right thing."

Fred Weisman has tangled with insurance companies for more than fifty years. He says some people mistakenly believe insurance companies are there to help their customers.

"The whole idea of an insurance company is to make money. What's the bottom line? When you are in that kind of situation, where money is your guideline, it doesn't matter how much you screw anybody, or what you hold back. Don't tell 'em your company is built on a significant manner on fraud."

Fred says he gets a lot of satisfaction from serving the public.

"They are dealing in situations they couldn't possibly handle in any way for themselves. So you have an opportunity to do something for somebody. That is the pleasure of representing the victim of injury, or the family of a victim of death. You are doing a job for somebody."

Fred has earned a place in the highly respected International Academy of Trial Lawyers. He has come a long way from the days of shagging pop flies on the outfield grass. He has the gift. He has the confidence.

"If you have to be looking around, and your eyes show that you are really not believing it, you're dead. The juries pick that up."

Ken Ehrlich, class of '60

"Justin Timberlake's manager was nearby and as soon as I heard about Rihanna not coming, at the time, they said she had been in a car accident, I went to this guy whom I have known for a long time, and I said I think I am going to be in trouble, and I may need some help. Let's start thinking about what we can do."

Ken Ehrlich is Executive Producer of the Grammy Awards on CBS. On February 8, 2009 he was hoping he wasn't going to be tossed a curveball like this, but he had to be ready just in case.

"Justin was already on the show, cause he was doing a number with T.I., so it wasn't a big leap. And we went to Justin and figured we wanted to do "Let's Stay Together," if Al Green would do it with him. Then I called Al Green's manager and we got Al Green in. Then we got Keith Urban, and it just kind of came together. It all happened within the space of two, two and a half hours. We left the stage after the rehearsal less than two hours before it was actually on the air. It was the second number in the show, so it was on the air just a few minutes after eight."

Chris Brown would turn himself into police. Rihanna says she had been assaulted. Because of her injuries and her trauma, she lost her high-profile slot on television's top musical showcase.

"One of the things built in, is they are live shows, and things happen. Maybe the closest thing to this was when Pavarotti got sick and didn't perform. It was in 1997 and then Aretha filled in for him, but that happened when we were already on the air. I didn't even know he wasn't coming until we were on the air. I guess if you can get through that one, you can get through this one. You kind of think back to those things and you figure you have to do something."

Ken Ehrlich is too much of a pro to press down firmly on the panic button in situations like those. This was his twenty-ninth year presenting the Grammys.

"It's always fun. Sometimes a little trickier than others, but always fun."

Ken is perfect for his role because he loves music, all kinds of music. Most people in their mid-sixties would be out of touch with the new sounds out there, but Ken stays plugged in.

"I like it. I still find it fascinating. I still find so much of it good. I had a great time this year with all four of the hip hop segments we did. I love "Swagger." I think it's a great track. I loved "Dead and Gone," the Justin Timberlake, T.I. song. I loved "American Boy." I think it's a terrific song that was performed by Estelle and Kanye.

"I like a lot of it. There are all kinds of music. There are all levels of it. As long as I can keep listening to things that are of interest to me, it's easy for me to stay with it. I don't ever feel lost.

"The only time I really felt lost at any time in my career may have been a couple of years when punk rock first came in. It was pretty jarring to my ear. I had grown up with classic rock. There was melody and it was guitar-driven, but it was guitar-driven with soaring guitar solos, and here was something that was just not. It took me a little while to hook into the Clash. It took me a little while to hook into the Sex

Pistols. It took a little while to find something in there that I actually found good, that I understood, but that's the last time I listened to music that I felt was alien.

"Even when hip hop came along, there were still antecedents that came from another place that I found familiar and interesting to my ears."

Ken grew up a short distance from Cleveland Heights High. He was two blocks away on Washington Boulevard. Art and Lucille were his parents. Art owned a business called Ohio Wiping Cloths.

"I learned a sense of humanity from him. There was a sweetness about him. My dad was an incredibly warm person. He was just the greatest guy in the world. My brother and I just grew up with really good values. We got a compassion for other people. An understanding there were people who didn't have as much as we did. We had an appreciation for what we had.

"My parents taught me to be honest. It was very important in our family. There were times when I wasn't, and I found out that honesty is the best policy. They were kind of strict. My mother was tough on us, both on my brother and me."

One of the lies Ken was able to get away with, had to do with his nightlife. Art and Lucille Ehrlich may have presumed he was headed to a Heights High basketball game, or joining some buddies at Mawby's for a burger that was buried under a pile of grilled onions. He was instead heading over to a place called Gleason's Musical Showbar.

"It was on Woodland somewhere. We could go down there and we would be the only white people there, and it wasn't a problem. Everything was great. I remember seeing Ray Charles there. I remember seeing Chuck Berry and Bo Diddley when they played the club.

"I do ask people like Smokey Robinson, I ask people like B.B. King, who I know played it, if they remembered it.

"There was a place called the Baby Grand which was at E.55th and I think Carnegie. It was a tiny little club and it was mostly piano players. I saw Ray Charles there. I was fifteen or sixteen. My parents never knew about that. It was as close as a white person could get to the black culture. Those places weren't upscale. The people weren't dressed to the nines. They were workingman's places. It was wonderful. There's no place like it anymore, no place like it."

Ken says a lot of the musicians from those days have fond memories of playing at Leo's Casino in Cleveland back in the '60s.

"I was pretty much gone from Cleveland at the time of Leo's Casino."

So how did he even hear about these inner city nightclubs with those wonderful entertainers?

"There were some summers I worked at my father's business. It was an industrial wiping business. We handled cleaning supplies for car washes. I wound up filling forty pound boxes, twenty-five pound boxes and fifteen pound boxes full of rags. You worked with people and got a pay envelope at the end of the week. I'll never forget that. On Friday's we would get these envelopes and maybe there was forty dollars in the envelope.

"There were all African Americans who worked with me, and that's where I learned to understand and respect their culture. That's were I got my love of black music. We would stand there working with Cliff and Richard. They would play WJMO all day. We would hear B.B. King and Big Maybelle. I was introduced to incredible music. Cliff and Richard would tell us about the places where we could hear their music."

Cliff and Richard had no clue back in those days that the boss's son, the guy they were packing rags with, would go on to work with all of the greats in the music world. Ken had listened to what Cliff and Richard said and had become a disciple of their music.

When Ken wasn't working at his dad's business, he covered Heights High sports teams for the school newspaper and also wrote sports for the *Sun Press*.

"I wanted to be a reporter for a while. I worked at WHK. I worked at the radio station. Nobody in the country had ever done high school sports on the radio before, believe it or not, or if somebody did it, nobody knew about it. I went down to WHK when I was a junior. I went into the boss. I set up a meeting with him. This was in the beginning of top 40 radio. It had just come to Cleveland. This was the first top 40 radio station. I went to this guy and I said you need me to be reporting the high school scores, the football scores Friday nights. I want to set up a network. I'll come in. I don't know what you want to pay me. I will come in on Friday nights. People can call in the scores.

"It had never been done in the country before WHK did it first, and then it spread all over the country. I never got a nickel for the idea. I got paid a dollar and a half an hour for doing it and all the records I could steal from the record library."

So this high school kid hustled his way onto the radio. He and his buddies hustled their way into the black nightclubs. Those high school years were great, right?

"I didn't have a very good high school experience. I had some friends I value. I wasn't totally unhappy. I wasn't really thrilled with it. I was not a very popular kid. I think there were a lot of kids that were not very nice to me. I couldn't wait to get out. I always wanted to get out of there. I wanted to get on with my life. There was a time in my life when I was bitter about my adolescence.

"The flip side of that is when I went to college, when I went to Ohio University. Some people would say, it was because I changed, opposed to them changing. It was probably a combination, but over the years people told me I changed.

"High school kids are a lot more cruel. At college, you reach a different level. I said to myself I am not going to be the Ken Ehrlich I was in high school. I started getting active, and I ran for this committee and that committee. I was president of my senior class and I ran for junior prom king and I finished second. I turned the corner. I had the opportunity to do that. Some of the people in high school who were really pretty mean to me, I am able to look back with a little more perspective on what high school life was like, because my life changed after that."

After graduating from Ohio University, Ken and his wife Harriet moved to Chicago. He got a job working in public relations. One of the clients was a radio station there. His connection with radio personality Marty Faye changed the course of his life.

"I wouldn't be doing this if it were not for him. I was doing PR for the station where Marty worked. I was over at the station one day. I had never done television. I had only worked at that radio station in Cleveland when I was in high school. He basically sat me down. He kind of liked me. I was pretty green. This was 1967 or 1968, so I was a few years out of college.

"He looked me in the eye and said, 'Look, I used to be on television in the '50s in Chicago. I am thinking about going back on television and would you be interested in producing my TV show?'

"I didn't know what that meant. I had no idea what he was talking about, but I knew enough to say yes. And I figured it out from there. That was it. None of this would have happened if I hadn't started producing this show. None of it. Absolutely none of it. I would have probably continued doing PR. I wouldn't have been very happy cause I don't think I was very good at it. I was a pretty good writer, but the rest of it kind of eluded me.

"I had a PR firm and I hated it so much. I couldn't wait until I started doing this. I can't thank him enough. He saw something in me I didn't even see in myself."

The Marty Faye Show was broadcast from a small studio in a downtown office tower. The station was a fairly obscure UHF outlet. But Marty Faye had outstanding show biz connections. Top name entertainers performing at Chicago nightclubs, would drop in and make an appearance. Tony Bennett and George Carlin were frequent guests.

"The most continuous through-line in all of this is Tony Bennett. Every time he would come to Chicago, he would do Marty's show, so I got to know him. Later on, Tony went through a period where there wasn't much going on for him. I don't think much happened for him in the '70s. Maybe I had him on another show or two, and probably not too much until the middle or late '80s. Then all of a sudden he had this resurgence. And every time I would see him, the first thing he would say to me, even to this day, 'Marty would be so proud of you.' The last time I saw Tony was a year ago at the Grammy show and he put his arm around me and said that.

"To have that continuity, that's really special. He never forgot Marty. There's a version of the song "Chicago," and Tony changed the lyrics to say 'The kind of town that Marty Faye could not shut down.' To this day, when I see Tony, that connects all of those thoughts for me."

Ken always maintained his passion for pop music. His next step up the television food chain would be a major leap. He launched a music program on WTTW, the PBS station in Chicago. At first, the show was titled *Made in Chicago*. It featured musical acts performing in concert. As the show developed, its name was changed to *Soundstage* and it was distributed across the nation.

Soundstage showcased concerts by Bob Dylan, Tom Waits, the Bee Gees, Muddy Waters, Al Green, Aretha Franklin and Harry Chapin.

"That show was pretty critical because that's when I really learned how to deal with talent. It was the first time I got to meet people who would come in and out of my life for years. People like Bonnie Raitt, People like Randy Newman. People like Barry Manilow.

"I met Dr. John. Dr. John has been one of the influential people in my life because he introduced me to New Orleans music, which I heard when I was growing up, but I didn't place it. We did a show called "Dr. John's New Orleans Swamp." It had the Meters and Earl King. That's when I met Professor Longhair. That became critical in my development. If you watch the Grammys over the years, the recent Lil Wayne performance for example, grew out of an understanding of New Orleans music. For the last part of his presentation, we had living legend Allen Toussaint and we had the Dirty Dozen Brass Band.

"In public television in those days, you had no budget. We had no money. I would go to the airport and pick these people up. I just got to know them. I think the budget for each *Soundstage* show was $30,000.

"Bob Dylan was on. One of the shows that got the show noticed was "The World of John Hammond." John Hammond was this legendary record producer for Columbia Records. He worked with everybody from Bessie Smith, Billie Holiday, to Benny Goodman, to George Benson, to Bob Dylan. He discovered all of these people including Bruce Springsteen. We did a show that honored him. A whole bunch of people came back and Dylan did that show. That's where I met Bob. We worked together several times after that. He's interesting."

The program developed a strong national following, but after three seasons, Ken thought it was time to move to Los Angeles and get into the mainstream of the television world.

He developed a reputation for producing entertainment specials featuring the big names in music. His credits include producing shows for Faith Hill, Celine Dion, Elton John, Ricky Martin, Shania Twain, Christina Aguilera and the Spice Girls. Toss in producing the Primetime Emmy Awards and you can see he keeps his plate full.

111

With decades of putting on the Grammy Awards, Ken has perfected the technique of pairing-up artists to present once-in-a-lifetime collaborations that have become the trademark of the show.

"In my mind, they all work. You don't have a problem putting Beyonce' and Tina Turner together, and knowing it's going to work. Or Beyonce' and Prince. The classic thing I did a few years ago, Springsteen, David Grohl, Steven Van Zandt, Elvis Costello. You are not going to miss there.

"The trickier ones are the Foo Fighters and Chick Corea. I loved it and thought it was wonderful. A lot of people thought it was great. We don't do them purely for effect. We do them because I try to and find some musical connections between the artists. I think they have certainly become a signature part of our show. I think it's one of the reasons people can tell a difference between the Grammys and other music shows."

Ken says artists clamor to be on the Grammy Awards. Perhaps in the early days it was a little more difficult to convince them to perform with other musicians.

"Now artists will say, 'Hey I've got a good idea, how about I do something with this person or that person?' So it's very open. In any given year when we start the show with a blank piece of paper, it's really not hard to look and see people who could be collaborative together.

"I have abandoned things in the past because I may have thought they would be good ideas in the beginning, and then they really didn't feel right. But for the most part, I think they are great fun to do. I think they are fresh for an audience to see.

"I can't tell you what it was like walking into the Jonas Brothers set-up before Stevie got there. And then when Stevie walked in, to look at those kids and see the adulation, and the love, and the respect they had for him, and then being brought into that family.

"They were so receptive and so open with him. I loved to watch that and I think it was the same thing watching Beyonce' when we did Prince and Beyonce' together. I mean here was the master. I mean she never thought she would ever wind up doing a duet with Prince. It's great fun and it really creates new music."

If Ken Ehrlich was star-struck he wouldn't be able to get his work done. Working with the top names in show business is for Ken, just another day at the office. Paul McCartney was doing a run-through before the 2009 Grammy Awards broadcast. He turned to Ken and asked how the rehearsal went. Ken said it went fine, but he told Sir Paul he was still disappointed about something. Over the years, Ken has requested that performers on the Grammys scrawl out the lyrics of one of their songs. Ken keeps these treasures as mementoes of the shows. Paul had failed to deliver in the past. He knew he was in the Ehrlich doghouse. He grabbed a piece of paper and wrote the lyrics to "Blackbird."

"As far as performers who knock my socks off, there are more of them than you would think. Although you try not to show it, because you are working with them on a collaborative level. I've worked with Paul four or five times now. It's still a thrill every time. It really is.

"We are the same age, and in 1964 Paul McCartney was one of the best known people in the world, and I was a struggling college graduate. Now it is 2009, you find yourself working together. You find yourself suggesting things. You find yourself on that kind of level, and it's pretty heavy stuff. You can't help but be overwhelmed by his presence."

Ken says the Grammy performers are artists he admires. He never takes them for granted. He says he has gotten to the point where he can be pretty honest with the artists.

"I had Chris Martin of Coldplay tell me the other day, cause they finished their rehearsal and they asked me how I liked it. And I said I liked everything except the end. I said there is no ending to this song. I said there is nothing there.

"So he said, 'Yes I know, I know.'

"I said no, I don't think you know. Otherwise you wouldn't end like that.

"He said, 'Well we gotta work on that.'

"They walked away. We finished our rehearsal on Saturday. On Sunday they ended their song with this glorious little a cappella harmony thing they did at the end of "Viva La Vida."

"I said to them that was really terrific.

"He said, 'That's what we love about working with you is that you will tell us when you think we are wrong.' And I do. I don't think I always did that, but over a period of time when you work with these people, you know number one, you're not on their payroll. You don't have to be political. You just tell 'em the truth."

Ken says he has developed that over the years. He says early on, he might not have bothered to go up to Prince and suggest that he do a different song for the Grammy Awards.

"But certainly in the last ten or fifteen years, at least, maybe more, there's just not enough time to work your way through the nuances and the little bit of this and little bit of that. You say it. Let's get on with it."

Paul McCartney isn't Ken's only connection to the Beatles. In 1978 he did a Ringo Starr TV special and worked with not only Ringo on that show but George Harrison as well. He also did a tribute to John Lennon. He worked in collaboration with Yoko Ono on that program.

"It was the first show done at Radio City after 9/11. We originally were scheduled to do the show the day after 9/11. It turned out to be a pretty amazing show musically. It was so emotional. The story was so tied in to New York City."

In doing the Grammy Awards and the Emmy Awards, Ken's work is under the microscope. Critics are always ready to bash a program for being just another awards show. If Ken comes up with an original approach, other critics complain that he went too far. Veered too far away from the routine presentation.

"Sometimes I just think those who can, come and do. Those who can't, critique. I've lived by that for a long time and I'll continue to live by it. Whether they are great reviews or bad. That's my credo."

A show like the Grammys is supposed to draw in a large diverse audience and keep that audience, even though the program is presenting differing styles of music that cut across all sorts of taste.

"Without compromising it, you try and make it as accessible as possible. You try to think of the broadest range of viewer. You don't want to alienate either end of the audience. You don't want to alienate kids by making it too general. But you don't want to alienate an older audience by making it too young.

"From year to year, what we do is, sometimes more successfully, sometimes less, this year probably more, is we carefully built a show that either end of the spectrum isn't going to say, 'We don't want to watch this, we are going to go somewhere else.'"

The music industry is struggling lately. Exposure on the Grammy Awards is perhaps more important than ever.

"There's a huge discovery factor with the Grammy's. Even though we feature a lot of mainstream artists, they are artists people have seen before. The way we present them and what they do on our show, I believe opens them up to people who either weren't really fans before, or even aware of them before.

"I can tell you this year's show is going to spark a huge sales bump for the Jonas Brothers because of what they did. Them singing a Stevie Wonder song with Stevie Wonder, as big as they are to their audience, it's going to be huge this week because of who they opened themselves up to on the show. Same way with a number of other artists. I've always approached the show, that it's about building careers, not selling records. At the end of the day, people discover much more about an artist than just their latest hit."

Yes if Marty Faye was alive today, he would indeed be proud of Ken Ehrlich. So would Cliff and Richard, the guys from the wiping cloth company. They opened Ken's mind to an appreciation of popular music. For much of his career, Ken has been presenting that music to fans across the world, and presenting it in spectacular fashion.

"It's been a good life."

Ruth Malaney Vick, class of '36

"We were very fortunate. My father was able to keep his employment. We weren't terribly affected by the bad times. That was very lucky."

Ruth Malaney Vick was indeed lucky that her father was able to keep his house on Hyde Park Avenue in Cleveland Heights. Some of her friends were forced to move out of their homes during the Depression. Her dad, Martin Malaney was in a Depression-proof industry. He was the advertising manager for the Loew's Theater chain in Cleveland.

He had to take a pay cut back during the Depression, but held on to his job. Even with the rough economy, people still flocked to the movie theaters. It was a chance to escape from their woes.

"Oh yes, I went to a lot of movies. The price was right."

Not only did Ruth, her twin sisters Ethel and Elinor, and her mother Loretta get to see movies free, but they got to meet a celebrity or two along the way.

"Jimmy Durante. He was very prominent at the time. I remember he signed one of his pictures for me. It said, 'Don't let any other star steal you from me.' He was a nice guy."

Martin Malaney's friends called him Mac. He impressed the big shots with the theater company back in New York.

"He was full of ideas. He was a real idea man. They wanted him to come work in New York. My mother didn't want to move, and he honored her wishes."

Ruth went to Boulevard, Roosevelt, and then on to Heights High. Cain Park was literally in her backyard as she was growing up. Actually it wasn't even a park back in those early days. Ruth and her friends would play in the big ravine that was there.

"My twin sisters were identical. They were five and a half years older. They were great sisters. They spoiled me rotten. They would argue like the dickens, and the next minute they'd be going out the front door, arm in arm, the best of pals. They treated me like I was a doll to play with.

"It was a great area to live in. We could just zip down to Lee Road and go to the library. I enjoyed it immensely. We did have a good time growing up."

Ruth remembers sports were big at Heights High.

"We were very competitive. Everyone wanted to beat us and not many schools did. Cleveland Heights and Shaker Heights were mortal enemies. I was proud of the school."

Because of her father's job, the family got to visit all of the Loew's Theaters in the area. The Granada was at West 117th and Detroit on the border between Cleveland and Lakewood. The Granada was what was called an atmospheric theater. The entire theater was like an elegant garden.

"It was quite spectacular. It had a blue ceiling with sparkling lights that went on and off. That was quite an effect."

Martin Malaney played a role in the development of Sweetest Day in the early '20s. It was an event organized by Cleveland candy makers. The idea was to present sweets to the people in our lives we may have taken for granted. The sick, orphans, the elderly and even the neighborhood newspaper boy.

Big movies stars of the day like Theda Bara and Ann Pennington came to Cleveland to pass out candy.

"My dad had boys from a high school on the West Side come down to a matinee and he gave them boxes of candy."

Sweetest Day has evolved over the years to more of a romantic observance. The third Saturday of October is a day to give candy, flowers, and a card to someone you love. The original intent of the day has faded. Sweetest Day is most popular in the Great Lakes region, but it is said to be spreading across the nation as people move to other places.

Ruth Malaney's dad played an important role in the movie business in Cleveland, but unlike so many movies made in those days, there would be no happy ending to his story.

"My father died at a very young forty-three. He had gallstones, which nowadays would be a cinch, would be no problem at all. In those days, a lot of things were waiting to be discovered."

How did Ruth's mother deal with the tragic death of her husband?

"In those days, you coped. Whatever came along. You stood up to it. That's it. She was very strong. We had to overcome obstacles. Whatever came her way. She would handle it."

Ruth's sisters were students at Flora Stone Mather College at the time. Ruth was still a high school student when her dad died. Fortunately before he died, Martin Malaney had made a financial decision that paid dividends for his family.

"My father was a very smart man. He knew the banks were in a bad way. So he took the money out of the bank and paid off the mortgage on the house. So the house was free and clear. That was a Godsend. He had the forethought to do that."

Shortly after Ruth graduated from Heights, the amphitheater at Cain Park was completed. The days of the ravine were over.

"That was the place to go. My mother wasn't thrilled, though. There were a lot of people milling around. People were running around and making disturbances, as she would call it. But I certainly enjoyed it."

Ruth also enjoyed her days at Playhouse Square.

"That's where all the excitement was. Everybody just gravitated downtown. Herman Pirchner's Alpine Village was across the street on Euclid Avenue."

Ruth Malaney went to business school at Dyke. Her life was changed forever the day she went to the swimming pool at the Alcazar Hotel in Cleveland Heights. She met a lifeguard there named Joe Vick.

If you were in trouble in a swimming pool, you would want Joe Vick to come to your rescue. Swimming was always a big part of his life. He was in his early twenties when he earned a spot in an extravaganza called Billy Rose's Aquacade. The show featured a large cast of swimmers, divers and dancers. It was the featured attraction in 1937 at the Great Lakes Exposition along Cleveland's lakefront.

Joe was a swimmer in the show. Billy Rose lined up Johnny Weismuller, Esther Williams and Eleanor Holm to star in those water spectaculars. Rose put on hugely successful Aquacades after the Cleveland run at the 1939 World's Fair in New York and in San Francisco at the Golden Gate International Exposition. Joe Vick traveled with the show.

He and Ruth got married and went on to be the proud parents of seven children. He made sure his children were competitive swimmers. Joe stayed in great shape throughout his life by doing laps almost every day. Even after retiring from Allstate, he continued swimming, and he became a familiar figure at Richmond Mall in Richmond Heights. He was a dedicated mall walker.

Ruth and Joe's daughter Loree became a well-known reporter and anchorwoman at Channel 8 in Cleveland. In the days when Loree was anchoring the noon news, like clockwork, Joe would find his way down to the electronics section of the Sears store in Richmond Mall just before the newscast would get underway. He walked up to every one of the television sets on display there, and made sure they were all tuned to Channel 8.

So you could say that Ruth's father, husband and daughter all found their way into the spotlight in one way or another. Since her dad played a role in establishing Sweetest Day, it was no surprise Ruth turned out to be one of the sweetest graduates in Cleveland Heights High history.

Barry Gordon, class of '66

Barry Gordon knows psychologists often get a bad rap. They are frequently the butt of jokes.

"A lot of them are not so grounded in their own lives. They can still do pretty well as therapists. Some are not as solid and grounded as they could be. It's not as easy to find solid therapists as it should be."

Barry is as grounded as a person can be. He is genuine. He has a sincerity about him. It is easy to see how people can open up to him and spill out their problems. He has a general practice. He sees adults for the most part, but some adolescents. He often sees couples, and has a specialty of sorts. He does a lot of work with men who have issues with their fathers.

Baby boomers were often ignored by their dads when they were young. Dads often made their jobs their top priority.

"In the '50s, we still had that expression, children should be seen and not heard. We did not relate to kids as having feelings and needing help to work through issues. Now how do we look at kids? We look at kids so dramatically differently."

Barry was president of Student Council at Cleveland Heights. He was a leader and a role model. His grades were excellent. He often had a broad smile on his face. Few at the school had any idea his childhood was a difficult one. His mother Leah died when Barry was three and a half years old. Barry's brother Norm was six. His brother Howard was nine.

"When my mother died, the adults around me didn't have the concept I might be scared. I might not know what to expect. I might not understand things, and I would need help. They looked at kids as a blank slate, and you just move along. You move as you need to. You don't need guidance. It's not a good idea to talk much about those feelings. It will just go away."

Barry was left with only two flashes of memory of his mother. In one of them, he can picture his mother handing him a little pad of paper to draw on. He also remembers going into her bedroom the day she died. He can't remember if he actually saw her in the room that day. Leah Gordon had fled Poland in 1937. She got out at a time it was getting difficult to leave Europe. She had stomach cancer. Her health declined. She was only thirty-five when she died.

Barry's father tried his best to care for his three young sons. Hy Gordon worked as a carpenter. He contacted Jewish Family Service to get caregivers.

"There would be a parade of people. There were inconsistencies. We got bad people. After a year and a half of that, he realized it wasn't going to work. He couldn't get reliable help, so we went into a foster home."

Fortunately all three boys were placed in the same home. That was at least one constant for them. Barry, Norm, and Howard lived with that family for three years. They moved back in with their Dad after he remarried. That marriage would not last long. Hy Gordon divorced and bought a home in Cleveland Heights. The boys stayed with him, although life was not easy.

"He was not a good parent. He wanted to take care of us, but he really didn't know how to take care of us. He didn't know how to parent. He had a bad temper. He was impatient. I think it was very difficult to be a single parent. I think he was overwhelmed.

"We got a lot of help from neighbors. More than we got from family. Help from the parents of our friends. We helped each other. I was probably raised more by my older brother, my middle brother Norm, than by anybody else."

Hy Gordon had come to this country from Poland after World War I. He never wanted to be a carpenter. His dream was to be a teacher.

"Because of the language issue, he really couldn't succeed at that. He was not a happy guy. I think what we really resented was his temper and his way of handling things. When he got angry, most of his conflict was with my oldest brother Howard.

"When he got angry with Howard, he might punish us all by not shopping. He might not grocery shop. We really got scared there might not be any food. Sometimes we would spend our own money to go get milk, so we would have milk with the cereal.

"He would eventually get over it, or we would learn to soothe him enough to get past the latest conflict. I don't think we ever resented him for not being a softer guy, or more nurturing, or more understanding. It was the negative attitude that was so hard to put up with. He was really abusive. Verbally abusive, and sometimes physically abusive with my oldest brother.

"Over a period of years, I found a different way to relate to him and started to understand him better. I understood his limitations and realized in some ways he couldn't help himself. It shifted from my kind of bitterness at him. In the process, he changed a little bit. He started to soften up. He tried to take more interest in me and my kids. So I was able to be at peace and I could feel sadness when he died."

Barry has relied on his personal life lesson to guide people through issues with their own fathers.

"I really try to get people to take the time to find out the context of their father's lives. If they can understand what their lives were like, they start to understand the father's behavior was really less about them. It was about the father's own life being acted out.

"When he was a kid, his family home had burned down twice and they had been uprooted. Then they were uprooted by the war, so they were refugees. Then he came to this country at twenty-three. He didn't speak the language. He was starting from scratch. He had so much insecurity. The one thing that kind of gave him stability was his work."

Later in his life, Hy Gordon came from out of town to stay with Barry's family for a visit. Barry's wife Eileen thought her father-in-law might want to keep himself busy during the visit, so she asked if he could build some window boxes. Barry came home one day and his father had been working on those window boxes.

"He actually comes up to me and he is glad to see me. This feels so different. It was so unusual to see him acting warm in that way. He walks in the house and we are talking about my day. I said this is so nice. We will have dinner and this is going to be kind of special.

"I'm starting to say something to him, and I realized he is not there. I look out the back window, and I see he has gone back to work on the window boxes. My initial instinct was to get angry. Like the old feeling, there he goes again. He really doesn't care about me. And then something clicked. I realized this isn't about me. This is about how driven he is to get the job done. It all went back to his upbringing.

"So it was a turning point for me in understanding him in a different way, and letting go of my picture of him. I realized that the way he was functioning was coming out of his own experience. That's what I try to help people recognize. Talk to your father about his life and what he grew up with.

"One of the most potent questions I asked my dad was, 'When were you happy in your life?' Because he never seemed happy and his answer to me was, 'To tell you the truth, I never knew happiness.'

"Well that was profound to hear him say that, and suddenly it's not like he's always mad at me. This guy never knew what it meant to be happy."

Despite his problems at home, Barry was popular at Cleveland Heights High. He was elected junior class president, and the following year was elected president of the Student Council.

"Student Councils have become sort of irrelevant. At Heights in those days, it was kind of important. I think it was important for me on two levels. First of all, it gave me a real niche in school. By the time I was at Heights, I was the only one left at home. So I am living at home with my father, who is not a picnic to live with. My friends and school were really my safety valve. That is where I felt a sense of belonging. Where I felt appreciated. Where I felt liked."

Barry said he enjoyed being in a position of leadership. He liked that people looked up to him. He said it gave him a feeling he was making a difference. He said his brother Norm helped pave the way for him at Heights. Norm was president of his senior class.

Barry says Norm was an important person in his life. When Norm headed off to Harvard, Barry decided he wanted to follow him there as well.

Norm excelled at Harvard and went on to medical school at Case Western Reserve. He landed a fellowship at the National Institutes of Health in Washington, D.C. He was all set to be chief resident of internal medicine at University Hospitals in Cleveland.

Norm was married and had two young children. Before he took the job at the hospital, he was diagnosed with non-Hodgkin's Lymphoma. He was just twenty-nine years old when he died.

"I only had two choices. Either really screw up, or try to grow from adversity."

Barry made the right choice. He came back to Cleveland, got married, and began work as a psychologist.

"It is enormously fulfilling. I see a lot of people who are unfulfilled in their work. I feel every day is a day of growth for me. Every day something happens that enriches my perspective on life. I love what I do. I love the connection to people.

"You are being trusted with helping people in a way that is so satisfying. You see what happens over time. Seeing the results is enormously satisfying.

"Each appointment feels like a poem. I never know what's going to happen in the course of it. I know where we start. I know where I'd like to end up, but I don't always end up there. There's an ebb and flow. In the course of an hour, some moving things, some insightful things happen. I think everyone of those is like a poetic moment in time. It's a great privilege to experience that."

Barry is often asked how he can spend his days just listening to the problems of others. He doesn't look at it that way. He hopes to guide them through adversity. He feels he is engaged in a process, that most of the time leads them to a better place.

Normally Barry's patients visit him every week for several months and then the number of visits are scaled back over several more months.

"I have had people who I haven't seen for twenty years. They call me up and want to come in about something. That is so gratifying. There are a lot of people who rely on me over their lifetime. Not for a lifetime, but over a lifetime."

Barry says the role of psychologist has changed in recent years.

"There are all these limits as to what you can charge, invariably you wind up working longer hours in order to make the same amount. People have an image of psychologists as though we are surgeons or something, raking in huge bucks. If they knew the reality, we are lucky to be doing as well as the plumber. The restrictions and the amount of required paperwork, getting authorizations, has really changed the field. That has taken away some of the satisfaction."

Barry has seen countless people over his career. He gives a lot of credit to his formative years at Heights.

"I really think the quality of the education really helped. The quality was such, when I got to Harvard, I could do the work. I was prepared. I knew how to study. I had challenging courses. I think it was great preparation.

"I think the quality of the students at Heights was so good. We had so many bright kids. They were really challenging minds. I think that brought out the best in all of us. I think that helped people set their sights high.

"We knew we were at a good school. There were high expectations of us. The general sense was people's family's had high expectations for them. There was a culture that people felt they could do well in life, could do well in college. You could be successful and you ought to be pushing yourself in that direction."

Barry knows that when students arrive as freshmen at Harvard they sometimes feel overwhelmed. They wonder how they earned the privilege to be accepted at such a vaulted institution. He reflects on what a Harvard student told him back then.

"In his first year, he would look around and say, 'Why am I here?' The second year he would look around at the new students and say, 'Why are they here?'"

Tony Tomsic, class of '53

Tony Tomsic heard all of the hammering in the basement of his home on Keystone Road in Cleveland Heights. His father said he was building a stall shower down there. But when his dad took him down to inspect the project, the fourteen-year-old boy was thrilled to discover his dad had actually constructed a photography darkroom for him.

Tony's love of photography blossomed when he entered Cleveland Heights High. He enrolled in a journalism class and he signed up for the staff of the school newspaper, *The Black and Gold*. Zora Rashkis taught the journalism class and was also adviser to the newspaper.

"She was a big influence on me. She was very creative. She said she needed a picture on the front page of *The Black and Gold*. She asked me if I could think of anything. There was snow on the ground. I said let's take the staff outside. I said I'm going to have them, all at once throw snowballs at me. If they do it all at once, it will be a good picture. She encouraged stuff like that."

With that jumpstart from Zora Rashkis, you might say Tony Tomsic's career started to snowball. He would soon be on the staff of *The Cleveland Press,* and eventually parlay that into a second career as one of the most talented photographers at *Sports Illustrated.*

Tony Tomsic's work would grace the cover of that magazine more than thirty times. He never diminished the role of Zora Rashkis.

"You are looking at a screw-up here, who got straightened out by that lady. She taught me discipline. She never actually said 'Go follow your dreams,' but she may as well have. A lot of times, near the end, I wasn't in class. She let me go do something. If I had some idea for pictures, she encouraged me."

Tony's father owned a meat market on Hayden Avenue in East Cleveland. Tony worked there. With the money he earned, was able to buy a fairly-sophisticated press camera.

"I started shootin' it. All trial and error."

While at Heights High, Tony was smart enough to latch on to a mentor. He was at a Heights football game and introduced himself to *Press* photographer Fred Bottomer. Fred took Tony under his wing. He would invite him along when he shot Browns and Indians game at Cleveland Stadium.

"I learned from Bottomer. He treated me pretty good. I spent a lot of time with him. I took a picture at a Cleveland Heights basketball game. I was a junior and it ran in the *Press.*"

Tony looked older than he actually was. He admits he and Fred would discuss photo techniques from time to time at downtown saloons.

"That's when Payne Avenue was really jumpin'."

On one trip to a Browns game, Tony snapped a picture of Lou Groza kicking a field goal. He and Bottomer had stationed themselves in a photographers box that was attached to the side of the upper deck. That box was called the "sling." It was the only picture Tony took that day. More than fifty-five years later, it was published in a book.

Tony went to Ohio State, but grew tired of college life. He was anxious to get going in photography. His keen eye paved the way for his big break. He went to a high school football game and noticed the high-energy antics of the coach. His name was Lee Tressel. His son Jim would eventually become coach of the Ohio State Buckeyes.

"I saw this crazy guy on the sidelines and I thought this coach would make a hell of a subject. Not the football game, but the coach. I shot all the pictures and the *Press* ran them all around the page. There must have been eight pictures. He was going crazy."

Tony was only nineteen years old. The paper was impressed with his work. A week later, he was hired.

"I was told I was going to start at the bottom. The reason we are hiring you is, we looked at the ages of everybody in the darkroom and decided we needed some fresh blood. It was kind of an impulsive thing back then. I was told I was the last guy hired without a college degree."

Tony's primary role at the *Press* was shooting photos for news stories, but he got his share of sports assignments as well. He headed down to the stadium on May 7, 1957. Herb Score was set to pitch for the Indians against the Yankees. Normally, Fred Bottomer would be at the games, but he couldn't make it that night.

"Back then, the photographers are actually allowed to stand on the field, in foul territory. Gil McDougald is up. He squares away to bunt. I got ready to take the picture. He straightened up and he whacks the ball and it hits Score in the eye.

"I knew the minute the ball hit Score. You could hear it. I saw the blood trickle out of his ear. He was laying there. There was a vigil at the hospital. I didn't get the picture of him actually getting hit because I'm on McDougald."

Years later, Tony would be injured at Cleveland Stadium as well. The Browns would put on a pre-season football doubleheader every summer. Buffalo was one of the teams playing in the first game. Tony was on the sidelines when a defensive back took a cheap shot at tight end Billy Masters of the Bills. Masters was propelled right into Tony.

"When a guy is coming at you, you have two choices. Basically, you hit the deck or you sidestep him. I thought I could sidestep the guy, and I did. But that defensive back drove him right into me. He slammed me right under my nose and I flipped over backwards.

"The first thing I opened my eyes, there's a guy right in my face. It's Gary Collins of the Browns in street clothes. I don't know what motivated him, I think he just got a kick out of it. He always had a reputation of hating the press. He said in my face, 'I'm glad he hit you. That son of a bitch nailed you. Now you know how it feels.'"

Tony Tomsic was shooting news stories on the streets of Cleveland during some of the most turbulent times in the city's history. He was assigned to the Hough Riots.

"There's a guy in this building, and I hear bing, bing, bing on the street and on this car. I thought someone was throwing gravel. This guy is shooting a gun. I'm by this car. I'm in the open. From underneath this car, comes an arm grabbin' me and the guy says, 'Get your ass down here. This guy is shootin'.' He didn't kill anybody. They wound up getting the guy."

In April of 1964, Tony headed over to a school construction site on Cleveland's East Side. Demonstrators were opposed to the building of the new school because they felt it would only continue the district's policy of segregating students by race. Reverend Bruce Klunder was twenty-seven years old. He was a graduate of the Yale Divinity School and was head of the Student Christian Union in Cleveland. He was committed to the civil rights movement and that is why he played an active role in the school protest.

"It was one of the sadder days. Bruce Klunder lays down behind this bulldozer, which was the stupidest thing in the world to do. People were yelling and he got backed over on. I was right there when it happened. I took a picture of a woman screaming in the foreground. You could see Klunder's body in back."

The bulldozer operator said he had no idea Klunder was behind his bulldozer.

"They made so much noise and this poor driver, he sees the people in front, he's scared. He doesn't want to hurt anybody. His natural reflex action is to back the thing up. The crowd almost killed the driver."

Demonstrators at the site were also heaving bricks, bottles and chunks of concrete. Thirteen people were hurt. Eight of them police officers. Tony was standing right next to a plainclothes policeman.

"Somebody in the crowd is throwing bricks at the cop. The guy is doing it hand grenade style. Up and over. We are trying to watch where they go. One of them had circled around and hit the cop in the head. He went down. There weren't enough cops there. The horses weren't there yet. I guess I was scared. He went down. What the hell could I do.

"I took my jacket off and made a pillow for his head. He was just laying there. He was conscious, but I knew he was hurtin' badly. The horses came, and things got back under control.

"I left my jacket there. Two weeks later, I'm in the darkroom and I get a call from the city desk. I was told there are two gentlemen here to see me. It was two cops and they are holding my jacket. It's got a bit of blood on it. The cops are apologizing to me because they couldn't get the blood out of the coat. I started crying. I walked away. I just couldn't handle it. That could have been me."

Tony was told the officer hit in the head with the brick was never quite the same. He never patrolled the streets again, He was assigned to duties inside the police station.

"Everybody asked, 'Weren't you afraid for yourself?' I guess I was after the fact, but after seeing this guy down there, I thought, God, I was right next to him."

Tony thinks luck was often involved. Whether it came to escaping injury, or to getting the perfect picture. Another frightening situation took place in the Little Italy section of town. Protesters were up in arms about plans to integrate Murray Hill School. Pete Miller was also there. He was a news photographer for Channel 8.

"We were there when Pete almost got thrown off the roof. I got the hell beat out of me. We got cornered. I learned about mobs and crowds and how they develop. All it takes is one or two guys to get a crowd going. They had nothing better to do and they came after me.

"The camera flew down the street. About a half hour later, a cop comes up to me and he's got my camera. It's ruined, but the camera is not opened. So I said let's get this in the darkroom because I had been taking pictures as fast as I could before they attacked me.

"I didn't want to open it in the daylight and ruin the film. Another photographer, Bernie Noble got a hammer and large screwdriver. We went into the darkroom and Bernie said he is going to hold the hammer and I'm going to hold the camera. He said he's going to have to hit the camera pretty hard and bust it open.

"I said, 'I'm supposed to hold the camera with two hands, while you swing the God damned hammer in the dark?' Well we got it open, and the paper was able to run the pictures. You could actually could see those guys comin' at me. They all had their pictures in the paper. The police arrested them."

Tony says he wound up with a bloody nose. He says the thugs had threatened to throw Pete Miller off the third floor of the fire escape on the side of the school building.

Despite the brushes with danger, Tony says he cherishes his twenty-five years with *The Cleveland Press.*

"I had a fun time at the *Press.* I wouldn't trade those years even for the years I had with *Sports Illustrated.*"

The Cleveland Browns have never been to the Super Bowl, but Tony Tomsic has. In fact, he has taken pictures at each and every one of the Super Bowls. He has crisscrossed the country to cover college football games. He has been assigned to the World Series numerous times, and covered the Olympics. But it was one simple photo shoot at Jacobs Field in April of 1996 that really put Tony in the spotlight.

Sports Illustrated was putting together a story on Albert Belle. Some pictures of the Tribe slugger had already been taken in spring training. The article was going to talk about his uncontrollable temper. Mention the time Belle drove his SUV into a teenager near his home. Describe the time he flung a baseball into the stands right at a fan who Belle claimed was heckling him.

Belle was working-out before a day game at Jacobs Field.

"I had taken pictures of him before. I just walked right up to him and it was not a problem. He knew a story was being done by the magazine.

"They were stretching on the ground and I had a real long lens. The colors were all beautiful because he was in red. I'm looking at the color and shootin' his picture. I get the finger wagging at me, 'No, no, no.' So I backed off. I quit shooting him. I was standing on the track near the dugout and Belle was out in short centerfield.

"I hear the words, 'Asshole, I told you not to take my picture.' I wasn't sure I heard it, so I yelled back as loud as I could, I said, 'Could you please repeat that?' He repeats it, loud and clear.

"Next thing, I hear a crack behind me. If you have ever heard a baseball hit a seat, it cracks just like a rifle shot, CRACK. Then, the next thing I know, instinctively, I guess I saw one coming. I put my right hand up and the ball catches me on the hand.

"The ball hit me. I didn't think anything about it. I didn't see any blood or anything. I'm standing there, and somebody runs up to me, and says you better get inside so they can dress that. I said what are you talking about? I turned my hand over and it was all bloody. So they cleaned it and dressed it."

Tony was prepared to drop the matter at that point. He didn't press charges. He didn't seek out news coverage. He didn't hire an attorney. But word of the incident began to spread. A Boston sportswriter tracked him down, and wrote a story about Belle's raging temper.

Tony waited until the end of the year to file suit against Albert Belle. A few months later he was in Winter Haven, Florida for Indians spring training.

"Somebody is yelling, 'Hey, I want to talk to you.' It's Orel Hershiser. He says, 'I'm waiting for a call from your lawyer.' I said what are you talking about?"

It turns out, Hershiser had been standing next to Belle when he heaved the two baseballs at Tony. Hershiser said coming forward about the incident was the right thing to do. Tony told him he didn't have to get in the middle of all of this, but Hershiser was willing to tell what he saw.

"After Belle did it, Hershiser went up to him and said, 'You better go up and apologize to this guy, or it's going to blow up in your face.' Orel says to me, 'I think your lawyer ought to hear what I have to say.' So that made the case. There was no more dispute after Orel got involved."

At the time of the incident, Tony's beard was white and flowing. He was a large man with a substantial belly.

"Jose Mesa said, 'How in the hell can anyone throw a baseball at Santa Claus?'"

Tony says he came of age as a photographer when he was only twenty years old. It was at the height of the Cold War. The military brought an Atlas Rocket to downtown Cleveland and set it up on display, not far from the Peace Memorial. That's large statue with the arm stretching up to the sky.

Tony framed up a picture with the rocket in the foreground and the imposing statue in the background. He called the city desk.

"I think this will make one hell of a picture. I think we are talking page one here. You would have to run it the whole depth of the page."

Tony was thrilled at the response. The editor decided to totally make over page one in order to accommodate his photo.

"It was like one of those hold-the-presses situations. I was on cloud nine for several days. It was an inspirational thing for me. They took my word. It was pretty damn impressive. It made me try to think a little bit differently."

Tony's advice to young people interested in a career as a photographer.

"You gotta have a lot of belief in yourself. I never thought if it is a Saturday or a Sunday, or what day it is. All the years I was doing this, I never thought about that. You just do it until you get the job done."

The most frequent question Tony gets involves the *Sports Illustrated* Swimsuit Issue. He makes it clear he has never shot pictures for that issue. All of the requirements to shoot the girls in particular swimsuits, in particular locations, is too much for Tony.

"I'm a seat-of-the-pants photographer. If I have to think, I'm in trouble."

Steve Presser, Class of '76

Many people are familiar with Steve Presser's family. His grandfather William Presser was one of the patriarchs of the Teamsters Union. Jackie Presser was his uncle. Jackie became a powerful force with the teamsters as well. His grandmother Faye wasn't widely known, but was perhaps the most colorful one of all.

"My grandmother was a flapper. A gambler. A character. One wild woman. I think she gave birth to my uncle Jackie in a taxicab because she didn't want to leave a card game. She was a crazy woman and could cook up a storm. My grandfather weighed 325, my uncle was 350 and my father was 275. That was a lot of stuffed peppers, and kishka and Hungarian goulash in that household."

Faye Presser outlived her husband, but never really slowed down.

"She gambled away the family's money in the last years of her life, going down to gambling casinos in the Bahamas. She was a character and would make you laugh."

Perhaps it was Faye who inspired Steve. His mission in life is to make people laugh. He is the proprietor of Big Fun on Coventry. It's a store that is jam-packed with thousands of toys, gadgets, gizmos, magic tricks, collectibles and trinkets.

"All of it is fun, yet affordable. The motto is, 'Things you don't need, but gotta have.' I mean, who really needs my crap. I mean how many Whopee Cushions, drinking birds and fake dog doo, do you need."

It was a simple trip to Chicago that exposed Steve to the possibility of opening up his own fantasyland on Coventry. His wife Debbie had friends there, including a fellow originally from Shaker Heights. His name is Ted Frankel and he opened a store on the North Side called Goodies.

"When I walked in there the first time, I was overwhelmed. All of the toys I would try to find and collect, were right in front of me. It was like going and watching the *Wizard of Oz* on the big screen for the first time, and seeing it go from black and white to color."

Steve wanted desperately to open his own store back home. It would be a radical departure for him. After all, he had worked as a stockbroker for the previous seven years.

"I wore a suit and tie every day. The first two or three years were kind of cool, then it became, well it wasn't me. I felt bad for my customers when they lost money. I felt terrible about that."

Steve scouted locations. He found a building on Coventry. It had once been the home of the See-Saw bar.

"It had been vacant for four or five years. It was disgusting. I looked at the space and said this has great potential. I had this idea of transporting people to the past. I got the floor from bowling alleys at Kinsman-Lee Lanes in Shaker. The large showcases were from Taddeo Jewelers in Little Italy. The light fixtures were from Higbee's downtown. The back bar was roughly fifty years old, taken from a place on the West Side. The refrigerator was from the '40s, purchased from a Shaker Heights mansion. The drawers were the card catalog from the public library downtown."

Steve's Big Fun was taking shape. He stocked the store with treasures and then opened the doors in 1990.

"I tell people I went from stock to schlock. Ted had a sign in his store that says, 'Come shopping, leave smiling.' That's our mantra, we want to make people happy, make 'em laugh."

Laughter, practical jokes and outrageous stunts have been part of Steve Presser's life dating back to his high school days. He was involved in one of the greatest pranks in Heights High history. The transformation of the clock tower into a huge, glorified Mickey Mouse watch.

"Peter Cooper created the Mickey Mouse out of contact paper. He has gone on to be well-known artist. He is doing "Spy vs. Spy" for *Mad Magazine* now.

"Two guys actually climbed the clock tower in the middle of the night. My job was on the ground crew. We were across the street in the middle of the parking lot behind the Cedar-Lee Theater with a "jerry-rigged" laser. The lasers of today are probably the size of your pinkie. Back then the thing was probably three feet long and we "jerry-rigged" it so we could plug it into the cigarette lighter of my mother's car.

"My job was to shoot the laser through the trees onto the face of the clock to signal that it was okay, that there were no police around. That was the first signal. If the police were to come, I would shoot it back up there again. They would be notified and would climb down before the police got up there."

The guys up top were already hard at work. Steve and a female accomplice named Lilly were down below, keeping a watchful eye.

"All of a sudden, there's a tap on our window. It was a police officer with a flashlight. He shined it in. He says, 'What are you doing here?'"

Another officer arrived and they reprimanded Steve and Lilly for being out and about so late at night. They told them to go home. The officers never noticed what was happening to the clock tower. Steve regretted he had to abandon his post, but the project was a big success.

"The Mickey Mouse stayed up there for I think, twelve years."

Steve is not one to rest on his laurels or presume that his was the greatest prank at Cleveland Heights High. He says his efforts were topped several years after the clock incident took place.

"The kids took three pigs, real pigs, and painted the number '1' on one, the number '2' on the second one, and the number '4' on the third one. Of course teachers rounded up the three pigs. Number one, two and four. Then they spent hours looking for number three."

Steve has a serious side. After he graduated from the University of Michigan, he took a job at a center for mentally-challenged people.

"I worked there for two years in direct care as a group leader. I was a rehabilitation specialist. I have always had an affinity to people who have special needs."

Steve has remained a life-long friend to many of the people he worked with back then. His children got to know many of them.

"It opened my kids eyes up to how unique life is and how different it can be. How appreciative we can be for what we have and how it is to be involved with people who have different abilities and special needs."

Parents bring their children in to Big Fun and the kids think Steve is some sort of emperor of a magic kingdom. A prince of fun. Someone larger than life.

"It's like this little play world for me too. I'm a superhero to some kids. They look up to me and that's fine. But I always tell them and tell their parents, you better raise the bar a little bit if I'm your son or daughter's hero."

After a dozen years in the original location, Steve decided to move across the street into a storefront that had twice the space, and a basement for much-needed storage. If the small store was a draw, the larger one should be an even bigger draw.

"If you had a great childhood, why not relive it? If you didn't have a great childhood, why not have a better adulthood? Try to capture the past you missed out on."

Steve is the first to admit that being the ambassador of fun is oftentimes far more than fun and games.

"Owning your own little toy store, no matter how busy I look, or how big and successful it is, it's a grind and it's very difficult. It's not easy."

But Steve is on a mission to brighten the lives of his customers.

"I've made unbelievable friends. The strong majority, once they walk in the front door, they could be having the crappiest, shittiest day, and they 'Come shopping, leave smiling.' Like Ted Frankel says in Chicago, 'It's like a safe place on the Monopoly board. You can leave your troubles behind.'"

Steve wasn't looking for trouble, but thanks to a longstanding dream of his, he ran into plenty.

"I guess stubborn is in my blood. I'm nostalgic. I always liked cool family places and I became enamored with diners, years and years ago."

Steve's goal was to find an old diner and truck it back to Cleveland Heights. He was convinced the community would welcome it with open arms. He was able to secure a lot on Lee Road for his diner. An extensive downtown redevelopment project was underway in Atlantic City, New Jersey. Steve found a diner that had been most recently used as Lu-Chi's Chinese diner. The building had seen much better days. Steve was told he could purchase it for $8,000.

A company said it could lift the diner off of its foundation and place it on a flatbed trailer for $2,000. City officials told Steve they wanted the diner uprooted quickly. If it wasn't, it would be demolished.

"The first day on the job, the rigger calls us and says he can't lift the diner for the price that had been agreed to. He said, 'I'm going to lose money on this.'"

Steve asked what the revised cost would be, and the owner of the company said the new price would be $5,000. Steve was still waiting to make final arrangements for a trucker to transport the diner when he got a call from a city official who congratulated him on moving the diner. Steve told one of his middlemen that he thought someone had just stolen his diner.

"He called the rigger, and the rigger said, 'I moved the diner for you. I was afraid the city was going to destroy it. It's on my property. It's safe here.' They said it will be a little bit more money than we agreed upon. 'If you can pay me, I'll release the diner to your trucking company for $21,000.'"

Steve thought the rigging company was holding his diner hostage. The next month Steve received another bill.

"Twenty-seven thousand dollars total. A storage charge was added. Chutzpah. If that isn't the definition of chutzpah. I went nuts. We wound up spending a year and a half and $37,000 in legal fees too."

Steve says when the dust settled, the rigging company reduced its charges dramatically and paid Steve's legal expenses.

Steve tracked down a companion diner for his project. He would place the two diners next to each other with an enclosed lobby connecting them.

"Before we opened the place, we are probably $350,000 in the hole. We opened to great fanfare. The place was packed. Anyone in the restaurant business can tell you, running a place is the toughest thing in the world."

Steve's dream started falling apart. Fifteen short months after he opened the twin diners, he had to shut the doors. It was just before Christmas 2005.

"I had a talk with my staff. I literally was crying. I just told 'em I was so sorry. It was my dream of dreams, and it just didn't come to fruition. I had borrowed money from everyone to keep afloat."

Word spread quickly. Someone sent out e-mails and letters telling of Steve's plight. They explained that Steve had always been a friend who supported the community. People were urged to show up at Big Fun and give Steve the biggest day of business he has ever had.

"Sure enough, before the store opens, there was probably a hundred people outside waiting in line. Two little kids were selling hot chocolate. They made eighty-five dollars that they gave to me, and we had an all-time record at the store. I took that money and made good on all my restaurant employee's paychecks. They all had Christmas."

Steve lost everything. He said he had personally signed for everything. Six and half years of work ended in disaster.

"It's akin to going across raging rivers, through the desert, climbing the mountain, putting the flag down on the top of the mountain, and looking over the side and tripping and falling off. I made it to the top and I stuck the flag up there."

Steve, the laughing guy with the squirting flower on his lapel, had to adjust to this huge setback.

"It's very humbling. You go from opening up this spectacularly successful business, to something that was disastrously unsuccessful. You try, and you get back up. It takes years."

Steve Presser, a walking billboard for good times, was transformed into a symbol of failure.

"For the first six months after it closed, I would be at Zagara's grocery store, people would come up and they would say, 'I'm so sorry.' They would hug me and I would be like the guy who came back from a war. Somebody who lost somebody in God-forbid an accident. People couldn't even talk to me. They felt so bad. They would stare at me. It was really strange."

Steve was no stranger to the business world. What went wrong on Lee Road?

"Our costs were incredibly high. Everything from construction to management. We never got a hold of that. If you don't get control of your costs, it's a runaway train. We couldn't catch up to our debt. We kept chasing, chasing."

Steve said he learned about being more careful in business. He admits he let his emotions get ahead of him.

He drives by the diner numerous times every week.

"It's shuttered now and it hurts me. I looked at the diners as being my kids."

Karen Gogolick, class of '68

"We both do some rope tricks. He does a lot more than I do. He decided it would be good to walk on stilts and do rope tricks, so he designed a stilt-walking cowboy costume. He's eight feet tall. He does rope tricks and we do county fairs and state fairs. He spins a rope around kids.

"That spun off into doing parades, and now we have this elaborate parade rig, where I drive this covered wagon that looks like it is being pulled by an armadillo, and he walks on his stilts. That has become an income stream for us. Who would have thought parades pay people money to be in them?"

It has been a long, dusty trail for Karen Gogolick. She is probably the only Heights High graduate who dresses up as a cowgirl, goes on stage and yodels. She is one half of a rootin' tootin' duo called KG and the Ranger. Her husband Rick Roltzen is the Ranger. They are not based out in Wyoming. They live in Madison, Wisconsin.

"Our big claim to fame is we have won the harmony yodeling championship three times. There's an organization called the Western Music Association and we entered their contest three times over the course of six years, and each time, won the title. There really are better yodelers, solo yodelers, but we have something special when we yodel together, because we have a really good blend, and harmony yodeling is difficult. People tell us we have something unique when we do that."

It was a couple of serious injuries that changed the course of Karen's life. One steered her toward a career as an artist. The second injury guided her toward a career as a musician.

"If someone had told me that I'd make my living as a musician. I'd have laughed in their face. Never in a million years, would I have thought what we are doing now is possible."

Karen lived on Meadowbrook in University Heights. She was a student at Wiley. She was nearly twelve years old and was close to wrapping up seventh grade.

"I was in a serious accident. I was pinned under the rear wheels of a school bus in the parking lot. I didn't break any bones, but had extensive skin and muscle damage to one leg.

"All of the kids were running alongside the bus, kind of jockeying for the first seat. I was standing closer to the bus than I should have. I slipped in a puddle. The bus had come to a stop, but he pulled ahead a few feet. I fell under a wheel and the bus was still moving. The driver rode with me in the ambulance to the hospital. I was lucky it wasn't a lot worse than it was. I spent a month in the hospital and then spent the whole summer doing rehab."

Karen says that frightening experience turned her more inward. She became more intellectual. She restricted the amount of physical activity she did.

"That affected my personality. Someone brought me some canvas board and some paints. I looked out the tiny window of the hospital room and painted a tree. That's how I started painting."

When she entered Heights High she sharpened her painting skills in art classes. At the same time, she developed an interest in making jewelry. Her dad had a lot of tools in their basement. She got a small welding torch and some silver wire. She taught herself to solder and to make small pieces of jewelry.

"Somebody saw something I made and offered to buy it from me. From that moment on, I was hooked. Not only was it fun to make this stuff, but it dawned on me, I could make some spending money doing it.

"I loved making things and polishing them. To create portable art you could wear. You have something you can show off all the time. An oil painting is sitting on the wall and one person sees it every day. Jewelry you wear out in public and it gets seen all the time."

After Heights High, Karen enrolled in the Chicago Institute of Art. She realized the school offered little for students who wanted to be silversmiths or goldsmiths. She transferred to the University of Wisconsin.

After graduation, she got a job in Madison, Wisconsin. She says it was a "little hippie silver shop" on the second floor of a building. Karen wound up buying the business and made it more of a mainstream operation. She hired a staff to work with her.

"I was happiest when I ran the business myself. You wear a lot of different hats. The hardest part for me was dealing with the personnel, having employees and all of the tax stuff. I spent a third of my time at the bench doing what I loved to do best, and the rest of the time running the business."

Karen thrived on the creative end of the business, doing designs and coming up with ideas for her customers.

"I still to this day run into people who will flag me down and say you made my wedding ring, or they will stick their hand out and show me their ring. It came fairly naturally to me. It was a collaborative process between me and the customer. It was very satisfying."

But Karen had to step away from the career she loved.

"I started having physical problems. I had tendinitis in my shoulders and elbows. Nothing I did made it go away. It was the repetitive motions that were causing it. The choice was to keep the business and stop doing the bench work, and just hire that out to other people, or sell it. I didn't want to be an owner and not do any of the work myself, so I sold my business. It was hard. It was like a grieving process. It had been so much of my identity. I was the jeweler. I had no idea of what I would do after that."

For a girl brought up in University Heights, and then living in

Madison, Wisconsin, entering the world of cowboys and cowgirls seemed to be an unlikely next step.

"I always liked anything that had to do with cowboys. I remember being about five years old and piling up pillows off of our couch and piling them on the floor. I would sit on them like I was riding a horse. I'd ride my horse and watch Annie Oakley on TV."

Karen had dabbled in music during her Heights High years. It was a hobby. She played guitar and sang protest songs popularized by Joan Baez and Bob Dylan.

After the jewelry store closed, Karen would go to a coffeehouse in Madison. Once a month, they held a barn dance there. Musicians were invited to drop in and play. Karen played stand-up base. Rick Roltzen also played base. He met Karen there one night.

"I invited him to be in our band. We played music together for two years before we started dating. We got married in 1989."

Karen had found a creative outlet to replace her jewelry making. She couldn't work at the jeweler's bench anymore, but she could step on stage.

"We dress up like Roy Rogers and Dale Evans. We wear the fanciest cowboy clothes we can find. No sequins or rhinestones, but if you picture in your mind what Roy Rogers used to dress like, Western shirts with a yoke. Big hats and cowboy boots. Rick has this marvelous ear for harmony. He used to be in a barbershop quartet. He plays the guitar. I play the banjo and harmonica."

KG and the Ranger do 150 gigs a year. They play in concert halls, outdoor music festivals, schools, nursing homes, folk festivals and corporate parties. Yodeling has become a big part of their act.

"I heard yodeling and I thought I could do that. It's a quick flip back and forth between a falsetto voice and a lower voice. It takes practice and a voice that breaks easily. Most people, when they sing, they smooth over that break. When you are yodeling you don't.

"It was unique for Roy Rogers and the Sons of the Pioneers to do two, and three part yodels in their songs. It's a myth that cowboys yodeled to their cows."

Karen says the yodeling in Switzerland and Germany is different than the yodeling they do. She says the techniques are similar, but the melodies are different. Swiss yodeling has a little different characteristic sound. It was used in mountainous countries to communicate from hill to hill because it carries. The sound penetrates more than a shout would.

"It was probably performed here in a vaudeville act by German or Swiss performers, and the cowboys picked it up and incorporated it into their music. At the time, it was called hillbilly music. It wasn't called cowboy music, or Western music. There was no country music industry. Cowboy songs were played on the radio. They were mixed in with the pop music. The music done by the Sons of the Pioneers was a blend of swing, it had some jazz chords in it, and it had the cowboy theme.

"I think Roy Rogers and the Sons of the Pioneers created what we call Western music. The three, and four part harmony singing that the Sons of the Pioneers were known for, really started off with them. Before that, there were yodelers like Jimmie Rodgers and Gene Autry, but the Western music came hand in hand with the cowboy movies. The movies were so popular they needed five or six songs for each movie, so the repertoire started growing. It was a symbiotic thing. The movies and the songs came together."

Karen and Rick got the opportunity to meet some of their heroes. Patsy Montana became famous in the '30s when she recorded the song, "I Want to be a Cowboy's Sweetheart." She was eighty years old when they met her. Karen says Patsy was the first yodeler she listened to.

In 1994, Karen and Rick traveled to Tucson, Arizona where they went up on stage and sang "Happy Trails" with Roy Rogers and Dale Evans. It was a reunion concert with Roy and the Sons of the Pioneers. It turned out to be Roy's final public appearance.

"He looked very much the same. He was smaller in person than you would think he would be. He was immediately recognizable. Very slender, with those high cheek bones. His singing voice at that point was a little rough, but as soon as he started yodeling, you realized he was one of the best yodelers there ever was. His yodel was still terrific, even in his eighties. He was a little forgetful on the words. He did a nice job. It was nice to hear him."

Karen says Dale Evans had always been one of her favorites. She said Dale portrayed a very independent woman on TV. Dale wasn't the "poor me, I have to be rescued type of character."

"She was always the one who had an idea, or went off on her own and did this and that. I seem to remember on the show, she ran a café. She had a business. She was the proprietor of the Eureka Café."

Karen actually wept when she first saw Dale Evans in person.

"She was a terrific singer. She never really wanted to be in Westerns. She wanted to be a cabaret-style singer. She really had the voice for it. She was quite remarkable.

"When I was a kid, I didn't miss a Roy Rogers and Dale Evans show. The music, I think it was in my brain. I wasn't conscious of having listened to that music as a kid, but when Rick and I started learning the songs, there was a familiarity to them. It was like, oh, I've heard that before. It was something very comfortable and familiar about the music. It must have been from seeing the movies and the Roy Rogers show on TV when I was little."

Physical limitations forced Karen out of the art world, but not entirely.

"I do all of the art work for the act. The posters and the promo materials. I use my business skills, cause we are self-employed. I do all of our taxes and the business stuff. I'm our agent. I wear three different hats."

But the hat she enjoys wearing most is the hat she wears up on stage.

"We had a bumper sticker that read, 'We Brake for Western Wear.' There are catalogue stores and when we are on the road, we try to stop and shop. It's half the fun of doing the music we do. The music is interesting, but dressing up like a cowgirl is really fun.

"It's not only the music, but the history that interests us. It's a very wholesome, satisfying kind of show to put on. We don't have to worry what age our audience is. It works for two-year-olds to hundred-year-olds. It's an uplifting, happy kind of music. We teach a little bit about where these songs come from. We are on a mission to keep a tradition alive."

Karen still remains shy and inward, nearly half a century after that bus accident sent her to the hospital.

"My personality changes when I'm on stage. I'm a ham. That's the hardest thing about doings the bookings, because I'm kind of shy. It's hard to blow your own horn."

Thomas Smith, class of 2002

"He had hit his girlfriend. His girlfriend's brothers had come back and shot him."

Thomas Smith is glad his father took him to work that day. His dad is an undertaker and he wanted to show his son that a nineteen-year-old boy's life had ended senselessly in violence.

"He had several bullet holes in his body. That showed me that life can be short."

Thomas lived on Newbury Drive in Cleveland Heights. During his middle-school years he wasn't a bad kid, but his parents worried he might fall victim to some bad influences.

"I was just doing immature things."

So a trip to a mortuary served as a wake-up call.

"It was life-changing having my father in the funeral business. Like every child, I had a couple troubles growing up. Looking at that boy's body, was the most eye-opening thing. It wasn't that old people were dying. People in their eighties and nineties dying. This was a kid dying. He was barely old enough to vote. There's no comin' back."

Thomas realized he was going to focus on his studies and his interest in varsity sports at Heights High.

"I am not going to make the most of this by just jacking around and doing what I was doing. If I didn't change, I was going to wind up like that guy."

Thomas made sure his years at Cleveland Heights High really paid off.

"I really enjoyed the school. It put you in a real world situation. There was diversity there. There were people who did well there. There were different kinds of environments. I think it was one of the most rewarding experiences I had. The type of classes they offered. I took an anthropology class. I took a political philosophy class. They offered Latin. Heights High was known for its music department."

Thomas was a student at Heights when he made a career choice.

"I was president of the Future Educators of America. Getting involved with FEA, with the clinics and the events they had across the state, inspire you. I got experience teaching. I taught a motivational class at John Carroll for kids from East Cleveland. I'm glad I got involved. Otherwise, I wouldn't have felt as strongly as I do about education. Being a member of Future Educators of America probably did make my career choice for me."

Thomas went to Bowling Green State University. That's where he met Nicole Schamp. They are engaged to be married. Nicole studied fashion in college and she was offered a job as a buyer for Zappos.com in Las Vegas. Thomas liked growing up Cleveland, but he was willing to uproot. He landed a job as a history teacher at Clark High in Vegas.

Thomas played football at Cleveland Heights High and was also an accomplished member of the school wrestling team. He made it to the state wrestling tournament in Columbus in his junior year.

He was on the football team at Bowling Green. For his first year there, his coach was Urban Meyer. Meyer is the Ohio native who has gone on to capture national championships as coach of the University of Florida.

"It was cool. It was really interesting. He was a good motivator. He took a good approach. He related to players really well. He kind of took you to the point where you might break, and then he uplifted you. He was the kind of guy people would run through a brick wall for. The best thing I learned from him was that playing football wasn't as important as graduating and getting your degree.

"You learned discipline. Your learned to be on time. You learned how to work hard. He taught us if you feel like doing something, you should just do it. I can always say that Urban Meyer was my coach. He could really recruit. When he brought me up to Bowling Green, he assured me that things would be okay without my family there. He brought me into their family."

Thomas also received plenty of guidance from Larry Hoon, his wrestling coach at Heights High.

"He taught me to deal with situations that might make me uncomfortable and find a way to come out okay. He taught me that everyone was our teammate. He got us involved with community service. On Thanksgiving Day, wrestlers would rake leaves for people in the neighborhoods who weren't able to do their own yard work."

Thomas is not much older than some of the students in his history class at Clark High. He also serves as an assistant football coach and an assistant wrestling coach at the school.

"I enjoy the coaching part of it. You see kids in the classroom, they might give you a hard time. On the football field or the wrestling mat, you get to see different sides of those kids. You get to see the real personality come out. Some kids are really shy and quiet. They don't say much, but you get them on a football field and they can knock kids heads off."

Being a high school teacher and a coach in Las Vegas presents some unique challenges to Thomas.

"The parents aren't as involved as much as they are back home. You go to any Friday night game in Cleveland, and you would see the stands full. No matter who they are playing. No matter how bad the team is. Over here, you just don't see that. You'll just see a bunch of kids in the stands."

Thomas says lifestyles are just topsy-turvy in Vegas.

"The hotels and casinos are the main business in Las Vegas. Some kid's parents will be working from eleven-thirty until seven in the morning. Something we don't have to deal with in Cleveland. There's just not a lot of parental involvement in anything. That's just the nature of the town.

"A lot of things are more accessible in Sin City. One of the local high schools started a drug testing program because they had a heroin problem. The parents are working unusual hours. There are no recreation pavilions here for kids to go and burn energy. The town is adult-oriented. A lot of the kids work. Many of them don't get off of work until eleven or twelve at night."

Keeping students on track and motivated is not easy.

"That's the thing about Vegas. It's like no other place in the world. The kids all want to leave because there is nothing for them to do. I tell them the hard part is I can go down on the strip today and if I get a valet job at Ceasars Palace, I could be making twice as much money as I am making now. The kids see that, and say, well if a valet parker makes $50,000 a year, why am I working so hard in school. I can just go work in a casino and make an excellent amount of money."

Thomas tries to point out to his students, if they are not thrilled with living in Las Vegas while they are in high school, chances are they won't like it any better ten years later. So, if there is a chance they will move away, they have to get a solid education.

Thomas says he would love to come back to Cleveland Heights someday, but because of Nicole's job, they are limited in the number of places they can live. He wants to make sure she is happy.

"To be a good teacher now, it takes a lot of patience. You have to be patient with the kids. You have to be patient with the administration. You have to take everything day by day. You have to care. I think there are a lot of teachers who don't care about the kids. I care about them and I want to see them succeed.

"I care because with a lot of the students, I see a reflection of me in them, of how I was when I was that age. I want to steer them down the right path for society, for our country. I feel I have more of an obligation to help steer them in the correct way. I think there has to be a turnaround somewhere."

Perhaps that turnaround will begin step by step, in Thomas Smith's history class, or on the practice field after school. The teachers and coaches at Heights helped guide Thomas. He doesn't diminish the role his father played.

"I am grateful for my father being a big influence in my life. He definitely steered me the right way, especially when I see these kids out here in Vegas. Kids out here are different than Midwest kids. Their parents work all hours through the night. This is a twenty-four hour town. It's quite obvious a lot of kids don't have a fatherly influence. I am really grateful I had it in my life. If I can be more like my father, I think I'll be okay."

Leonard Kolod, class of '51

"I've had one wife, one job, and one house."

To hear about the constants in Leonard Kolod's life for the last five decades, you might picture a rather bland, predictable fellow. But Leonard has an adventurous side. His Heights High class has been holding a reunion every five years for the last twenty-five years. Leonard has hopped aboard his Harley-Davidson motorcycle to travel to all of them.

So how big of a deal could it be to ride from Beachwood to Landerhaven? Well that would be a fairly easy cruise. But Leonard lives in Brentwood, not Beachwood. His cross-country drive from Los Angeles, is about three thousand miles.

When he was a student at Heights High, Leonard owned a Cushman motor scooter. He left it here when he moved to the west coast to attend UCLA. He went on to became a successful lawyer. He specialized in real estate and estate planning. One night, on his way home from his office in Beverly Hills, he noticed that a gas station was renting motor scooters. He drove one home and a passion was rekindled.

"It all came back to me. I had no fear. I drove it home in evening rush hour traffic."

A few days later, Leonard bought a motorcycle. He continued to upgrade and went on to buy five Harleys over the years. His brother-in-law was also a biker and they would set out on rides to Mexico, New Mexico and Washington state. Trips that would total out to be two thousand miles.

When he posed the idea of riding his Harley to his Heights High reunion, Leonard's wife Bobbie was supportive.

"She encouraged me. She said you can do it."

Leonard was fifty-five years old when he made that first trip to Cleveland.

"The first trip is always the best. It was really an adventure. I didn't have a cell phone then. There wasn't a large network of dealerships and I had problems with that bike on that trip."

After riding here for his reunion in 2001, Leonard wound up in the hospital for treatment of a blocked artery.

Five years later, his trip back to L.A. featured a real scare. He was traveling through Montana. A company called Big Sky Asphalt had just repaved a road that morning. They put gravel over tar. There was no warning about the condition of the road as Leonard approached. His Harley lost traction and Leonard was thrown to the pavement. He was able to continue on to Salt Lake City, but he had torn a ligament near his left ankle. He was in pain and had to have the bike shipped back to Los Angeles.

Leonard's class will have another reunion in 2011. He will fly to Cleveland for that one. On a long-distance trip to North Dakota in the summer of 2008, Leonard ran into some trouble. He nearly collapsed while riding through Nevada.

"I can't handle the heat, and I can't make the trip to the reunion without going through heat."

For much of his childhood, Leonard lived on Cummings Road near Thayne. While at Heights, his family moved to a bigger house on Severn, just off of Taylor. When he returns for his Heights High reunions, Leonard strolls down memory lane.

"I always walked the neighborhoods. There was something that compelled me to do that."

Leonard might have ridden his Harley from California to attend reunions at Shaker Heights High. His father Ruby had looked at properties in Shaker. He was a wealthy man and could have purchased just about any house in Shaker Heights, but homes there had deed restrictions saying they could not be sold to Jews. Ruby Kolod could have fought that, but in the end, decided he didn't want to go where he wasn't wanted.

Ruby Kolod was born on the Lower East Side of New York City. When he was twenty-one years old, he and a friend decided to move to Cleveland. They paid fifty cents each for a ticket on a Greyhound bus.

His first job in Cleveland in 1931 was trying to peddle bags of coal. It turned out to be a mild winter, and the business venture turned out to be a bust. But Ruby Kolod started making connections with Jewish businessmen in Cleveland. They got involved with a gambling club out in Geauga County called the Pettibone Club.

"The guests back then would get dressed up. They went for the good food."

Leonard said his dad's good fortune was possible because Ohio did not have a state law that outlawed gambling. Local option prevailed. Counties that wanted to have gambling were allowed to have it. The Pettibone Club was a huge success in the post-war years. Leonard's father had hit the jackpot.

"The governors changed. It went from (Thomas) Herbert to Frank Lausche. He wanted to stop it. He couldn't get a law to stop it, but he could harass people. He would have the state fire marshal raid the place to check fire extinguishers. The state troopers would stop cars on the road for safety inspections. It was a whole system of harassment to keep customers away."

The crackdown by Governor Lausche would change things in Ohio and indirectly start a new era in a sleepy frontier town in Nevada. Ruby

Kolod and his partners Maurice Kleinman, Sam Tucker, Lou Rothkopf, and Moe Dalitz saw a dim future in Geauga County.

"The governor squeezed them. They saw the handwriting on the wall. Luckily, there was a place, Las Vegas, where it was legal."

Wilbur Clark built a place in Las Vegas called the Desert Inn. He went broke and his hotel was on the market. The Cleveland partners found their toehold, their next enterprise. Ruby Kolod was younger than the others. He was a working partner. He ran the casino at the Desert Inn. It was his baby.

"His name was paged every five minutes."

Leonard's father became a Vegas pioneer. A shrewd businessman who helped lead the way in the transformation of a desert crossroads into a booming, glitzy city.

"He wouldn't believe it. He couldn't imagine this. He couldn't have foreseen this. The highways, the airport, those buildings. All of the people who live there. It's a huge community now."

Leonard Kolod had a front-row seat to the development of a boomtown. His father was there at the beginning of a gold rush.

"When we would be there during the Golden Age it was magic. The first era, I like to call the Old West. It was like the last frontier. The original Vegas."

"I call the second era, which was my father's era, the country club era. There was the Sands, the Sahara, the Desert Inn, the Riviera, the Thunderbird. No one questioned that the Desert Inn was the king of them all. They were luxurious, but they were like a country club."

"A third era was the corporate era. Hughes bought them all up and they were run in a corporate way, and whenever they did an addition, it was just blah."

"The fourth era is the theme park era. The Luxor, New York New York, Circus Circus, Caesars Palace, Mirage, Treasure Island."

"There's a fifth era going on now, It can be called the opulent era. You are talking about the Wynn, the Venitian, the Palazzo. They are just like palaces."

Leonard has fond memories of his father.

"What he was, and what he said, really made me. There's no question he was of another generation. He had biases. He was opinionated. He could have a temper. I loved him."

Ruby Kolod was one of eight children. His wife Esther was one of five children.

"He supported everybody. He was a patriarch. He had great common sense. He never graduated from high school, but he had street sense. He loved doing for people. He wouldn't let anyone do anything for him. He could go any place he wanted for free, but he wouldn't do that."

Leonard says a favorite story of his, shows the character of his father.

"We were walking along the boardwalk at Coney Island and some bum came up to my Dad. Dad smoked Lucky Strikes. The guy said can you spare a cigarette? Dad reached in and gave him his pack. As we walked on, I said dad, he just asked you for a cigarette. Dad turned to me sternly, and said, 'If you need a cigarette, you need a pack.' I always remembered that."

"He had a theory, when people ask for something, they were asking for the minimum they need, and if you give them more, they would get great joy.

"When you come from nothing, he was raised on herring and black bread, you can turn out one of two ways. When you start with nothing, you can become very greedy and tight, or you can become real generous and get joy out seeing people get things dad didn't have."

Ruby Kolod was a man of fierce determination. Leonard said it was common for his father to visit them in Los Angeles. He would normally arrive on Friday afternoons, but for one visit, he arrived early in the morning. He asked Leonard to take him to the Bank of America at Santa Monica Boulevard and Beverly Drive.

"The night before, a guy had been at the limit of his credit at the casino. My dad told him to give him a check for ten thousand dollars, and he extend his credit by that amount. The guy said he didn't have a check, and my father said I will let you fill out a cashier's check."

Leonard dropped off his father at the bank and he went in to cash the check. The teller told him the account had insufficient funds to cover the check. Ruby was not about to give up. He went to Leonard's law office and placed a call to a vice president of the bank. He knew the bank executive and he requested a favor. He wanted to know how much money the man had in his account. The vice president looked it up and told Ruby there was nine thousand in the account.

Ruby and Leonard return to the bank.

"Dad takes a deposit slip, writes one thousand dollars on it, and he hands the teller ten, one hundred dollar bills. The teller stamps the deposit and dad then produces the check. The guy goes back and then gives dad ten thousand dollars cash. Dad says nine thousand is better than nothing."

Plenty of excitement in Ruby Kolod's life, but Leonard said his dad paid little attention to his own health.

"He ate steaks at midnight. He had a lot of stress. He smoked about three packs a day. It was too late when he tried to take care of himself."

Ruby was only fifty-seven years old when he died. It was just four short months after Ruby and the other Cleveland partners sold the Desert Inn to Howard Hughes in 1967.

It was Ruby who had told Hughes he had to vacate the penthouse of the hotel because high rollers were coming in for the Christmas and New Year holidays. Ruby wanted the penthouses for the regular special guests. Hughes didn't pack his suitcases, he reached for his checkbook instead.

At first, Ruby Kolod thought Howard Hughes was buying the Desert Inn, merely out of spite. Hughes must have been angry about being told to leave. But Hughes would then go on to purchase other Vegas hotels.

"Dad said, 'If I knew he was going to buy more hotels, we could have got a lot more money out of him.'"

Leonard has led a comfortable life in Brentwood. Movie star neighbors have come and gone. Leonard has stayed in the house he purchased for less than fifty thousand dollars nearly fifty years ago.

"I retired a long time ago, and I did it on real estate, not stocks. I never really liked stocks. They aren't making any more real estate, but they are printing a lot of stock certificates. Also, when you get up in the morning, your land is still there."

Leonard left Cleveland Heights a week after he graduated from Heights High. His dad had taken over the Desert Inn a year before.

"I'm really a Cleveland guy. I still am. I've been here for fifty-seven years. I talk Cleveland all the time here. I remember the shame I had in my fraternity house in 1954. I was a junior. I bet everything I had on the Indians. They lost four straight and I had to hide out."

Looking back on his early days.

"I had a great junior high and high school life. The fun, we were out all the time. I loved it."

Jimmy Polster, class of '69

Heights High students will remember Jimmy Polster as the saxophone player for Papa's Bag. His group played hits from the '60s, soul music, James Brown, the Beatles.

Jimmy has worked a series of day jobs over the years, but music is still a part of his life.

"It's like my golf, or my bowling. It's a chance to party a little bit, and make some music."

He is a proud member of a group called the CruiseMasters.

"We played this gig. It was in Akron in the middle of this huge cornfield. A reunion for Firestone High. A member of the class was Chrissie Hynde from the Pretenders.

"I said something over the microphone about Chrissie Hynde

being here, and all of these girls, a posse around Chrissie Hynde all night long, came up to me and they go, 'Don't say her name. She doesn't want any attention drawn to her.' I could tell they were the mean girls, who probably didn't even talk to Chrissie Hynde when she was in high school.

"Later on, I said to Chrissie why don't you come up and do a song with band? She goes okay, comes up and sang a song with us. She danced "Hava Nagila," she sang "Hava Nagila." She was having the time of her life.

"The funniest thing of all happened when the job was done. We broke down all of our equipment. We loaded it up. And we are walking by, and she is standing there with her whole posse and she goes, 'You guys goin' home? You want to grab a cup of coffee or something?' She says that to us. We said no thanks, we gotta go. It was the night we blew off Chrissie Hynde. The girlfriends are, 'Oh my god. It's the chance of a lifetime.'"

When Jimmy was a student at Cleveland Heights High, his older brother Paul enlisted in the Marines and shipped out to Vietnam.

"I was pro-war because my brother was in Vietnam. At the time, 1969, everything was changing. Things in my opinion would change in Ohio later than on the coasts. The anti-war movement was underway in 1969. In Cleveland Heights, it really wasn't. Within two years, though, everyone was a hippie."

Jimmy enrolled at Kent State University in the fall of 1969. He met Liz Troshane there. She was from New York City and her politics were more Left-leaning than Jimmy's initially.

"She was really anti-war. Within a period of a year and a half, I went from being totally in support of the war, because of my brother, to being anti-war. I was engaged to a gal from the Students for a Democratic Society. Liz was radical. Her best friend was Alison Krause."

Alison was one of four Kent State students shot and killed on May 4, 1970 during an anti-war demonstration.

"I happened to be with Jim Levine, a friend from high school. We were having lunch. The riots had been going on all weekend. When lunch was over, he said let's go see what's going on. He told me he wanted to stop in the restroom first. I said okay, I'll wait for you.

"As we were approaching the lower hill, we heard the volley of shots. Jim looked at me and said they had to be blanks. When we got up there, we saw everything that was going on. We saw one person laying there bleeding.

"It was, oh the war hits home now. Of the many people who were injured and killed, some weren't even taking part in the rally, they just happened to be there. I didn't find out Alison was dead until later that day. I was really upset. I knew her very well. Liz and I used to double date with her all the time. Alison wasn't particularly radical, just a hippie.

"To send in soldiers with live ammunition, it was wrong. Although someone did burn down a government building. So the line has to be drawn somewhere. The heartland at that point began to change in terms of where the country was going, and I think ultimately ended the war.

"I get emotional just talking about it. When you really think about it, it hits pretty close, and it seems like yesterday."

The Kent campus was closed after the shootings took place. Jimmy returned that fall for his sophomore year. He decided, however, he didn't want to be on campus for the spring. He and a friend took off for Europe.

"We were hippie backpackers. My hair was long. I had to cut my hair at the border going in to Morocco because they didn't let longhairs in. While I was there, I started thinking twice about getting married to Liz while we both so young. We eventually broke things off."

Jimmy spent his summers working at U.S. Steel. His earnings there went a long way toward paying for his tuition at Kent. Jimmy and his friend Kenny Kushner got a Volkswagen bus and decided to take a trip out East. They actually wound up at the music festival in Woodstock by accident.

"It was pretty heavy. We planned this summer trip. We were going to go to Toronto and Montreal. Kenny also had some people he knew in Long Island. We hadn't even heard of Woodstock. While we were on the road, we heard there was a music festival in upstate New York. We wound up getting directions and going there."

Jimmy looks at Woodstock as a cultural and political turning point.

"It was clear, things were different after that. I became a hippie. I saw Santana. In fact. I'm told I'm in the movie. I don't even know if it's me. It sure looked like me. I had this big 'fro then. People say, 'I saw Woodstock and you were in it.'"

There was no mistaking it was Jimmy Polster that night on stage at Cleveland Heights High. It was February 21, 1968. The Turtles were performing at the school, and Jimmy's group, Papa's Bag, was the opening act.

"That was pretty amazing. At the end of their performance, they trashed all of their equipment. Pushed over the amps and all of that on stage as part of their show. They were brand new, Vox, state-of-the-art, big amplifiers. The manufacturer must have given those away. Take this stuff and we'll have our name behind you on stage.

"They came up to us after the show and they said, 'Come here you guys. You want to buy this stuff? Give us two hundred bucks.'

"It was a great deal. The equipment probably still worked just fine. We didn't care. We didn't want it. We can't do that. We'll get busted."

Jimmy actually began playing in a band during his junior high days. His run with Papa's Bag and the CruiseMasters stretches for more than forty years now.

"I'm not really a good musician, I'm really not. I can barely play that saxophone. I'm more of an entertainer. I'm like the DJ. Like I was with Papa's Bag. I get people up on stage. I get 'em to do line dancing, play tambourines, celebrate their birthdays.

"We have been lucky to pull this off all these years. I get people doing circle dances, the "Hokey Pokey," "Hava Nagila." I've had Hell's Angels actually dancing the hora to "Hava Nagila.""

Papa's Bag was a prolific group in the Heights High era.

"I remember one August, we played sixteen gigs at the Executive Club. We played so many Bar Mitzvahs and confirmation parties."

The CruiseMasters play at area nightspots now. Their groupies tend to have a bit of mileage on them.

"The Savannah in Westlake is one place. The crowd is old people. The crowd is our age and oftentimes older. They party like they are nineteen years old. They call that place and another place out that way, the Viagra Triangle."

Jimmy could not have survived on just the income from his music career. He worked as a social worker after leaving Kent. He helped set up a food co-op. He organized a child care center. He helped build a recreation facility. He realized he didn't want to continue with social work.

"I went to New York state and started building one-of-a-kind pieces of furniture. I was a cabinet maker for twenty-five years. I always liked to work with my hands. I eventually moved back to Cleveland and opened a shop in Murray Hill."

Jimmy thought he would try something else. He began selling vinyl replacement windows.

"It was what they call a one-time close. Those types of in-home sales. They are the guys who won't leave your house. They will stand on their head to get the sale. I'll drop another ten percent to get the sale. It's a special kind of skill. I was able to be successful at it for awhile.

"I can develop a pretty quick rapport with people. There are all these scripts you are supposed to use. I don't care if you are selling something for five dollars, if someone doesn't trust you, they are not going to buy anything.

"So what I would try to do is find some commonality between the person and me, instead of some sales pitch. I'd see their kid is in the military, I'd say, 'My brother was in the military.' It would have to be genuine. I wouldn't talk sports because I'm not a sports guy. If I see an old piece of furniture, I'd establish I was a cabinetmaker. Establish some sort of credibility.

"I wasn't like the hard kind of closer, where a lot of these guys just beat the people up until they'll sign. I was much more come-in-through-the-back-door. Ultimately, I don't think you can sell something unless you believe in it. I believe the product was pretty good. I didn't think I was ripping anyone off."

After six years of selling windows, Jimmy moved on to working as a salesman for a roofing company.

"I wasn't very successful. I didn't know anything about roofing."

But that job gave Jimmy the germ of an idea.

"When I first started, they gave me a digital camera and a twenty-five foot ladder. They said climb the ladder, go up on the roof. Bring back the pictures, and we will tell you what to do.

"I figured why not just put a camera on the top of a pole. I actually invented that. I am patenting it now and I have some investors. You don't have to look in a camera to take a picture now. You can use my device to take pictures down a chimney, under water, or in a crawl space.

"I wasn't successful with the job, but it allowed me to come up with this device."

Jimmy Polster keeps plugging along. He does his best to hit all the right notes. He is toying around with various names for his invention. Among the possibilities are The Long Shot, The High Pod, and of course The Pole-ster.

Rita Abrams, class of '61

"If you met Erik, you would think he is the most jaded, cynical guy in the world, and when he was mixing the song, he told me his eyes got teary. He said it was either going to be a total bomb or a worldwide smash hit."

Erik Jacobsen was a respected music producer. He put together the group The Lovin' Spoonful. He did the song "Spirit in the Sky" with Norman Greenbaum. He has worked with Chris Isaak and Tim Hardin. Jacobsen has credentials.

When he hooked up with Heights High grad Rita Abrams in 1970, it would be the first time he worked with a schoolteacher and a bunch of children.

"He's such a hard-boiled guy on the outside, yet inside he's such a sentimental guy. He's probably the only producer in show business that would have been interested in that song."

The song was "Mill Valley." It was the name of the delightful San Francisco area town where Rita Abrams had settled. She was a kindergarten teacher there. She wrote the feel-good song on Christmas Day 1969.

I'm gonna talk about a place that's got a hold on me
A little place where life feels very fine and free

"I was walking through Mill Valley. I was in love with the town and it suddenly occurred to me. It would be a nice town to have a song about. I had been told about this producer Erik Jacobsen. I kept running into him and people said he would like my song. He listened to it three times and said, 'Let's do it.' He took it to this business meeting of Warner Brothers. All the guys stood up and gave it a standing ovation. They put a rush release on it and it went all over the world."

Where people aren't afraid to smile
And stop to talk to you a while

The record label on "Mill Valley" said it was performed by Miss Abrams and the Strawberry Point Third Graders. It became an anthem of sorts. An upbeat, toe-tapping, face-smiling song featuring all-American children who lived in this idyllic Bay Area community. A brotherhood-of-man type song in a part of the world where flower power had blossomed.

And you can be as friendly as you want to be

"It was absolutely dazzling. It was a very heady experience. I kind of forgot who I was for a while. We had recorded it with kindergartners in a kindergarten class and when we listened to it, they mistook yelling for singing. Erik enlisted the third grade class and they were perfect for it."

Talkin' bout Mill Valley. That's my home
It looks as pretty in the rain as in the sun
And there's a mountain that belongs to everyone
And there are creeks that run on endlessly
And trees as far as you can see
It makes you feel as if your life has just begun

The song took off. Warner Brothers sent a film crew to Mill Valley in mid-summer to film a music video of the song. This was of course before the MTV generation. The video has surfaced on YouTube.

"The film was taken by this young filmmaker hired by Warner

Brothers who happened to be Francis Ford Coppola. I never even knew he was involved until two years ago when the producer told me."

There were twenty-three students in that third grade class. All sang for the recording and many appeared in the accompanying video.

"The kids got some pay, they got some gifts. The school got some gifts. The kids got tape recorders."

Those kids are now forty-seven or forty-eight years old. The Internet has sparked so much interest in the song now, Rita is hoping to write a book about the "Mill Valley" song. She is trying to track down those kids who performed on the record and show pictures of them from back then and from now.

"I am trying to corral them and get them to collaborate with me on the book. I have been going after them with a vengeance."

Rita remembers the day that video was shot. It was the Fourth of July, 1970.

"There was one time during that day, they were filming me, I sat down on a bench and I was dizzy. It was almost like I was going to faint. It was almost a delirious type of experience. People following you around. I was at the peak of all that new-found fame. For a while, I became so self-centered, self-oriented. There was nothing else in life except that song, and people around me contributed to that because that's the only thing everybody talked about."

Rita Abrams did a guest shot on the *Smothers Brothers* television show. Quite a leap for a young woman who was accustomed to playing in front a group of kindergarten kids. Rita's song transported people from all over to the world to a happy place called Mill Valley. The song was like a two minute recess from the cares of the world.

Some years before, Rita wasn't exactly a hit with George Strickling, the director of the Cleveland Heights High Choir. She auditioned, but was told she wasn't quite ready for the highly acclaimed choir.

"It was really kind of a heartbreak. Everybody was really shocked I didn't get in. As it turned out, I think I was better off being in Girl's Glee Club. I loved it. We sang with the Robert Shaw Chorale. Clair T. McElfresh, the director, got us to sing at rock and roll concerts. We sang with Marv Johnson and Gene Pitney."

Rita says she had a brush with fame long before the "Mill Valley" days.

"I started writing songs when I was fourteen. I had a girl's singing group and we almost got to make a record. We did make a demo and gave it to disk jockey Bill Randle. It got very exciting for a while, but then nothing happened."

The name of the group was the Lollipops. The song was called "It's Almost Summer." Abby Zimbalist and Phyllis Lyons were members of the group. It fell short of fame.

Rita put together a girls band in Boston when she was a graduate student at Boston University. She was earning a degree in special education and was hoping to become a music therapist someday. When she graduated, she moved to the Bay Area and landed a job at Strawberry Point School.

When the song came out, the school office was flooded with phone calls from reporters all over the country. The record was a hit, yet sales were not spectacular.

"It was what they call a turntable hit. It was very popular. People would walk into the store to buy it. They couldn't find it."

Rita thought she should take things to the next level. If the single attracted so much attention, how about doing a complete album.

"Whatever royalties there were from the single went in to making the album. Forty thousand dollars, which at the time was a lot of money. The album is still in libraries across the country."

Rita Abrams was by no means through with recording. If a kindergarten teacher can make records, a veterinarian certainly can too. Dr. Elmo Shopshire's name may not ring a bell, but every Christmas we are all familiar with his voice. Dr. Elmo came out with a novelty record called "Grandma Got Run Over by a Reindeer."

That classic put Dr. Elmo on the map and led to years of collaboration with Rita Abrams.

"I love Elmo. He's wonderful. We have been working together for over twenty years."

They have produced some two dozen novelty CDs. Some have a holiday theme. The Halloween recording is called "Dr. Elmo Sings the Boos."

"I've been delighted and amazed how well they have sold, especially since they have been distributed by SONY BMG. Elmo is a wonderful guy. He is honest, sincere, incredibly hard-working. On stage, he comes to life. He's a wildfire on stage. He's an electrified performer, but he is very humble man. He still worked as a vet until a couple of years ago."

Rita Abrams has always stayed busy. She writes musicals for the stage. She has written a musical based on Jane Austen's *Pride and Prejudice*. She hopes to get a theater company interested in producing it.

She has written a musical based on the book, *Men Are from Mars, Women Are from Venus*. It has been presented in Las Vegas. She has joked about changing the title to *Men Are from Mars, Women Are from Cleveland*.

She has presented a satirical revue that pokes fun at Mill Valley and Marin County. That one is called *For Whom the Bridge Tolls*.

"I always have a creative passion, always needing to create and produce. It's my motivation. I have always retained a sense of wonder. I have more of a sense of wonder than when I was young. If you see all of life as a miracle, then you are forever young. The truth of my life is that I have been very lucky and I do have a good life. I'm divorced and because I'm so in love with my work, and I get so much reward from writing music, writing shows and writing comedy, that is kind of my partner in life now."

After "Mill Valley" was placed on YouTube, Rita started getting e-mails. One came from a veteran of the Gulf War.

"He said he had been in a foxhole and he was terrified for his life and this song started running around in his head. He felt like it saved his life. It gave him a sense of calm. It got him through."

I know there may come a time I'll have to leave Mill Valley
And every memory will seem like make-believe
And all the good things that are mine right now
Will call to me and ask me how
I could have left them all behind
How I could leave Mill Valley

Rita says she was shopping in Whole Foods recently, was approached by a young girl who recognized her, and told her she loved the song.

"Some had never heard the song. They are hearing it for the first time and they are so excited about it. There was this saying, 'Know your own bone, gnaw on it, bury it, and dig it up again.' That really resonates with my career."

It's hard to believe that "Mill Valley" is a forty year old treasure now.

"That was a time of innocence and that was a long time ago. Everyone will tell you the town is a lot more crowded now. There's a lot more traffic. Fortunately, esthetically it hasn't changed much because local government has been rigid about building requirements. The town hasn't turned into a little L.A. In the center of town, there used to be businesses for the people. Now it's more high-end, boutiques and galleries. Expensive clothing shops. So it's not as folksy as it used to be. When I wrote the song, it was the tail-end of the hippie era. There was a much more free-wheeling spirit than there is now."

If the town has changed a bit, Rita Abrams is pretty much the same.

"I've never become jaded and never become as sophisticated and worldly as I should be. I'm not a Pollyanna at all. I'm basically a positive person. One can feel very old, or one can feel very lucky to be alive and well. That's how I feel."

Bud Weidenthal, class of January '44

"He was somebody you looked up to."

Bud Weidenthal was among the first to interview Sam Sheppard. No, it wasn't after Dr. Sam was accused of murdering his wife Marilyn in their Bay Village home in 1954. It was thirteen years earlier at Cleveland Heights High."

"Sheppard was seen as the big man on campus with the letter sweater and the girlfriend named Marilyn. He was on the track team. Four guys went to Columbus and won the state championship. Sheppard was the quarterback on the football team. He was a great basketball player."

Bud Weidenthal was the guy with the pen and notepad. He was a sportswriter for *The Black and Gold*, and interviewed Sheppard several times for the school newspaper. There was plenty to write about. Sheppard was named the school's outstanding athlete. He was chosen most likely to succeed. He was class president all three years at Heights.

"In my relationship with him, which was not intimate, there was nothing that would indicate trouble ahead. He was a hell of an athlete. The guys in the letter sweaters were school leaders. Sam was one."

Fast forward to a July morning in 1954. Bud Weidenthal was now a reporter for *The Cleveland Press*. He came to work early that day and was sent out to Sam and Marilyn's lakefront home. Sam maintained an intruder had knocked him unconscious and had killed his pregnant wife.

"I covered the killing. I happened to be on the city desk."

It would immediately turn into one of the most sensational murder cases in U.S. history. A young doctor from a prominent family, suspected of murder. His high school sweetheart the victim. Rumors that Sam and Marilyn had both strayed from their marriage vows.

"I have no idea."

Bud did not wind up covering the trial for *The Cleveland Press*. He never formed an opinion about whether the one-time high school superstar was guilty of murder. But his boss at *The Cleveland Press* certainly did.

Louie Seltzer was short in stature, but a powerful driving force behind the success of his newspaper. He led the crusade to arrest Sheppard following the murder.

"There were front page editorials. The assumption was they were written by Seltzer himself. It said, 'It's Time to Bring Him In.' It was before Sheppard was arrested. They felt Sheppard was being protected. They may have over done it. I'm not sure."

Sheppard was convicted of the killing, but the verdict was overturned more than a decade later. It was determined that Sheppard had been denied a fair trial because of the pre-trial publicity and the "carnival atmosphere" that prevailed in the courtroom.

The role of *The Cleveland Press* and its editor Louie Seltzer came under plenty of scrutiny. The handling of the Sheppard case may have been a low point for the paper, but Bud Weidenthal maintains there were many high points. He worked for the newspaper for thirty years and was one of its biggest supporters.

"I was deeply enchanted with the *Press,* which I thought was a great newspaper, and I still do. When they went after a story, they went after a story. The *Press* was the largest and most influential newspaper in Ohio. They had a circulation 100,000 more than *The Plain Dealer*. They knew and understood what the public wanted in a newspaper.

Bud says *The Cleveland Press* was a working-class newspaper. It was geared for blue-collar workers and their families.

"They were the *USA Today* of the twentieth century. It was readable. It was short. You were only able to have one story on page one that continued on to an inside page. There were short sentences, understandable, written for the average working guy.

"Ninety percent of the staff were Clevelanders. They knew Cleveland. They understood it. They knew the neighborhoods. They didn't bring reporters in from God knows where, like *The Plain Dealer* did. They were fast and they knew the territory."

Bud gives all the credit to Louie Seltzer. He was the guiding light, the champion of the newspaper.

"He was absolutely energetic, absolutely enthusiastic. He reminded me of a football coach. Every morning, at the end of the editorial meeting he would say. 'Okay guys, go out and get 'em.' You felt like you were in a football game.

"He never fired anybody. There was just something about him. Scripps-Howard gave him complete control of the paper. They were making big money. They had a circulation of 400,000. Louie had a band come marching down the newsroom when he passed 400,000.

"Its penetration into the blue-collar neighborhoods was a reflection of Seltzer's attitude. He never let us forget who we were writing for, who we were writing about. We weren't *The New York Times*, we weren't *The Plain Dealer*, which was stiff and boring. We remembered who our audience was, and if you see *USA Today*, that was the idea the *Press* had."

Bud knew that the *Press* had a winning formula.

"Good graphics. Graphics were very important. Pictures. Large pictures. Anything that made it easier for the reader. Most of our stories were not on the intellectual level, but on issues that people had to deal with.

"The penetration in Garfield Heights, Maple Heights, Parma, Strongsville, and Brunswick was incredible. Seventy percent of the residents of Garfield Heights subscribed to the *Press*. It wasn't one of those nose-up-in-the-air publications."

You could say that printer's ink ran through Bud Weidenthal's veins. His ancestors came to Cleveland way back in the 1840s. His grandfather, Maurice Weidenthal was the theater critic for *The Plain Dealer* and also served as that paper's city editor. His grandfather's brother worked at *The Cleveland News* and another brother worked at *The Cleveland Leader.*

"When my grandfather was in the business there were seven daily newspapers in Cleveland. He and Marc Hanna were very close. My grandfather was on the train when McKinley ran for President in the 1890s. He wrote a long article about it for the *Saturday Evening Post.*

Bud's father William ran the Weidenthal Publishing Company. It was located on Bolivar Road, near the site where Progressive Field now sits. It printed community papers like *The Shaker Sun,* and also put out *The Jewish Independent.*

William Weidenthal was only in his forties when he died. It was January 1931. Bud's mother Evelyn suddenly had to raise Bud and his twin sister. They were only five years old. Evelyn tried to run the printing business on her own, but during the Depression it was difficult for any business to make a go of it. She sold the company after a couple of years.

The family had been living in a house on Euclid Heights Boulevard, between Woodward and Superior. Like many other families during those tough times, the Weidenthals had to give up their home. They moved into an apartment further west on Euclid Heights, between Lancashire and Hampshire.

Bud befriended a couple of classmates whose families also had to move into those apartments. When they got older, they would hop on their bicycles and ride up Washington Boulevard to Heights High. They were students during the outbreak of World War II.

"Amazingly. the war didn't really affect us as much as it should have during our high school years. There is something about being that age. It wasn't as frightening to us as it should have been. I think a lot of us thought we would go in the Army, but the war would be ending soon."

When Bud graduated in January of 1944, the war was still raging. The morning after his graduation, Bud and several of his Heights High friends went downtown and got sworn-in to the Army.

"I went through eight weeks of training, which was kind of abrupt. I had never held a gun in my hand before."

Soon he was with General Patton's Third Army. He was in the Moselle Valley, near the border between France and Germany.

"I thought it was pretty there until I started hearing those funny noises. Incoming mortar rounds. Our task was overtaking the fort in the city of Metz. That had never been taken in history. I wasn't a line soldier. I was in the communications area, about a mile from the front lines. I was awarded an Air Medal for flying in a Piper Cub during the battle for Metz. We dumped ammunition and food to soldiers. We got Air Medals. We were the first infantry guys to get Air Medals."

The time in Europe was tough for a kid fresh out of Heights High.

"I became a man. I was a guy from a naive, kind of superficial Cleveland Heights High School experience, to being in an infantry unit with rednecks from Missouri, Oklahoma, and Kansas. It was quite an experience. I grew up. I became another person.

"Seeing some of your friends killed and seeing some the devastation of those cities, it was awful. When things got rough in Europe, they pulled 'em right out of college and they had practically no training. They were sent to Europe and they put them in infantry units and some of 'em only lasted a few days and they were gone."

Bud spent two years in the service and then went to the University of Michigan. When he graduated, he landed a job at the *Press*.

"I started out as a copy boy. I did that for eighteen months. I made thirty-five dollars a week. I then worked on the city desk for four years. When I was a kid, I was intrigued by crime. I spent a year at the police station at E.22nd and Payne. The *Press, Plain Dealer* and *News* each had its own office there."

By the mid-fifties, Bud was covering University Circle and the culture beat for the paper. In November 1966 a woman named Marjorie Winbigler was headed to Severance Hall. She was a member of the Cleveland Orchestra Chorus. While walking near the Wade Park Lagoon in front of the Cleveland Museum of Art, a man dragged her into the bushes, raped her, and murdered her.

"It was a bad scene. It made people afraid to go down there for the concerts. We looked into the lighting in the area, the police coverage, and wrote about the extent of crime in University Circle."

Bud says the crusade by the *Press* led to some changes there. Lighting was improved. University Circle formed its own police force. Patrols were stepped up. The *Press* was a watchdog in the community.

"When Joe Cole was buying the *Press*, I saw the handwriting on the wall. I left in January 1981. He closed it down in June of 1982."

Bud had moved on, but he shed a tear when the paper folded.

"There goes a great institution. There's no question about it. That was Cleveland."

Bud Weidenthal is concerned about the erosion in the newspaper business.

"I don't think it's a twenty-first century industry. People are lured away from newspapers by technology. You don't see many young kids reading newspapers. It's a tragedy in my opinion.

"If you watch the news on cable television, you are certainly being shortchanged. It's not journalism. It's one hundred percent opinion, with the exception of CNN which tries to be a news show."

So ask this grizzled newspaper veteran just how society can function with a lack of information.

"The fact is we are not functioning."

Earl Stein, class of '67

"I felt lucky I didn't get killed and I felt lucky he didn't get killed."

Earl Stein will forever hold a place in Cleveland Heights High lore. It was a Friday night in the fall of 1965. The Shaker Heights football team had traveled to Cleveland Heights to play the Tigers. This was definitely a rivalry game, even still, violent confrontations after the games were pretty uncommon.

After this Heights-Shaker clash ended, Earl and some buddies were hanging out in the school parking lot. He doesn't recall anything unusual taking place there.

"I said to my friends I have to get up early in the morning. I'm taking my college entrance exams, so I'm just going to walk home. They stayed. I lived a fifteen-minute walk away. I lived on Cedar Road. It was an easy walk for me and I started to walk.

"I was wearing a Heights High letter jacket from the swim team. I was pretty proud of it and I was just about to Taylor Road and I turned around, and I see a gentleman running towards me. The next thing I know, he jumps on me. There was an altercation. We started to fight. One thing led to another. I was stabbed in my chest and in my leg.

"He jumped into a car. I wound up staggering in the street. Somebody stopped their car and they took me to Doctors Hospital at the top of Cedar Hill. That's when I called my parents. They came down. Luckily, I was okay. I believe he was arrested down the street.

"I was probably pretty stupid to walk home alone with that jacket on. Apparently he told someone I beat him up in the parking lot and he was looking for revenge. I weighed like ninety-eight pounds in high school. I wound up with knife wounds and bruises, facial bruises."

News of the attack on Earl Stein spread quickly. People heard the description and fashioned a visual image of the assault. Many assumed the attacker came running at Earl with his knife drawn and started slashing at him. Now, more than forty years after the altercation, Earl sheds some new light on the incident.

"It was actually my knife. I don't know what possessed me to have a knife and I didn't know anything about knives. For some reason, I had a knife in my pocket that night. I had to go to some kind of hearing and I was interviewed about the fight. In hindsight, I probably should have taken a bus home, or waited for my friends. I never did take that entrance exam the next morning."

As it would turn out, Earl would spend much of his adult life working with knives. He was a counterman at the famed Corky & Lenny's Deli on Chagrin and went on to become one of the owners.

"I worked there from the time I was ten years old. I was a busboy, a fountain boy then I worked behind the deli counter. Corky Kurlander, one of the founders, is my uncle. Lenny Kaden was bought out about sixteen years ago. So now the deli is owned by Corky, his son Kenny and me."

The first Corky & Lenny's was located at Cedar-Center. It became a landmark and a Cleveland institution. The owners opened the second location on Chagrin Boulevard. For a time, both were in operation. That led to some confusion.

"People would come in say, 'I'm supposed to meet someone at

Corky & Lenny's.' Lots of times they were at the wrong Corky & Lenny's. We had a direct line. We'd call over there and I'd say, are Mr. & Mrs. Jones there? They'd say hold on. They'd come to the phone and they would laugh about it and they would say, 'I told you to meet me at Corky's.'"

Now with just the Chagrin location in business, there is no more confusion. The morning crowd at Corky's comes in just like clockwork.

"People who come in the morning are usually older, retired people. They don't have much to do. They sit around and they talk politics. Unfortunately, that group is getting older. They move to Florida. Some have passed away.

"By eight or nine, some of the business people come in. You see architectural drawings open up. Not as often as you used to, unfortunately. There are deals being done. I would say to them I won't charge you for the breakfast if you give me ten percent of the deal. But now it's more likely I'm charging for the breakfast, because the deals aren't so good anymore."

Earl sells a staggering 4,000 pounds of corned beef every week. Few customers realize it's actually imported.

"It's made in Detroit to my specifications and my flavor profile. It is shipped here and we cook it here. Some places buy corned beef already cooked. They heat it up. That's not good. The meat can be very tough and people don't like it. Ours is cooked tender and soft. It has a lot of flavor."

Health-conscious customers have changed their ordering habits at Corky's. A lot more turkey is being sold now. Amost half of the sandwiches sold these days are turkey. People are ordering far fewer hamburgers and more turkey burgers.

"I used to buy just regular corned beef and then I'd trim out all of the fat. Now I buy two kinds. I buy the first cut, and I buy the regular. I'm seeing more and more lean cuts being purchased."

Some customers steer clear of corned beef these days, but Earl is convinced there will always be a strong market for it.

"People just love corned beef. My attitude is always moderation. I wouldn't eat it for breakfast, lunch, and dinner, but you could have it once or twice a week. I have healthy foods. I have fruits. I have salads. I have egg-white omelets. You can get a bowl of soup."

Earl has tweaked the menu. Some regulars might say the servers haven't changed much. Some have been on board for decades. Waitresses at Jewish delis have a reputation of being business-like, to the point of being gruff, or even somewhat rude.

"Every so often, a customer will come up to me and they say, 'We had a nice server. We're not used to that.' I don't think it's that so much. It's the frantic pace. The servers are probably doing more than they should be doing. If I was really smart, I'd have runners running food. I'd organize a little bit differently. I've never been able to figure all of that out.

"If all of their tables get seated at the same time, it's pretty much just putting out fires. If the store is not too busy, then I think people get better service and have a better dining experience. I get very few complaints."

Corky's used to be a popular late-night hangout. Now it closes at nine o'clock on weeknights and eleven o'clock on weekends.

"To stay open to take in two hundred dollars, doesn't even pay to keep the lights on. People used to bowl. I was in a bowling league. You would bowl until eleven at night, then go to Corky and Lenny's for dessert until one in the morning.

"Your staffing is always an issue. Getting good help is an issue. Your overhead is always an issue. It's getting harder and harder. Every five years, your rent goes up. Your utilities go up constantly. Food costs go up constantly. You have to maintain that balance. What prices you are going to charge."

Walk into Corky & Lenny's, and the first things you notice are the showcases filled with a tantalizing variety of rich pastries. Earl is proud that most of them are made right there in his kitchen. He says he gets his bagels come from Bialys in University Heights. And the rye bread comes from Pincus Bakery, also in University Heights.

"A good rye bread is most important to a deli."

Earl was a diver for the Heights swim team. He claims he was overshadowed on the diving board by teammate Joe Frischmann. Yet Earl continued diving at Ohio University. He says he decided to give it up after he cut his leg on a diving board. He thought that was a signal to call it quits.

After graduating, he went to work at Corky's. A customer who owned a paper bag company came in one day and told Earl he was looking for a salesman. He said the job paid ninety-five dollars a week. Earl didn't see much of a future at Corky's at that time, so he took the sales job.

"I was a traveling salesman for about a year and a half. I hated selling. I wasn't very good at it. If it was an existing customer, I could deal with it, but there was a lot of cold calls, and after a while, I would pull up in front of a store, I would look out of my car window, and say they probably don't need anything today, and I would drive off. I decided this was not exactly going to be the career for me."

Earl returned to Corky's to work at the new deli on Chagrin. He took off again to run the Rapid Stop restaurant at Shaker Square. His father-in-law then got him involved in a video distribution company. When Lenny Kaden indicated he wanted to retire, Earl was invited to rejoin Corky's. This time as one of the owners.

It's a daily challenge. Earl's peaceful nature and calm manner help to keep the daily routine to a dull roar.

"It's a business and you are taking care of as many as one thousand people a day. You get one complaint. I think that is pretty good."

Earl says when one of his class reunions is approaching, classmates will ask him if he is planning to attend.

"I say why should I come to the high school reunion? Everybody comes here."

Earl's two children have helped at the deli over the years, but Danielle now lives in Chicago and works for a company that runs charter schools. His son Jared is traveling the country as the musical director for a show called *Spring Awakening*.

"He went to musical theater school at N.Y.U. His passion was theater. I wouldn't discourage that just so he could join the family business. He conducts the orchestra and is responsible for the integrity of the show."

Earl's wife Nancy ran the Crohn's and Colitis Foundation here in Cleveland for ten years. An organization important to the Stein family. Earl dealt with ulcerative colitis since he was ten years old. The condition flared up when he was in his mid thirties. He was on a heavy dosage of medications.

"In 1988 I had my colon removed. The surgeon created an internal pouch to replace my colon. He was able to construct something out of a section of my small intestine."

Sadly, because of all of those medications, Earl developed avascular necrosis.

"The joints of my hips just dried up. I have had hip replacement surgeries in 1988 and 1989. I had to replace one of those artificial hips in 1999 and the other one in 2007."

Earl is not the kind of guy to complain a lot. He presses on. He is grateful for life's blessings.

Earl Stein says his Uncle Corky has taught him to be patient, how to step back when tempers flare.

"In the kitchen in the summertime, it can get unbearably hot. You have the dishwashers back there. You have the cooks back there. It's 100 degrees outside and 120 degrees in the kitchen, so people sometimes lose their temper. Things get a little out of hand. Your first reaction would be we won't tolerate this. Get out. You're fired. Sometimes it's best if you pull that person aside, take five minutes, have a cold beverage and then come back to work."

After all these years, Earl denies that he has grown tired of the place.

"It's always exciting to be there, because there is so much going on there all the time. You never know who is going to come in. Friends, relatives, celebrities or politicians. It's a great place to meet people. Our old slogan was, 'From a bagel to banquet.' The new slogan is, 'Where people meet to eat.'"

Harold Mendes, class of '45

"I used to ride my bike there in the winter. Rain, snow we were there."

The year was 1942. Harold Mendes would ride that bike from his home on Baintree Road to the Pick-N-Pay grocery store on Coventry.

"I worked in the produce department in the basement for three years. I used to work from eight in the morning until eight at night on Saturdays. It was a long day. We made thirty cents an hour. By the time I left the job, we were making sixty cents an hour. That was considered big dough."

Harold didn't just stumble upon that job in the produce department. His father Joe was one of the founders of the Pick-N-Pay chain.

"He was a buyer. He picked out locations. He was a vice president. He started out candling eggs. It started out as a company called Cottage Creamery. Then they opened Farmview stores before they became

Pick-N-Pay. The grocery business was different in those days. It was a lot smaller."

Like other students at Heights High, Harold relied on his bicycle to get around during those World War II days.

"We didn't have cars to run around in. There were shortages of all sorts of things. Things were rationed. Gasoline wasn't around. You got four gallons a week or something like that."

Harold wasn't a rebellious teenager. Few students were back then.

"We did our homework. We never got in trouble then. Very few people talked back to our teachers. Teachers were the boss. I think the only trouble I had at Heights was, I was slumped in my chair at some sort of assembly and Mr. Flint, Roy Flint, he was the assistant principal, he was a tough guy. He took a couple of us and threw us out."

During the summers, Harold helped the war effort.

"I worked in a couple of war plants. I worked in the Willard Storage Battery plant one summer. Packing battery acid for overseas shipment. And then another summer I worked in an Army warehouse which was an old May Company warehouse on Payne Avenue."

When he finished Heights, he signed up for the Merchant Marine Academy. He worked on ships for one year. Then he spent a year and a half in the Army before getting a college degree at Western Reserve.

He went back to Pick-N-Pay for a time, and then launched an advertising business with a high school friend. That led to a job as a manager of a Muntz TV store in Pittsburgh.

"We advertised televisions for 99 dollars. It was a step-up operation. The average sale was three hundred dollars for a console. It was a good product."

In 1956, after that venture failed, Harold and a friend drove to Mexico. Two weeks later, his friend came back to Cleveland, but Harold wasn't finished traveling.

"I just kept driving. I didn't know what the hell I was doing, and I drove all the way through southern Mexico and then in Guatemala, Honduras, Nicaragua, Costa Rica and then Panama."

While he was in Panama. A friend from Cleveland called him with a business proposition. He was shocked that his friend was able to track him down.

"He knew I was down that way. He figured I would be in some

cheap hotel. He said he met some guy last week in Indianapolis. This guy sold whiskey barrels and tanks to make wine. He said these guys think they can sell these tarpaulins they make for export."

So there in Panama, while clinging to a telephone in a hotel lobby, Harold Mendes' life was changed forever. He was about to take a step into the world of importing and exporting products. His friend shipped a catalogue to him in Panama.

"I went to the U.S. Embassy and picked up the catalogue. A few months later, on my way north. I made a few sales. I actually got an order. I sold a car dealer in Honduras in Tegucigalpa a couple of thousand dollars worth of tarps, and from there I ended up in the export business."

Harold made his way back to Cleveland and launched his international trade business by importing auto parts and car stereo components. Tape players were the primary product. Most of the merchandise came from Japan. He served as a middleman for a Japanese manufacturer and a Cleveland outfit called Tenna Corporation.

"We did about $17 million of business and I was getting one percent."

Mendes Incorporated became export managers for companies that didn't have their own export departments. A chance meeting one day helped solidify his company's standing. His friend Bill Heller was hosting a businessman who was here from Japan.

"I was importing some brass tubing from Germany and Bill said I think this company has a metals division, why don't you talk to 'em? We ended up importing brass tubing from that Japanese company for many years. It's strange how one meeting on a street corner can change things."

Harold was playing a role in an industrial revolution of sorts. As the imports started trickling in, America's position as a manufacturing giant was beginning to weaken, one boatload at a time.

"At that time, there was probably more of a feeling of Americanism, or whatever you want to call it, but attitudes change. Today, it's hard to find anything made here. We were a little niche company. We imported a few things. Importing back then was almost a dirty word. Well nothing from Japan can be good because all they make is toys. China was the same thing. But that wasn't the truth. Things changed. Look what's going on in China today. Your shoes are probably made in China, and the quality is good. There's no complaint on most products."

Harold Mendes, who not too many years before was trimming lettuce in the basement of that Pick-N-Pay, was now a player in international trade.

"I think we learned by the seat of our pants. You learned about the different financing arrangements. Learned about credit. Knockin' on doors. Learned about mailing. You learned about promotion. Of how to promote yourself. Getting publicity releases into magazines. Getting into trade shows."

Harold had to earn the trust of business people halfway around the world.

"A lot of it is just based on relationships, where people trust you. We are middlemen. We don't make anything, but getting things from point A to point B, takes a little bit of experience."

Things could get complicated. Even though Harold's company wasn't involved in manufacturing the products, he still had to stand behind what he sold.

" We still maintain relationships with some of the Japanese we did business with forty years ago. I had a friend visit here just last summer whose little Japanese company, when we started with them, they were a trading company. They ended up doing two billion dollars worth of business. It's called Tokyo Electron Laboratories They make radios and car stereos."

Organizing a class reunion takes a lot of work. In most cases a committee is selected and there are numerous meetings held to iron out the details. The Heights High class of 1945 operates in a different manner. Harold Mendes is the committee.

"I did everything. Making out the invitations. I did the whole thing. It's easier not to have a committee. There are no decisions to be made. This is it. Don't have to worry about what you are going to eat, because I called the shots."

Yes, Harold has seized total control of his reunions. Not only is he willing to put his money where his mouth is, but he is willing to host the gatherings at his house.

The most recent reunion was in the summer of 2007. It was a celebration of the classmates reaching age eighty. Harold's rustic home sits on a heavily-wooded, ten-acre lot in Moreland Hills. A long time ago, this beautiful property was a hunting lodge. Harold provided the food and drinks. Classmates could bring dishes or bottles if they so chose.

"We didn't charge anything to anybody. People brought things. I think I ended up with more whiskey than I started with."

Harold said after that gathering, he got a call from one of his classmates in Florida. She told him she had a great time and can't wait for the next reunion. Harold said walking is difficult for her, but the reunions are important to her.

"Some of the best friends we make in life, we make during our high school years. I think since my high school days, I have made two good friends. That's it. Only two that I feel very close with."

Harold laments that more than half of his former classmates are dead now. It is getting more and more difficult to reach those who are still alive.

"Unfortunately, as you get older, you lose some of your old goombahs, your old friends. There aren't too many left."

Harold worked hard to provide a wonderful home for his wife and three children. He wonders how many young people have an eye on their future. His early years were far different.

"In those days we weren't so fast to spend money. We didn't have that much. Today there are so many kids who have no ethic of money at all. Whatever they have, they spend."

Susan Wolpert, class of '76
Ray Lesser, class of '74

Every month, more than 70,000 people go to their mailboxes and find the latest edition of the *Funny Times*. It's a publication jammed with dozens of humorous cartoons and a monthly ration of satirical columns. Garrison Keillor, Dave Barry, and Tom Bodett are among its contributors.

The editorial offices of the *Funny Times* are just a few steps away from Cleveland Heights High. They are on the second floor of the building that used to house the legendary Meyer Miller shoe store.

Susan Wolpert and Ray Lesser are the creators and driving force behind the *Funny Times*. They launched the magazine in 1985. For the first four years, it was distributed free on the East Side of Cleveland. When not sifting through hundreds of cartoons and submitted articles,

Susan and Ray would work the streets, trying to drum up advertising for the fledgling publication.

Susan said, "You judge your self-worth on whether you made a sale. You shouldn't, but you do. You are dependent on making money from one group, but making a product for another group."

The modern day *Funny Times* carries no advertising.

Ray worries that advertising is a corrupting influence.

"You have these advertisers supporting our popular culture. Rather than have the television shows people would really want to watch, you have the television shows advertisers are willing to advertise on. People so much want things for free, they are willing to sacrifice their taste and the quality of the things they see, because they'd rather just get things for free."

The laughs in the *Funny Times* are not free. A one-year subscription costs twenty-five dollars. Susan says a lot of people buy gift subscription to the magazine, just before the holiday season.

"We are in a culture where you have to give a holiday gift, so we take care of it for them. It is something that will lift people's spirits. They are not going to be sad."

Ray describes Susan as a humor consultant. Perhaps an unlikely role for her.

"She's hilarious. She's very funny, but she doesn't like funny things."

Susan said, " I wasn't one of those people who read the comics. I don't like funny movies."

"She doesn't watch funny television shows. She doesn't watch television at all. She doesn't read funny books."

Susan said, "I'm serious. I came up with a new tag line last year for the *Funny Times*. Seriously funny."

It took some serious work to get the *Funny Times* up and running in the early days.

Susan said, "We did all the layout. We didn't have any publishing experience when we started. We weren't making very much money at all. We bought health insurance, and then we were definitely not making a living. We always said we had Blue Cross to thank for our business. Once we bought the insurance, we couldn't afford our business, so we thought we would pursue this one idea of making it a better paper, and marketing it nationally. If that would work, fine. Otherwise, we would pitch it. But it was a hit immediately. We did direct mail, we made up a mock issue and sent it around."

Within six months, Susan and Ray had amassed 10,000 paid subscribers.

For the last five years, Susan has relinquished some of her involvement with the *Funny Times.*

"I work on social change and transformation things. Mainly in the city of Cleveland and beyond. Israel-Palestine peace, political campaigns. We are just doing a tree-planting project in Cleveland Heights. We are planting fifty trees that will grow up to be big hardwoods."

Susan and Ray credit Cleveland Heights High for their ability to think freely.

Susan said, "We both went to the New School. There was this alternative school at Heights. Alternative education was popular when we went to school. At first, they had something called Flex. It was an English and social studies program for two periods a day.

"Then they started a full program and they had three hundred students and ten teachers and a wing of the school. The idea was students would be responsible for their own learning. We would make up the classes ourselves. We would tell the teachers what to teach. We could do independent research. Do internships. It was really an exciting time."

Susan is disappointed the New School faded away.

"Everything is oriented now toward passing the proficiency test. Students have to do all the curriculum."

Ray says the Cleveland Heights environment helped shape him as a free thinker.

"To me, what makes the graduates of Cleveland Heights High so great is not that the school is great. The school has had its ups and downs. There have been some great teachers there over the years, but it's really the community of Cleveland Heights is a great community that attracts a lot of amazing people to live here. We have such beautiful houses, beautiful parks, really interesting businesses that over the years, have mainly been owned by independent owners, small business owners."

Ray and Susan's small business is now approaching a twenty-five-year anniversary.

Ray said, "People who have subscribed include Hillary Clinton. She was a subscriber when she was still the wife of the governor of Arkansas. And then we got a change of address to the White House for her.

"Steven Spielberg was a subscriber. His sister bought him a subscription after reading about us in *The Washington Post*. His sister was the person who wrote *E.T.*"

One could say the *Funny Times* is a publication for people who have moved on from *Mad Magazine*. It certainly pokes fun at serious topics. It takes a head-long dive into politics and it favors the Left.

Susan said, "I think we might be the only Left publication that is profitable. There are many progressive people who buy the *Funny Times,* but we aren't really recognized by the progressive press as being a progressive publication, because we are not serious. The Left has to be really serious about everything that is going. I think that has been getting in the way of progressive ideas, because they are so serious. They don't know how to live."

Ray said, "Most humor which is left-leaning, or progressive, comes from people who are poor. People who are downtrodden. The humor that they make is about the people who are up there running things. Humor is kind of repressed anger, a different way of venting your frustration.

"You are attacking the people in a way that you can, with words or pictures. When you really can't do anything else about your situation because you are under their thumb. If you are making fun of billionaires, powerful politicians or Hollywood stars, or people who are rich and famous, you can holler left-wing, but it's really making fun of power. It tends to be funnier and better received by the masses.

"Right-wing humor seems to be made by a few people who are kowtowing to rich people and they are making fun of poor people. How funny is that? Who is their audience? Do you want to make fun of poor people or sick people? It's not that funny."

Susan says they are not into frat-boy humor. They don't like mean humor.

"We find ways to show what is wrong with the system, without losing our humanity. Humor is a way people can look at a dissonance in their world, where what people say doesn't match the way it is, or what we dream of doesn't match the way it is. Or we put ourselves into different types of behaviors that don't make any sense. So humor is a way we look at that, and actually get a little bit of freedom. I mean, think about your own life, when you are having conflict, and can get to the point of laughing at it."

Ray and Susan have not been laughing lately about the cost of doing business. They say they have been hammered by postal rate increases and production costs. Since they carry no advertising, they can't bellyache about a downturn in advertising. They relish their independence.

Ray said, "We are able to have viewpoints about the news you won't find in mainstream media, because we don't have advertising and we are independent. So we don't have big brother looking at us and breathing down our necks, saying you can't make fun of that. We can do whatever we want. That gives us an edge over most others."

The *Funny Times* is gaining some promotional exposure on its Web site. With many people turning to the Internet for news, Ray and Susan have an added challenge of keeping the humor fresh in their monthly publication.

Ray said, "The hard part is trying to predict what is going to be funny in ten days. By the time I read it and it goes through the layout process, and gets printed and mailed, there is this lag time. So much humor, especially political humor is so topical. If you watch the *Daily Show* from two weeks ago, it's not funny anymore. It's only funny the same day. It's only funny for a couple of days and then it's not funny anymore. We don't like to be like that."

To hedge their bets somewhat, Ray likes to have a fair amount of what he calls evergreen humor. Items that will remain funny for a long time. Cartoons that have a long shelf-life.

When Ray and Susan are about to go on vacation, they often send a card to subscribers in that area. They invite them to meet them. It's a unique way to meet their customers. At one point, they thought the *Funny Times* could be used as a vehicle to market humor material.

Ray said, "This was before Amazon.com. We said we should just sell humor books, cartoon books. We should have a humor section, just like the humor section at the bookstores. Sell the humor books of our writers and cartoonists. That was sort of successful for a while. Not long after we started doing it, there started being Amazon.com and they sold everything we sold for forty percent off. So it was kind of tough to compete with them."

In any given issue of the *Funny Times,* there could be as many as one hundred contributors, including writers, editors, and cartoonists.

Susan said, "Most cartoonists are either syndicated or self-syndicated. Self-syndicated means they have created their own network and they have contacted people and sent out their works."

Ray added, "The way most people make a living these days as writers and cartoonists, they have to have more than one place they publish. There are very few people whose work only appears in one publication. It would be impossible to make a living doing that. There are a few cartoonists who make their living selling to the *New Yorker.* The *New Yorker* pays about five hundred dollars per cartoon, so they sell all their rights for five hundred. We just buy one-time rights for cartoons."

So what has been the secret to the on-going success of the *Funny Times?*

Susan said, "We are good editors, and that is why we have been successful. Probably because I didn't like humor, things had to be very funny to make me laugh."

Ray said, "We do very well in isolated areas with cold winters. Somebody said they summer on an island off of Maine. They know this lobsterman there. He brought over the *Funny Times.* He cuts out the cartoons and shows them around."

Susan says her experience at the New School at Heights High helped make the *Funny Times* a reality.

"I have always been extremely self-directed. By having that experience at Heights High, for me to do things I wanted to do then, was very positive for me. I regret there aren't more alternative schools. The idea there was to create lifelong learners. If you want to be my friend, you better keep on thinking."

Ray thinks much of the humor out there today is misdirected.

"All of the humor on television, making fun of women, making fun of various different races. Humor that is accepted by great big corporations, that you can put on television. You watch some show that is supposed to be funny, and where is the joke? Why are they making fun of these people?

"They don't want to make fun about what is really angering people, and what is really upsetting people. Let's just make fun of J Lo, or Britney Spears to distract people. Humor that distracts people.

"People get brainwashed by the advertising because we are that kind of animal. They go out and they buy all this crap the advertisers want 'em to buy. So we have this consumer society. We are just consumer driven. As long as we keep buying the stuff the advertisers sell, they are going to keep putting out all those shows and those magazines that attract the minds of the people that are easily brainwashed.

"Our publication is only for people that don't care about it. They buy it. They want to pay for it. If they don't want it, they don't pay for it."

Ray and Susan are a couple of analytical, deep-thinkers who make their money by trying to make people laugh. They admit subscriptions have leveled off somewhat, but they hope their publication is recession-proof.

Ray said. "We think we are like a bar. You know the secret of a bar, don't you? When times are bad, people go and drink because they are miserable. When times are good, they want to drink because they want to celebrate. It's the same thing with humor. People want to laugh, whether the times are bad or good."

Al Gray, class of '45

"The car was still there. There were footprints in the snow to the garage. He had slept there that night to avoid people. One or more people he thought might be coming to look for him."

December 7, 1952 has endured for more than half a century as Al Gray's personal day of infamy.

"He went to the corner store to get a cigar and he never came back."

Al's father, Robert Gray was sixty years old. Perhaps his dad bought that cigar that night and went into his car to smoke it, as he pondered his future. How long did he sit in the car? Did the bad guys track him down? Or did Robert sneak away before dawn and just keep running for the rest of his life?

Al Gray thought of his father as a pioneer of sorts. Robert Gray played a major role in helping Jewish families make the migration from Cleveland's Glenville neighborhood up the hill to Cleveland Heights.

Al was just four years old when his own family moved from Glenville to Desota Avenue in 1932.

"He moved probably fifty percent of the people who moved from Glenville up to the Heights. He made a real business out of it."

But after a successful run, things started souring for Robert Gray. He lost his business. He was out of work and didn't seem very motivated to find another job. Al's mother Lottie had to find work to keep some money coming in.

"Unfortunately, he loved to gamble. He had been done-in by gamblers, because he disappeared in a fashion, if you thought about it, indicated it was not his choice to go away from Cleveland."

Al was twenty-four years old when his father vanished. He was in law school at Western Reserve.

"I ran ads all over the country. I didn't have any real money, but I wrote letters, placed ads, contacted police departments as far away as Los Angeles."

Al was haunted by his father's disappearance all of his life. Were gamblers to blame, or did Robert Gray just decide to abandon his wife and two sons? Al wondered if it had been a mistake for him to have confronted his father about his mid-life crisis.

"I said I was the one who drove him away, because he was gambling and not working. At that point, the business had shut down. He was driving my mother up a wall. I used to shout at him. It was a tough period for all of us."

Al never let go of his guilt. It didn't matter if it was real or imagined. When he reached age sixty, he suffered a setback. Mental problems took control of his life.

"That put me in the hospital when I turned sixty, which is called an Anniversary Syndrome. I went into the hospital the same age he disappeared."

Al spent three long years recovering from his mental difficulties. He never heard a word about what happened to his father. Despite his father's problems back then, Al knew it was uncharacteristic of his father to just run away.

"I really think the bad guys took him."

When Al was a student at Cleveland Heights High he was a writer for *The Black and Gold* newspaper, and also worked on the staff of the *Caldron*, the school yearbook. He enjoyed writing, but a teacher at Roxboro warned him in the ninth grade, that earning a decent living as a journalist would not be easy.

The teacher's name was Walter Kincaid. He was Al's social studies teacher. He was talking to the students about choosing a career path.

"I was interested in journalism. He helped me to understand journalists of that day were underpaid. The average journalist in those years was making 900 dollars a year. Doesn't that sound unreal? And he brought that to my attention. He gave me a sheet that had that information on it, and I can remember saying to myself, I gotta look for something else."

World War II was still going on when Al graduated from Cleveland Heights High. He enlisted in the Navy. His mess hall assignment helped him reach another career choice decision.

"Young, smart, Jewish guys thought about becoming doctors. In the Navy, when I was in boot camp, I worked in the kitchen with chicken gizzards. I sure didn't like that. I couldn't face up to the fact of going to medical school."

The war soon ended and Al Gray's military career was a short one. While a student at Western Reserve, he started shaping his career goal.

"I had seen lawyers in the movies. I had developed a respect for lawyers and the law."

Al was only twenty-three when he earned his law degree at Reserve. He fancied himself as a talented lawyer.

"I could talk the game good. I could talk to the judges good. I knew 'em all. Courts were smaller. It was a friendlier environment."

Al had a successful career as a lawyer. He didn't get married until he was forty-seven. A few years later, his wife Anita gave birth to a daughter. Al decided to take down his shingle. He wanted to spend all the time he could with his family.

Even the most successful of lawyers would have a tough time shutting things down at age fifty, but Al certainly had something to fall back on. As a young man, he picked up on the importance of buying stocks. He had a gift for it. He had the insight and the moxie to take a chance when others might shy away.

He bought his first stock while he was in law school. Al spent 378 dollars on Republic Steel stock. It was just before the outbreak of the Korean War. Al said it was a very good time to buy a stock.

" In 1952, I bought a very important foreign stock, which nobody in the United States was buying, called Royal Dutch Petroleum, which was the owner of Shell Oil here."

Al would buy ten shares at a time. He would spend just shy of three hundred dollars each time. Soon, he had a couple of hundred shares.

"Nobody was buying foreign stocks in those days. I also learned about borrowing money to buy stocks. My biggest success of the early years was in Japanese stocks. I was a real pioneer. I went to Japan as part of an around-the-world trip. Seven weeks in 1962. Everybody thought I was a little crazy. I loved the idea of going to foreign countries. I always did."

Back in those days, most Americans still hung to the belief that anything made in Japan was inferior. Al had a different perspective. He gobbled up stock, getting in the ground floor of Sony, Hitachi, Matsushita and an insurance giant called Tokyo Marine.

"I didn't sell them for twenty-five years. They became the hub of my investment world."

Al Gray has ridden the highs and the lows of the stock market. Some with less nerve would have bailed out when they were ahead, and Al Gray has been far ahead. But he continues to watch the trends and buy stocks.

"In my market activity, some would say it is a gamble. I say no. You make the percentage plays that make it less than a gamble. Do your best to take advantage of the information that is available and do wise investing."

Al says he has taken a bath in the stock market in 2008.

"We live in a growth world. I think timing is very important. I just wouldn't run willy-nilly cause the market is down. I'd get some good advice in how to do it."

Over the years, Al Gray has been eager to share his fortune with others. He has been an active supporter of the Cleveland Heights High Alumni Association. He has been honored by the Case Western Law

School for his ongoing contributions. He has been active in politics, hosting fundraisers for candidates. He has made contributions to religious organizations and countless charities.

He has been saddened by the rapid decline of the Cleveland area economy.

"I think it's the great challenge in the world to be optimistic about the community's future because of the departure of employers. The fact so many companies have either closed, or moved out of town. I think it's a terrible negative. We have suffered an enormous amount."

Al Gray has been among the fortunate ones. He has not suffered. His home in Moreland Hills looks like it could be in Beverly Hills. The flowers and shrubs are expertly manicured. A pond sets off the peaceful backyard.

Step inside the front door and visitors are taken aback for a minute or two. Al Gray is a collector. He holds on to memories. He displays trinkets that remind him of his interests. As it turns out, Al is interested in just about everything.

Display cases are filled with things like fossilized dinosaur eggs, moon rocks, autographed baseballs, sports jerseys, books and pictures of Hollywood legends. Works of art are prominently scattered in every room. Every flat surface is covered with magazines, notes, and letters. It is the kind of disorganized chaos that most women would be reluctant to tolerate. Al lives alone. His marriage ended in divorce. His two daughters live nearby. Al became a grandfather for the first time at age 80.

So why does this kind-hearted man with so much on his plate, stay so involved with his high school?

"I love it. I have wonderful memories."

He attends all of his Heights High reunions. Groups of friends also get together on a regular basis.

"I've always believed in staying in touch. I think it is one of the greatest experiences in life to remain in touch. You don't live with 'em day by day, but it's nice once a year or three times a year. You have the opportunity to share some experiences."

Al Gray thinks his years at Heights High set the table for his eventual achievements.

"You just had a positive feeling about the schooling you were getting.

I think the education was outstanding. I think I had a wonderful opportunity as a result of being a good, but not phenomenal student."

Al Gray estimates the enrollment at the high school was one-third Jewish back in those days.

"I would say the atmosphere was not as smooth as you would like it to be. There was a great deal of anti-Semitism before the war because of the Depression and the Jews were among those blamed for the Depression."

Life took some unexpected turns for Al Gray over the decades, but he always found his way. He took risks with the stock market. He borrowed huge some of money to buy stocks. He was confident his moves would pay off. But during his school days, he did play one thing right down the middle.

"I wrote the speeches for both of the candidates running for school president. I knew one of them was going to win."

Ruth Rivin, class of '69

"Life threw them some really big challenges. She was in a really serious car accident two months before they were going to get married."

Ruth Rivin is an executive producer with a company called LMNO productions in Los Angeles. She has been the guiding force behind countless documentaries on A&E, Discovery Health, TLC, and Lifetime. Her latest program focused in on Jamie Parks and his wife Lynn.

"Lynn's car accident was back in 1987. It left her in a coma for seven months. She had brain stem injuries. When she woke up, he didn't even know if she would remember him. When she did remember him, she told him to leave, to move on. She said she'd be a burden to him. Jamie said no, he was staying with her.

"She said if you want to marry me, I want to walk down the aisle. He said okay, fine. Whenever you are ready, you can walk down the aisle. It took seven years of rehabilitation therapy to be able to barely walk down the aisle with the support of her dad and her brother."

Jamie Parks was a letter carrier and a dedicated long-distance runner. He didn't want to just leave Lynn at home while he went running, so he started pushing her in her wheelchair while he ran. They became a fixture in their Tinley Park, Illinois neighborhood. Jamie became stronger and stronger. They would do 5Ks, then 10Ks and eventually started doing marathons.

"She was never supposed to be able to have a baby, and she had a baby. Then she started holding the baby in the wheelchair while they were running. It was just a beautiful love story. A story about commitment and adapting to what life throws at you. It just touches you. Their inspirational story makes you appreciate the simple, important things in life, like relationships, love and health."

Jamie decided the 2008 Boston Marathon would be the couple's last marathon. Ruth and her crew put together a program for Discovery Health called *Marathon Love*. It showed Jamie and Lynn preparing for the race in Chicago. The crew followed them to Boston to capture the drama of their final marathon.

"Everyone who has seen this special has been profoundly moved and I realized there really is a hunger to hear these kinds of stories. We always hear so many bad stories, so many negative stories in the news, but people see this story and they just respond so strongly to it. It has inspired me to keep telling these kind of stories."

Ruth Rivin says she loved her years at Cleveland Heights High. She was a high-energy person back then, but still is amazed she found the time to do everything she did. For her, Heights was a stimulating environment. It sparked her creativity.

She was a physical education major at the University of Cincinnati, and minored in modern dance. When she finished college, she founded the Peanut Butter and Jelly Dance Company. The dancers would visit elementary schools and introduce the students to modern dance. They had a grant from the Ohio Arts Council. Ruth says parents and teachers would often tell them after they performed that they should put their dance programs on television.

She says that planted the seed for her to do something on television. When Ruth and her husband decided to leave Cincinnati and move to Los Angeles, she thought it was a perfect time to make that career switch.

She went to an employment agency and was chosen for an entry-level job with a news syndication service called N.I.W.S. That company would solicit news stories and five-part series from television stations across the nation. It would then feed those stories to subscribing stations that were looking for additional content for their news programs.

"I learned the ropes. It was an entirely new career for me. I started learning how to write short, two or three minute long news pieces. I was able to see news stories that were submitted by reporters from all over the country. The reporters thought their stories could air nationally. It gave me this great overview of what kind of work was being done, and the approaches used by everyone who was telling stories. We dealt with a lot of specialty reporters, like medical reporters, business, and consumer reporters."

N.I.W.S. had a six-year run. One of the reasons it shut down was because of the growth of CNN. Local news departments had the opportunity to use stories provided by CNN and there was less of an urgent need to use a service like the one Ruth's company was providing.

Ruth moved on to LMNO Productions. Her assignment on her new job was to pore through footage from an old TV program, *Kids Say the Darndest Things*. Forty years earlier, host Art Linkletter would have laugh-filled conversations with children. It was a popular segment on his show *House Party*. LMNO was reviving the concept. This show was hosted by Bill Cosby and it aired on CBS.

"What we did every week on that show, we had a section where we would pull together some of the old segments from the old *House Party* shows, and we would actually track down some of the kids that were on that show. We brought them into the studio. That was my job on the show, to screen the old *House Party* clips, and put segments together.

"I tracked down some of the kids who were now adults. They were so thrilled. It was one of those wonderful memories for them. It was a little piece of their childhood. To see the clips of themselves when they were children was great because they weren't able to record those shows at home when they first aired."

Ruth says Art Linkletter would make guest appearances on the new show, and would interact with the grown-ups whom he had interviewed decades earlier.

"He was as sharp as can be. Art was still funny. He had amazing stories. His history goes back to the earliest days of television. He was so unpretentious. He didn't want a limo. He drove himself to the studio.

"Bill Cosby was phenomenal with the kids. He got down to their level and had wonderful conversations. It was a joy to watch him work."

When that show came to an end, Ruth started putting much of her energy into hour-long, documentary-style programs. She won several awards for a program called, *A Face for Yulce*. It was the story about a twelve-year-old girl from Indonesia who was burned when a kerosene lantern exploded in her face. Her face was burned and left disfigured.

"She was flown to Los Angeles to be treated by the doctors at the Sherman Oaks Burn Center. They transformed her face. We followed her on her entire journey. We had a camera crew in Indonesia in this little village and followed her travels to America, her year with the doctors, and the return to her family.

"She was a sharp little girl. Even the doctors said she never complained. She went through a lot of difficult surgeries and treatments. Her injuries were some of the toughest, most painful anyone can deal with. She never cried. She was just strong. It was another inspirational story of what the human character is capable of when people are put to these severe tests. She's doing great. She looks great."

As an executive producer, Ruth oversees a project from start to finish. She does the initial research, the shaping of the creative content of the show, and the on-location production. She oversees the writing, the editing and all the final stages of post-production. She is in charge until the final master of the program is turned over to the network. She admits there are pressures along the way. Her supervisors have to approve of each step along the way.

"I think I have a pretty good sense of storytelling. I like to tell stories and I think I have an eye for what a good story is. Once I find a good story, I know how to tell it. It always come down to that for me. Telling the story. Honing the story.

"I try to make the part of TV I contribute to, something I can be proud of. Something that is informative and entertaining. I don't necessarily defend the whole industry. I know there are a lot of good programs out there. I think it is a great medium for educating people. Everybody has to pick and choose what they watch. You may have to look to find quality programming, but it's certainly out there."

Ruth has been with LMNO for fifteen years. With each project, her confidence grows. She takes increasing pride in her work.

"Every time I make a program, you go through a period of everything feeling a little chaotic, unformed and unshaped. Then, there's that blank-page moment, that writers go through, where you can't imagine how you are going to get to the end of it. Now that I have been through it, so many times, I have the confidence it will take shape and will become a show. I'm able to start on the path now with a little more faith. You get a little better and a little more efficient."

From time to time, Ruth is given a project and she has some initial reservations about it. Perhaps she is not enthusiastic about topic.

"I just set one foot in front of the other. I have had shows where I have said I am just not into this subject, or wondered how I am going to tell this story. I guess I have a natural curiosity about things once you start going down the path. You meet some people who are involved in whatever the subject is, and you find they are pretty interesting people, and there is something interesting about the subject. The things take shape. It is a pleasant surprise. I manage to find something in every program that I really enjoy sharing with other people, and I know they will enjoy hearing about it too."

Marathon Love was in a sense, a marathon for Ruth. She had produced another show about Jamie and Lynn Parks ten years before, when they ran their first marathon race. They stayed in touch over the years. The Parks handed over their home videos to Ruth so she could incorporate them into the latest project.

"Their first reaction was, 'I can't believe you watched all of those hours of our home movies.' I went through hundreds and hundreds of hours of their home movies to select the moments we included in the documentary They were kind of astounded with that.

"Their whole family watched the show and loved it. It's very gratifying. Usually, I feel there was something I should tweak. Surprisingly on this one, I felt it was perfect. The network gave me a lot of independence on this one and we made the show I wanted to make."

When she was a senior at Heights High, Ruth Rivin was president of the Swim Cadets. She had to provide the creative direction for the swim pageant that was presented. She looks back at that now as great training for a television producer. Once an organizer, always an organizer.

She is never sure what the next project will be. A proposal has been tossed on her desk. It is for a program for the Science Channel called *Meteorite Men.*

"It's about these two guys who scour the earth looking for buried meteorites. They are really colorful characters. They are digging these rocks out of the earth that have been there for thousands of years. Rocks that came from outer space, and all of a sudden, these guys open up this interesting world."

It sounds like a story worth telling, and Ruth Rivin is just the person to tell it.

Cathy Cofield, class of '79
Barry Cofield, class of 2002

"We went to the Super Bowl. It was amazing. For the last few minutes, when they won the game, we were just on pins and needles. Afterwards, we all went on the field. It was just wonderful."

Cathy Cofield's son Barry was in the Super Bowl in his second year with the New York Giants. He was a sports superstar at Cleveland Heights High. He played football, basketball, baseball and ran track. At Northwestern, he was able to concentrate on football. He could have gone to college just about anywhere.

"He got offers. The mailbox would be filled. I have shoeboxes full of them. Offers he got from colleges. He and my brother went over all of the offers and they met with different scouts and such. My brother felt Northwestern would be good for him.

"Me, I was thinking, I hope he goes to Ohio State, because that's close. But there would have been a lot of competition at Ohio State. He went to Northwestern and he stood out. He started as a freshman."

Barry said, "My football coach at Heights, Mike Jones, was a tremendous influence, and is still a part of my life. He is a role model as a family man and as a professional. He played a large role in my choosing Northwestern University. He encouraged me to go to a school where I could stand out and not get lost in the mix. Northwestern's coaching staff included several Ohioans who made me feel at home."

Cathy says her son started getting noticed by pro scouts while he played for Northwestern. She says Barry had his sights set on the NFL.

"I think he really tried. He had his heart set on it. I think that was his goal. He would tease people. People would say what's your major? He'd say football. Deep down inside, he thought it could happen."

Barry said, "I didn't seriously think about my prospects in the NFL until my junior year of college. It was more of a dream than a realistic destination until then."

Cathy said, "On draft day, we sat around waiting. He turned the TV off, cause he couldn't take it anymore. He was taken in the fourth round, the second day of the draft. As soon as his name went through, everybody's phone started ringing. Text messages started coming through. People were congratulating me and congratulating him. His agent called him. Coach Coughlin called him."

Barry said, "Draft weekend was the most nerve-racking time of my life. There is the incredible uncertainty of where you will end up living and how much money you will make. That is if you are lucky enough to be drafted at all. When the Giants called me, I had given up on watching the draft and was watching a movie with my wife Kendra."

The fact that the New York Giants would start Barry Cofield as a defensive end as a rookie, is a testament to his abilities. Of course, his starting assignment came as no surprise to his proud mother.

"I thought he was immediately going to play, but he told me later, even though he was picked, he still had to go there, work out and try out and earn a spot, but we were blessed he started."

Cathy had some dreams for Barry at the start of his pro career.

"When he got drafted, I said I hope he makes it to the Super Bowl in his career. And it happened in his second year. I mean, it's been amazing."

Cathy was a single parent when she raised Barry. She always supported his interest in athletics. She did her best to attend all of his games at Monticello Middle School.

"I think I did quite well as a single parent. I had support from my family. But to have him turn out so well, that makes me the proudest. How did I do that? Just a lot of love, a lot of love."

Barry said, "My family put more emphasis on academics. Athletics was like a cherry on top."

Cathy transferred to Heights High when she was in the eleventh grade.

"It was a big difference from John F. Kennedy. I was a High Stepper with the marching band at Kennedy. I had to give all of that up. When I came to Heights, I didn't get involved with anything. I wish I could have gone to Heights earlier. They had this awesome curriculum. So many different classes.

"I did work-study in my senior year. I used to work up at Halle's at Severance."

Barry had little time for a job while at Heights. Sports took up most of his time all through the high school years.

He said, "I really enjoyed Heights. It was a great cultural mix and I have still have friends I talk to regularly."

Cathy took a job at the Cleveland Clinic and has now moved on to the Metrohealth Medical Center. She verifies a patient's insurance coverage before surgeries are scheduled.

Her friends at work were well aware she is a Super Bowl mom.

"They had decorated my cubicle. They had footballs. They had pictures from the Internet of him and hung them all around. I had a football hanging over my head from the ceiling. One lady had made a little caricature of him. They call me the Super Bowl mom at work. I'm still basking in the ambiance. I'm still living in the glory."

Barry said, "I don't think I fully appreciated playing in the Super Bowl until I missed out on it in the '09 playoffs. The Super Bowl was another dream come true that I will treasure forever. The circumstances surrounding the game made it perhaps the best game ever. Beating an undefeated team in the fourth quarter was unreal."

But when was it that Cathy Cofield had an inkling her son was destined for greatness?

"I think it was when I started looking up to him. He like surpassed me. He started wearing size 15 shoes. We had to special order his shoes. I said this kid has to do something special, if nothing else to afford his own shoes and clothes. He grew up so fast.

"In fifth grade, his muni league flag football coach thought he showed a lot of talent. Barry really seemed to enjoy it when he was on that team."

Barry was getting plenty of notice as an athlete at Cleveland Heights High. His mother says he didn't think he was a big deal.

"He was fairly shy and quiet, even with him playing the sports. He started dating in the eleventh grade. Kendra Armstrong was from the Monticello neighborhood, but she was a student at Regina."

Barry and Kendra went on to get married.

Cathy was, and still is Barry's biggest fan. She tried not to miss a game at Monticello or at Heights.

"He kind of knew where I sat. He could look up and see me most of the times in my usual spot. At basketball, I was there and had like eight pom pons, waving 'em. I was just proud of him."

In October 2008, Barry came to Cleveland Stadium when the New York Giants faced the Browns.

Barry said, "I had over seventy people at the game. It was a great feeling to have so many family and friends see me play against my favorite childhood team. Family and football are the top two things in my life right now."

"He was excited. Originally he kind of hoped he would play for the Browns at one point. Maybe some day, he will. I'm a Browns fan unless they play the Giants. I had to root for the Giants that night and I had to take a lot of flak. We were clapping and whooping and hollering."

Cathy has the NFL Package, so she can watch all of the Giants games on her TV at home in Cleveland Heights.

"In between plays, friends of mine will call and say did you see that? Did you see what he did? It's exciting. I'm still floating on a cloud. I haven't come down yet."

Cathy turns to the Internet to read about what Barry does both on the field and off the field. He takes the time to do a lot of charity work.

He visits children in the hospital whenever he can. He stays active in Cleveland during the off-season.

Barry said, "New York has so much money flowing around here, I feel the Cleveland area is more needing. I recently got involved with the Pop Warner Football League in Cleveland Heights and an AAU basketball team in the area."

"He's always been a good kid. I'm so happy for him. I said to him do you realize you are a celebrity? He's modest. He knows he gets the attention, but he's a modest kid."

Barry Cofield has always been aware of the importance of his education at Cleveland Heights and Northwestern.

Barry said, "The balance of academics and athletic competition at Northwestern is unmatched. I also loved my teammates at Northwestern. We had a quality group of guys that I wouldn't trade the world for. Northwestern has a beautiful campus and I enjoyed my time there."

Barry learned early on that life can sometimes take unexpected turns. Barry and the other members of the Northwestern football family were stunned when his coach Randy Walker suffered a fatal heart attack at age fifty-two.

"Coach Walk was a disciplinarian who taught me how to be a man and a professional. He was a great family man and a dedicated coach. He did good things at Northwestern and will be missed by many. I only hope when I leave this earth, people will care as much as they did when Coach Walk passed."

Cathy beams when she talks about Barry. "He knew he had to get good grades to stay on the team, but it's not like I ever had to chastise him or chase him. He would work. He would make good grades. He's been a blessing to me. He's been a good kid. He's so deserving."

Cathy says Barry's days at Heights High provided a great foundation.

"He had a lot of support there. A lot of friends encouraged him. His teachers and the coaches, they took a liking to him. Academically he did well, and with the sports he did well, too."

The New York Giants fans are latching on to Barry Cofield as well.

"They seem like they love him from what I have seen on the Internet. We go to the games and usually you will see Strahan jerseys, or Eli jerseys. I see a lot of 96's for my son. I'm really ecstatic. All I can do, is smile."

Barry knows pro athletes have a responsibility. He said, "I believe all athletes should have a code of ethics. Have a way of carrying themselves in the public eye. Whether we like it or not, kids look at us as role models. I do, however, see some merit in Charles Barkley's desire for parents to be their children's number one role model."

Cathy said, "I've always tried to support him in whatever he wanted to do. I've always encouraged him to make good grades."

Cathy wasn't a devoted student of the game, but has learned more and more about football over the years.

"He's taught me things. I've learned different things about sports. Sometimes I ask him questions. He says, 'Mom, I've been playing football all these years and you should know this by now.'"

Barry should have many years of pro football ahead of him.

"Life after playing football is hard to imagine after all of these years in the game. I could see myself doing some broadcasting. I have seen the terrible hours that college and pro coaches have to work. The only thing I am sure of is, I don't want to sit in a cubicle. I want to interact with people."

Alan Schonberg, class of '46

"I had a Swedish nanny. We had a chauffer. We had an elegant apartment on Riverside Drive. We had a cottage on Long Beach for the summers. We were at the top of the world."

Alan Schonberg's parents were married in Cleveland. Soon after, one of Alan's uncles married into a wealthy family in New York City. He called Alan's father Julius and pitched an idea. If he moved to New York, they could launch a business.

"They had a cloak manufacturing business. Ladies coats trimmed with fur collars. They made a fortune. They did magnificently during the '20s."

Students of history can tell you the problem with the '20s is that they were followed by the '30s.

"My father lost everything in the Depression. By 1933, my dad was broke. Bankrupt and broke. That's why we moved back to Cleveland.

My dad's cousin loaned him fifteen hundred dollars and with that he bought a six thousand dollar home on Antisdale Road in Cleveland Heights in 1934."

Julius Schonberg had come full circle. His father had first settled here in the late 1890s. Julius and his three brothers and their father Abraham had all been peddlers back in Poland. Julius launched his first retail business when he was still a teenager.

"My dad opened a store. He was eighteen years old. It was in the wholesale district, which is now called the warehouse district on W. 6th Street. In those days, when you were eighteen, you couldn't sign a check, you couldn't sign contracts, so his father was the titular head of the business. It was called A. Schonberg Company. His father sat in the back of store and studied Talmud. West 6th was wholesale stores, up and down the street, both sides. Ninety-five percent of 'em were owned by Jews."

When Julius had moved on to New York for that ladies coats enterprise, the store on West 6th was left in the hands of his younger brother Sam. The ravages of the Depression swallowed up that business as well. So when Julius returned to Ohio, he had to find another way to support his family.

His cousin loaned him another fifteen hundred dollars and he opened a dry goods store in Cuyahoga Falls. Julius would make the drive every day from that house on Antisdale to the Akron area. Cuyahoga Falls was somewhat of a sleepy town when Julius first opened his store. Lots of farmers in the area. Husbands would bring their wives into town on Saturdays so they could shop.

"In 1939, the Akron rubber factories began to prepare for the war effort. All those farmers, their wives and their kids all went to work in the rubber factories and prosperity began to appear in Cuyahoga Falls."

Life back in Cleveland Heights for Alan was nothing like the luxurious life he enjoyed in New York City, but things at least had started improve for his family. Then tragedy struck.

"I was a happy-go-lucky little child. At age ten, my mother died. She had what they called in those days, a rheumatic heart. She died at age thirty-eight. She was a beautiful woman. She seemed to be universally liked. Very smart. A great mother."

Alan's aunt and uncle and their two daughters moved in with him and his father on Antisdale.

"I had a normal upbringing and a joyous upbringing. I loved my life."

Alan knows he could have been a better student at Cleveland Heights High. He says he worked pretty hard his first year, but for the last two years, he didn't bother doing any homework or studying. He was more interested in having fun. He headed down to Ohio State after finishing Heights, but wound up with pneumonia six weeks later. He returned to Cleveland Heights to recuperate and never returned to Columbus.

"I enlisted in the Army. I was in the 82nd Airborne. I went through jump school and I was sent to Germany as an occupation soldier."

Alan spent a year in the Army, but he didn't come rushing back to the United States. He landed a job in Germany working as a civilian employee of the U.S. Government. He would spend five and half years involved with running PX stores. During that stint, he began a courtship with a German woman.

"Maria was an extraordinarily beautiful young woman. She was one of nine children. Her father was never in the German Army, or involved in the Nazi Party. He was an alcoholic and her mother was not stable emotionally. Their house was bombed in '43 or '44. A couple of her brothers were in the army, the other children were all farmed out to other places. Maria was brought up in a Catholic convent by nuns."

Alan was a Jewish kid living in postwar Germany. He was involved with Maria, a German woman. Millions of Jews had been murdered by the Nazi regime.

"None of us coped with it. We just had to accept that it had occurred. The war was over. Germany was at its knees. It had no economy. People couldn't get enough to eat. They were in a pretty sad state. As an American, as a soldier and then a civilian, I had a great life. To me life was wine, women and song. I made a lot of money. Things were wonderful."

Alan was given more and more responsibility running those PX stores.

"I had all these Germans working for me, not one of them acknowledged they were ever in the Nazi Party. They were polite to the Americans. We employed them. Down deep, then and to this day, for what Hitler and the Nazi Party did to the Jews, I couldn't feel more hatred, but life goes on."

In 1952, Alan and Maria came to Cleveland. She converted to Judaism and they got married. They had four children.

"I went to work for Majestic Sportswear. We were one of the largest manufacturers of women's sportswear in the country."

Alan was a go-getter. He was named national sales manager of the company at age thirty-one. He worked for Majestic for ten years until he was thirty-three.

He then opened an employment agency in Cleveland. A couple of years later, Alan and a partner launched a company called Management Recruiters International. It was a headhunting firm. The company would recruit middle, to upper-level managers for employers. MRI took off like a rocket. At its peak, the company would have 950 offices across the United States and 250 more scattered across thirty-three nations.

"I put one foot in front of the other, day by day by day, and we built the company. I was able to surround myself with an operating staff of sensational people and work with great, great franchise owners who contributed mightily to the success."

Alan says many people are under the misconception that workers at a headhunting firm just sit around waiting for people to drop off resumes.

"The outside world might think we deal with unemployed people. We don't. We look for the best in the field. Every employer who has a need, there is someone fulfilling that need for another employer. That's who we look for. And so we purloin, if you will, steal people from company A and put 'em in company B. And now company A has an opening. We find them a guy in company C, and that's called executive search. Let's say Sherwin-Williams needs a controller. Glidden has controllers. We do the research to find out who is the best in the field."

Has MRI been raiding companies, just to walk off with their best and brightest? Alan doesn't look at it that way.

"It was in my opinion, a noble profession. Every employer who says, 'find me a guy,' has a check in his hand. He wants to give it to me, if I find that person, the right person. Every candidate you place, if we place 30,000 to 40,000 a year, you have enhanced his or her life. They wouldn't take the job if it wasn't an advancement."

Alan says more than one hundred MRI franchise owners have become millionaires. He says he never lost track of the need to do the right thing for his employees and the franchise owners.

"We have some offices doing three, four, or five million dollars a year. It's an incredible business for those who do it well."

Alan admits he was a late bloomer in life. It took him a while to see the light.

"If I have one lament, it is I didn't have the opportunity to mature in a college environment, and learn how to be a mensch. As a high school boy, I didn't learn that. It took me a long time to become a mensch. As I matured in the business, I found I began to discover my own humanity. I wish I had discovered it years and years before. I wish I had prepared myself for a contributing role in society."

Alan has definitely made up for lost time. His role with MRI is ceremonial now. He devotes most of time to philanthropic causes. He sits on the boards of numerous charitable organizations. He is involved with programs for students. He wants to inspire them toward success.

Alan says he was forty when he had a revelation. He figured out what life is all about.

"It put me in a different plane and a different perspective. From that point on, I always felt the more I could do for other people, the better off they would be, and the better off I would be. I saw things a lot differently."

Chuck Wien, Class of '66

Chuck Wien's family has been deeply involved in the carpeting business in Cleveland since the '60s. Chuck, and his father before him, never lost touch with the secret to success.

"The real secret to success, and there is no secret to it, it's pretty obvious. You have to take care of your customer, because this industry is so much built on referral and repeat business. Be there, persevere, work hard and take care of not only your customers, but your employees too."

Chuck's son Michael is a med student, about to begin his residency. It hasn't taken Michael long to realize many patients are getting shortchanged.

He told his dad, "Patient service in the medical field is extremely lacking. Maybe some doctors and some nurses are overwhelmed. Maybe there is no relationship there. Maybe they don't care."

Chuck says his son is a sensitive, caring individual. He always has been. Michael feels in his heart, it doesn't matter if you are in the medical field, or you are in the carpeting business, people should come first.

Marshall Carpet was started at Richmond Mall by Chuck's father, Marshall Wien. Chuck knows you can have strong management skills, but you have to make sure the employees feel they are a big part of the operation.

"We have had employees with us for a long, long time. They are really the backbone of our business. Is that a secret? No. But do all businesses have that? No. There are businesses that abuse their employees, that really abuse their customers. We bend over backward for our customers and do things we don't charge for. Do service calls where don't charge the customers anything. Years later, we take care of problems that are in the gray area.

"We do things for our employees, whether it's time off, days off. Whatever fits their needs and they appreciate it."

It's a formula that has worked for Marshall Carpet. The company is now beginning its fifth decade in Cleveland. This area hasn't exactly been a boom town. But Chuck says that can be okay.

"Cleveland is like a snail. It just plods along. Little dips. Little valleys. The cities that really spiked, have fallen the hardest."

Chuck says 2008 has been a definite challenge.

"We are feeling a downturn in activity, traffic, sales, customers, profitability, value. The pressures are there. The carpet mills have raised their prices tremendously, because it's an oil-based product.

"We are feeling the pinch now. If there is a commercial job floating around, maybe the rep would get three calls to bid on the job. Now he's getting seven or eight calls. The contractor is shopping for a low price as much as they can."

Chuck's brother Marc is also in the family business. He says Marc reminds him a lot of their father.

"My dad and my brother had these innate qualities of being a people-person. A man's man. Trying to be more than fair to people. I saw that with my father. I see that with my brother.

They have a certain likability which you just can't teach. You either have it or you don't have it. Charisma. People like you, and want to like you. They are engaging people."

Chuck downplays his own personality and his sense of humor. After the economic downturn and the collapse of the stock market, he liked to share a quip from a friend.

"He recalculated his retirement recently, and felt that if he worked for ten years after his death, he will be okay."

Chuck joined his dad's company right after completing Ohio State.

"My dad actually needed somebody at that time. I didn't know where or what I was going to do. I thought I'd give it a try."

Now nearly forty years later, Chuck is wondering when he can retire. Does he have an exit strategy?

"Berkowitz-Kumin." That's the name of the Jewish funeral home in Cleveland.

Chuck knows the floor covering industry has been changing dramatically in recent years.

"We have already seen some falling out in our industry. Falling out of family businesses. Small chains. You are not going to lose Home Depot or Lowe's, but we lost Buddy's. Lost some small family stores. Almost all of the department stores have gone out of the business. May's, Higbee's, and Macy's used to sell and install carpeting. They have gotten out of it. We have seen manufacturers close factories in our industry."

Chuck says his carpet business is labor intensive, so customers aren't inclined to shop for carpet on the Internet and then try to find someone to install it.

He says he picked up his work ethic from his father.

"He worked two jobs. He would work wholesale during the day, and retail at night."

He says his mother Mindell was a strong, guiding force as well.

"Our mother pushed us more to go to college, to stay in school. She was the disciplinarian of the two. She was a PTA mom and an involved, full-time mom. She was a very opinionated person. She wasn't shy about expressing an opinion, whether she was confronting a teacher, a guidance counselor, or a rabbi. She would stick to her guns and hold to her opinions.

"When my mom passed away, she was eighty. She traveled, did

things, She was active. Went to plays. She was comfortable within herself. She was able to handle being a widow. It wasn't going to stop her from being as happy as she could be.

"My daughter was sixteen at the time my mother died. My daughter's friends were at the funeral. The rabbi eulogized her, and right after, one of my daughter's friends came up to us and she said, 'When I die, that's the kind of eulogy I would like. I would like my life to be like your mother's.' Here is a teenager grasping what a wonderful life my mother lived."

Chuck admits the social life at Heights High was more of a priority than the schoolwork was. His friendships from then are as strong as ever. He says they are more lasting than the friendships from college.

"Good memories. I have nothing but good memories."

One of the most important lessons from his parents. "It's not always the length of time you live, but how you live your time."

Eric Silverman, class of '87

"If you let things weigh on you, it's just going to chew you up and spit you out. If you have to lay off thirty teachers, you have to take it as it is. Otherwise, it's going to burn you up."

Picture someone on a school board and you think of a middle-aged person or even a retiree. Someone who has finished a solid business career and is trying to give back to the community. Eric Silverman has been the exception to most perceptions.

"I've been doing this for fifteen years in one capacity or another. I'm forty now, I'm still perceived as the kid. For years and years and years, I've always been the youngest person in the room."

Eric hadn't been out of Miami of Ohio too long when he decided to run for a seat on the Cleveland Heights - University Heights school board in 1994.

"Nobody thought I'd win, including my parents. I researched every campaign for the previous fifteen to twenty years. I did my homework, I did my research. I found my voting base, which voters would be most apt to support me. I went door to door for four days a week for the entire summer.

"There were seven people running. I had the second-lowest budget and the second-highest vote total."

Eric Silverman was re-elected four years later. In 2001, he thought he could defeat longtime incumbent University Heights Mayor Beryl Rothschild. Voters were not interested in changing mayors.

During his eight years on the school board, Eric certainly did not blend into the woodwork.

"This is nasty work and hard decisions, and if you think you can close your eyes and just wish good things happen, it doesn't work that way. If you are upfront with the people, it works a lot better than trying to be polite and diplomatic. If you are the youngest person in the room, you've got to have your facts straight. You gotta know what you are saying."

Critics of Eric Silverman's tenure on the school board thought he was brash, perhaps pompous.

"People come up to me and say, 'Are you Eric Silverman?'

"I say, maybe. What's the context? How do you know me? Do I have to put on armor, or are you going to say something nice?"

Eric now sits on the Cleveland Heights - University Heights library board. He is the driving force behind the Cleveland Heights High School Alumni Foundation. He earns a living working for the LNE Group. It's a government relations firm.

As he has grown older, Eric thinks he has toned down somewhat.

"You can't shoot from the hip. I used to shoot from the hip. Say whatever I thought. I wound up burning a lot of bridges. Sure, I want things to be my way, but I don't want to be like Attila the Hun. You've got to compromise. You are going to have to work for what you want. What is the common ground where everyone can walk away with something. I'm not going to stonewall someone. I'm not trying to screw you over. I'm trying to have us all benefit and win from this."

Eric Silverman hatched an ambitious plan to actually tear down the science wing of the high school. It was added on in the early '60s. His plan was to restore the school to its original grandeur. That costly proposal never got off the ground. Eric now hopes the Alumni Foundation members will come up with part of the money to replace the clock tower of the high school.

"It's the one part of the building that has been consistent. It's the district's logo. Let's see if the project resonates with the alumni. In the worst-case scenario, you take the thing down and put a small roof up. Theoretically, you could lop the thing off and put a little peak there and be done with it. To me, that would be a bad emblematic sign of decline."

The clock tower is in disrepair and rotting away. Ignoring the problem could lead to extensive water damage to the building.

"There has been eighty years of patchwork up there. It's been one patch after another, as opposed to, let's go back and start from scratch. The clock tower is the icing on the cake. If we did nothing, it would be a big disappointment. It would be like when they tore down all the four elementary schools and Roosevelt. When they replaced all the windows with God-awful, ugly ones.

"It would be like, the caretakers of our community, of our assets, saying we don't value anything. Unfortunately, this community has a long history of short-term solutions to long-term problems. It would bother me to see that. It would be the latest in a line of bad decisions. It's like death by a thousand cuts. You could have done something right.

"On a board, you shouldn't look at how decisions will affect people this year, or next year, but I'm more concerned about how it is going to play five, or ten years out. You look at the stuff they did in the '70s and you say how could you do this? This is so dumb. But if the tower is not replaced, it wouldn't be the end of us."

Eric Silverman helped launch the Heights Alumni Foundation. It was something you might expect from an older graduate, not someone a dozen years removed from his high school graduation. He puts together a newsletter and mails it out to 10,000 Heights alums. He sponsors a couple of annual fundraisers and he is deeply involved with the scholarship program that provides college money to graduating seniors.

"This past year we gave almost fifty thousand dollars away for scholarships. I enjoy it, and I believe in it."

Before Heights launched its alumni organization, Eric traveled to Lakewood High and talked to Tony DiBiasio who started that school's program. He knows the foundation can play a huge role in the community.

"It's a marketing vehicle for the district. The district puts out information about what's going on. The school district is always going to say something good. The alumni foundation says something, it is going to be viewed in a different light."

Operating an alumni group for the Cleveland Heights High has challenges.

"If it's a small town, it's relatively easy to get your alumni involved because it's a small town and everyone went to one school. Heights has so many eras, so many generations. You want to represent all of them, and you want to be respectful and present them all equally."

Eric finds he is on a constant crusade to battle stereotypes and misperceptions about the school.

"Almost every other high school on the East Side has a nice suburban campus. At Heights, it's right there at the intersection. You could call five police cars to Shaker Heights High, or Brush, or Mayfield and nobody is going to see them. The cruisers at Heights High, boom, you ain't gonna miss 'em."

Eric tries to convince older graduates to maintain their ties with the school.

"What has always been an issue for us is they say, 'It was always so good back then.' Oftentimes, people are looking through rose-colored glasses.

"When I tell people, academically, we are a better system now than when I graduated, or the buildings are in the best condition they have been in since the '72 renovations, which was just abject butchery, they can't believe it's true, but it really is.

"People don't want to, or can't see that because they drive past Heights at three o'clock in the afternoon, and that's the perception they have. A bunch of kids hanging out in front of the high school who happen to be predominantly African American. Those kids are probably waiting, like I did, to take the 7AX bus back to Noble and Monticello."

Eric Silverman and his parents lived on Delmore Road. Throughout his school years, he witnessed a steady out-migration of white families and an in-migration of black families.

"There was a friend of mine, whose mother was a teacher in the school district. They said they were going to move in the next year or two. I asked why."

He said, "You know."

"I said no, tell me. You are telling me your mother isn't a good teacher?"

"Another friend said they were leaving the district because of the quality of the schools. I said, don't say it's the quality of the schools. If someone is moving out of the community, I don't want them to say it's the schools. I want them to say, I'm not comfortable with the racial balance. I don't want them to have an excuse. If they are going to move out, they are going to have to confront the reason why they are going to move. I'd tell them, so it's your issue. It's not the quality of education."

Eric started standing up for Heights High and the quality of the education he received there, when he enrolled at Miami.

"When I was in college, West Siders would say, 'Oh, you went to that ghetto school.' I was like, what are you talking about? I'm better prepared for college than you guys are. When I was in high school I didn't really think I'm getting this great, phenomenal education, but when I went to college, I realized I was well-prepared."

Eric was twenty-four when he was elected to the school board. He had a mission.

"So many stupid things were going on. It just irritated me. I figured there was a better way to do things. There were moronic decisions, and coupled that with people saying you went to that ghetto school. The Heights schools got a bad rap because of stereotypes."

The Cleveland Heights High Alumni Foundation handed out sixteen scholarships in 2008. It hopes to present twenty in 2009.

Eric is now president of the Heights library board. He will probably weigh options for other opportunities. He has accomplished a lot. He has rubbed some people the wrong way. He has taken his lumps.

"I have heard no matter what people say about you, you always return phone calls. Of course I do. That's my job. If you are direct and honest with them, and listen to them, they respect that. Give people, even if it is bad news, they want good news, but if you give them the straight information they appreciate that. If you listen to what people say, and take what they say into consideration, that goes a long way."

Some might now look at Eric Silverman as a forty-year-old kid, but even his harshest critics will grudgingly admit, this kid has come a long way.

Shirley Allen Shatten, class of '45

Shirley Allen Shatten is a person who is undeserving of heartbreak, yet has endured far too much of it in her life. She had a rewarding career as an elementary school teacher, raised four sons, and even into her eighties, she devotes four days a week to volunteering and civic commitments.

Shirley says her years at Cleveland Heights High were wonderful. The first two years more so than the last. Her senior year upended by illness.

"I got rheumatic fever and I didn't graduate with my classmates. I was at home. In those days when you had rheumatic fever, you had to stay in bed. An English teacher and a history teacher would come to my house, so I could get my requirements. I wasn't happy. I had all these dreams in my bedroom. I was going to have chairs around and people were going to come and witness my graduation. Isn't that silly? I still remember that."

Shirley remembers doctors would come to her house in those days. She says one doctor made a house call while his driver waited outside in the doctor's limousine. The illness forced her to miss her prom. It also changed her plans for her first year of college.

"The treatment, that was before penicillin, was going to Florida. If you had any heart ailments then, you went to Florida. That's how I happened to go to college in Florida.

"I went to Rollins College which was a wonderful school in Winter Park, Florida. I had the best professors in the world because everybody who was also sick came down there to teach. I had professors from Dartmouth. From Williams College. I had professors from all over. It was unbelievable."

Shirley would have loved to complete her college education at Rollins, but her parents couldn't afford to keep sending her there. She moved back into the family home on Raymont Road in Cleveland Heights and enrolled at Flora Stone Mather College on the Western Reserve campus.

Shirley's father, Sol Allen was a pharmacist.

"Before the Depression, he owned four drugs stores. He ended up with only one. It was at E.77th and Lexington. He sold it the year before the Hough riots. He was beat up four times in the store. My mother begged him to sell."

Shirley said her father never complained about the Depression and losing the three stores he owned.

"My father was the most tremendously optimistic person. My favorite statement from him was, 'It's only money.' Money was not an important thing to him."

Shirley was a student at Heights High during World War II. She remembers all of the shortages. People couldn't buy new cars. They couldn't get tires. Everyone had to use ration tickets for food. Gasoline availability was restricted.

"It was horrible. I used to walk to school and look at the treads on people's tires. We had food stamps. We got a "B" sticker on our car cause my dad was a pharmacist. He qualified for more gasoline. I remember we once went for a ride and I felt so guilty. We went for a ride out on Chagrin River Road. I thought that's such a terrible thing to do. I didn't say anything to my dad, but I felt it was a terrible crime."

Larry Shatten served in both the Navy and Army during the war. He used the GI Bill to pay for his education at Western Reserve. It was there that Shirley Allen met him.

"He was having trouble with geography and somebody told him I was doing well in it. So, he called me up and asked me if I could help him with geography."

Back in those days not many women enrolled in college.

"When women went to college, they were going to be a teacher, or a nurse. No one thought of doing anything else. Maybe a social worker. I always wanted to be a teacher. It was a wonderful profession for me. I loved it."

In those college years, Larry Shatten still carried emotional scars from the war.

"He was first in the Navy Air Corps. He talked a friend into joining. They were taking off of one of those carriers, during training, and his friend crashed. Larry left the Navy and joined the Army Air Corps. Then he was trained as a navigator because he wasn't going to be a pilot again after his friend's crash. He felt responsible for that."

Larry was through with flying planes, but he never lost his passion for aviation.

He went on to get his law degree, but never practiced. Instead he opened an insurance agency. Shirley launched her teaching career at Roxboro Elementary in Cleveland Heights. The Shattens bought a small house on Wilson Mills Road in Mayfield Village in 1952. They had four sons. Tom, Richard, Bill and Bob. All were exceptional students.

"My son Tom was unbelievable. In kindergarten, he was reading at sixth-grade level. By the time he got to junior high, he said, 'Mother, there are kids here smarter than I am.'"

There may have been, but not many. Tom was accepted to Harvard. A couple of years later, his brother Richard would join him there as a student as well.

Shirley would become a teacher in the Mayfield district. Life appeared to be perfect, but then the tragedies in her life would take place. The first was the death of her husband.

"Larry got lung cancer. He was fifty-seven. He didn't even smoke. I think it was because of asbestos. It was before they knew much about asbestos. The office building he was working in, they were tearing it apart while he was working there. Another young man who was working there died. So, I think it was that asbestos."

Tom finished at Harvard and went on to medical school at Ohio State. He and his wife settled in Pittsburgh. His practice thrived. Tom Shatten had six other doctors working with him.

"Tom died in a plane crash. The last conversation with him, I said, Tom, why don't you wait until your kids are grown up before you start learning how to fly a plane? He said, 'You didn't let dad fly, and he died young.' That was his last statement to me."

Shirley thinks her husband's love of aviation had been passed down to Tom. She said Tom's wife had decided to buy the flying lessons for him, just before the crash.

Shirley said the investigation proved that the accident was his flight instructor's fault. Tom was only forty-one years old. He left behind his wife and their two children.

His younger brother Richard had gone on to the Harvard School of Business after finishing his undergraduate work. He returned to Cleveland and took a job with a consulting firm.

"He ran a thing called Cleveland Tomorrow at thirty-one years old. They were looking for someone in their fifties or sixties to lead it, and they ended up hiring him."

Richard Shatten quickly made his mark as the leader of Cleveland Tomorrow. A planning organization dedicated to mapping out Cleveland's future. He was a shining star. Someone who earned the trust and respect of the business world in Cleveland.

"At Tom's funeral, Richard began to run a fever. Then it was discovered he had this brain tumor. We don't know where it started. They said he could have even been born with it. He lived six fruitful years after he was diagnosed."

Even now, when a development project fails to get off the ground, or another company chooses to abandon Cleveland, Richard's name comes up.

"He's been gone six years, and there was an article a couple of months ago, 'If Richard was here, none of this would have happened.'"

Richard fought a good fight. He was only forty-six when he died. He left behind a wife and three daughters.

"He went to the best doctors. They couldn't operate. He died on a Sunday. He had just worked the Friday before. He had his secretary there that Friday. He was dictating things. His mind was still clear. He was never really sick."

Before he died, Richard had started teaching at the Weatherhead School of Management at Case Western. By that point, he wasn't able to drive a car anymore. At first, he would ride a bicycle to campus. Later, his daughter would give him a ride there.

"Losing one son was unbelievable. Then a second one. It was all very hard. It still is."

Shirley helps run a scholarship program at Mayfield High School. It honors the memory of both Tom and Richard.

She is involved with a reading program in Shaker Heights called Learning English as a Family.

"These are doctors and professors who come here from foreign countries, and one day a week, they come and we give the families four books. We introduce them to the books, and we talk about the books. The kids come back and they tell us which book they liked the best."

She takes part in program at Center School in Mayfield. Kids are taught how to make quilts.

She serves on boards and committees for both Mayfield Village and the Mayfield Regional Library. She gives tours of the Mayfield Wetlands. Shirley has lived in the same house for fifty-six years, but even at age eighty-one, it's unusual to find her there.

She gets together on a regular basis with friends who worked alongside of her in the Mayfield Schools. Many are twenty years younger than Shirley. And she has remained in close contact with some former first-grade classmates from Fairfax Elementary. She has known them seventy years.

You might say, Shirley has been moving forward, making friends, helping others, ever since she recovered from rheumatic fever. Life can sometimes throw you a curveball. In Shirley's case, life has attempted to strike out the side. She has shown remarkable resilience. Shirley has never lost track of the deep losses she has suffered, but has never stopped reaching out and striving to make the world a better place.

Robert Zelwin, class of '68

Robert Zelwin was humorous and had a pleasant, outgoing personality at Roosevelt Junior High. He was part of the in-crowd there. So how were his years at Cleveland Heights High?

"I didn't like 'em. I had a tough time. I went from knowing everyone and being fairly popular. I got thrown into the environment. I wasn't maturing physically or emotionally like some of the other kids were. I saw friends starting to shave. Some of the guys I was palling around with, started smoking dope. I wasn't into that. I had this fear about it. I became somewhat of a loner the last year or so of high school."

Classmates who see Robert now, are surprised.

"I was the fourth-shortest person in our class. I grew after I got to college."

At Ohio State, Robert had a growth spurt, topping out at five-foot-eight. He was six inches taller than his high school days. Robert was a good basketball player. His height was a disadvantage back then.

In gym class, they were choosing teams for a basketball game. David Liff was allowed to pick the players for his team. The teacher, Mr. Kuhnle told Liff he had the first pick. Liff chose Robert Zelwin. Robert was embarrassed when the gym teacher laughed out loud. He was puzzled by the choice of the shortest guy in the class.

"He didn't know I could shoot the ball."

Robert had tried out for the basketball team all through junior high. He was among the first cut.

"I never made the team and it was just devastating."

No matter where he went back then, Robert didn't seem to fit in.

"Remember Wally's Pool Hall? Wally would kick me out because I looked too young. I said, but I'm just as old as these guys and he said yeah, but you don't look like it."

Robert just attended his fortieth class reunion.

"I said to some of the girls at the reunion, see, I'm taller than you now."

Robert is an avid runner. He is in good shape. He has lost much of his hair, but really isn't concerned about that. He knows a lot of the guys he went to school are now worried about being fat and bald.

"Some guys who were like really cool, walked the walk. But now they are feeling the way I did in high school. They don't want to be seen. They have their own little insecurities."

Robert said some students used to thrive in cliques during those high school days. At the reunion, he saw evidence that some people still have to rely on those cliques.

"Some of 'em couldn't walk five feet without having that other person next to them. That insulation. I'm not worried about the past. I'm worried about the present."

You couldn't blame Robert's father Sam Zelwin for worrying about the past.

"There were many a nights, in the middle of the night, I'd hear my dad screamin' out. He had a dream about the war. We didn't ask. I'd hear my mom say, 'Sam, Sam. Wake up.' I don't know what the dreams were, but they weren't good."

Sam and Ida Zelwin had grown up in a village called Novogrudok.

It was in Poland. It would later be taken over by Russia and now is in the country of Belarus. As a young man, Sam was a kosher butcher. No surprise, since both his father and grandfather were butchers.

"They were quite well-off in Europe. Not only were they butchers, they had cattle. They raised cattle. They didn't have to buy animals for slaughter."

In 1941, the German Army stormed into the area and took control. At first, Jews were forced to live in ghettos. Sam Zelwin was among those who started hearing about the next step by the Nazis. Jews were being shipped to death camps. Young men and women fled to woods to escape the Nazis and map out ways to fight back.

"There were stories they were killing Jews and that's when they decided they are not going to sit around and wait to be killed. They escaped from the ghetto."

Four brothers from the Bielski family would head the underground resistance movement that was based in the Naliboki Forest. They fought for their own survival and tried to sabotage Nazi operations. One tactic was to destroy incoming Nazi supply trains. Sam Zelwin was one of the heroes.

"My dad wasn't afraid of anything. He lived out in the woods. He said it was cold. They built camps. I don't know, out of wood, or they had tents. There was like three years of that. He said they always made sure they had one bullet left in their guns in case they got captured. There were about a thousand people that wound up in the woods with him."

Robert's mother Ida was also one of the Jewish Partisans trying to stay alive.

"They married in the woods in 1942. They didn't have jobs. Their job was to stay alive. He said they still practiced their religion. But my dad said, one day, they were so hungry they caught a pig and they slaughtered that pig. He would tell me he always remembered how good it tasted."

Robert's mother told him the Partisans constantly had to worry about Polish people telling the Nazis about them. Concerned they would reveal where their camps were set up. Armed members of the group would sneak on to farms and forcefully confront the farmers.

"They would go village to village because they needed food. They would go to farms. They would be armed and they would go to farmers and say they needed food. If there was a cow, they would slaughter the cow. They would warn them, if you tell anybody about this, or who we are, we are going to come back, burn your farm down and kill you and your family. It sounds pretty brutal, but guess what, it was war. They took food. They weren't asking, they were taking."

Sam Zelwin told Robert that he and another Partisan went into a tavern in a village one night.

"They were sitting in a corner and these Nazi soldiers walked in and they started talking about the dirty Jews. My father said they left the bar and waited for them to come out and then they took care of them."

Sam Zelwin's parents and a six of his brothers and sisters didn't flee to the woods. He never saw them again.

Sam and Ida made their way to a displaced persons camp in Germany in 1947. That's where their first child Harry was born. They settled in Cleveland in 1949. Robert was born a few months later. Two years after that, daughter Ileen was born.

In 1985 Robert traveled with his parents to Washington, D.C. for a Holocaust memorial ceremony.

"This woman grabs me and takes me off to the side. She goes, you don't know me, and I don't know you. I just want you to know that what your parents did for people during the war, you should have the most respect for them."

Robert's father owned Sam and Jack's Kosher Meat market on Taylor Road. As a young boy, Robert had no idea his parents were heroes. At first, he was a bit embarrassed by them.

"My parents had an accent. It was tough. You went to school, they would come to school, and as a little kid, you felt a little inferior because your parents were foreign. Now I have so much respect for people that have come to this country, whether Russian or from Europe. I've got some customers from Romania. I mean they have accents, thick accents. I understand exactly what they went through. It makes me more empathetic to what they have been through."

Robert's father died in 2005. His mother died the following year.

"Now I am so proud of what my parents went through. I think it has taken all these years. As you grow up, you appreciate what they did for you and everything they sacrificed for you."

Sam and Ida Zelwin married in the woods. They survived the woods and were parents to three wonderful children. They loved each other, but especially in their later years, they would bicker.

Robert says his mother would always pester his father. She would "hock" him, as Robert puts it. Sam took the abuse, but would remind Ida that she "vill miss him vhen he's gone." She did. Robert said she died of a broken heart.

In his later years, well after his retirement, Sam's old butcher friends would call him and ask if he could come in to help out for the holidays.

Sam always thought this was a chance to sharpen his knives again, and if he was pressed, he would admit it was a chance to slip away from the constant "hocking" of his beloved Ida.

Ida would say, "Vy do you have to work? You don't need the money. I'm a sick voman. You leave me by myself."

Harry, Robert and Ileen knew exactly why their dad was reporting for duty. It was a chance to escape the constant needling. They told their mom they absolutely had no idea why their dad was heading to the butcher shop.

When a son loses his father, he is supposed to take part in a morning prayer service every day for one year to honor his father's memory. Robert's year ended three years ago, but he still goes to pray every morning. He helps the elderly, frail men step up to the bimah. He puts their prayer books away for them.

"My goal every day is to do something nice for someone. I know who I am. If something happened to me tomorrow, I could say I've led a pretty good life. I've done a good job raising kids."

Robert runs a janitorial supply business and a cleaning company. He has enjoyed being his own boss.

"I've got the ability to talk to people. To sell things. It's very satisfying. I can call my own shots. I can come and go as I please. It's very rewarding. I'm not money-driven. Some people, they can never make enough money. I make a pretty good living. I don't feel like I have to go out and kill myself to make money. I just like the liberty."

Robert and his wife Ronna have three sons.

"A guy said how are your kids? And I said, I am very fortunate. I've got nice kids. And he said, that's the best thing you can say, because I'll ask somebody else and they'll say, oh my kids are making this much money. Saying they are nice, that's so good to hear."

Robert and Ronna have a grandchild now too.

"I have people say to me, your grandchild is beautiful. I don't care how good-looking he is. I just want him to be a nice person, because if you are a nice person, you have inner beauty."

Ellen Heyman, class of '59

"It takes a lot of courage to come here for the first time. People will very often say, 'I've had your calendar for six months,' or 'I have been driving around for three days, and I finally had the courage to come in.'"

Ellen Heyman is one of the founders and the guiding forces behind The Gathering Place in Beachwood. It's a support center for people with cancer, and the members of their families.

"When you walk through these doors, you have to acknowledge you have cancer. It's an acknowledgement you need help, and that's a hard thing. We all want to be independent. We don't want to need help from anyone.

"We complete the circle of care. Focus on the psychosocial, emotional, and educational needs. The non-medical needs of those facing cancer. Cancer affects every domain of your life. When people hear the word cancer, the first thing they think about is that they are going to die. Cancer can be a chronic illness. People are living a long time with it, but once you get cancer, life is never the same."

Some people come to The Gathering Place to visit the library and learn all they can about the disease. Others come for counseling, or to take part in the support groups that meet here. Art therapy is offered. There are movement classes, yoga, Pilates and tai chi. Participants can get a massage, try reflexology, or Reiki. One of the goals is to reduce the stress of battling cancer.

"Very often, people come at the time of diagnosis. They come straight from the doctor's office and they need information. They are just stunned at hearing the news. That's a very stressful time. When they are getting treatment, there are a lot of concerns and stresses.

"Surprisingly, the time after treatment is a time of high stress. You know when you think you are done with treatment, that it's all over, and you can put it behind you. But what happens is, while people are being treated, they are in the hospital and they have this huge support network from the medical team, the nurses and doctors. When they stop treatment, they see their doctor once a month, then every three months, so that source of support isn't there.

"Initially there is support from family and friends. While you are going through it, everybody is there and rallying around. But when you are finished with treatment, people think you should be done. You are done with treatment and you should be done emotionally too."

Ellen Heyman looks back at Cleveland Heights High and thinks of herself as one of the least likely to succeed. She says she didn't study, and was basically a goof-off. The class clown. She says she was a dreamer and failed to buckle down. During those high school days, she injured a knee, and while in the hospital, decided she would like to be a nurse. She got a nursing degree from the University of Wisconsin.

She spent seventeen years as a psychiatric nurse at University Hospitals. It was in 1998 that she teamed up with Eileen Saffran to kick around ideas for a facility like The Gathering Place.

"We held our first meeting in October. It was a grassroots meeting with health care professionals, cancer survivors and community activists. The meeting was in the Jewish Community Center, in this little room, about fifteen people. By March, we needed an auditorium.

"Starting a non-profit isn't an easy thing. Very few are successful, but people involved their faith and their money. We raised a million dollars even before we opened our doors. It was a real cushion to get started."

Ellen says people diagnosed with cancer all cope with it in different ways. She says that's why it's important to offer a wide variety of programs and services.

"When you get a diagnosis of cancer, the loss of control is one of the biggest things that hits people. We are used to living our lives, knowing what's ahead, and setting goals. We have to throw the date book out the window when somebody gets cancer. You don't know when your next treatment is, you don't know what's coming next. There's a lot of uncertainty.

"There's a constant threat it's going to come back, or it's going to get worse, or you are going to die. So there's a lot of anxiety and stress that accompanies it. Some people do a better job of keeping it at bay. They have a little more denial and are able to go about their lives. But for many people, it's kind of with them. They wake up every day and they think about it."

The Gathering Place offers a number of programs for the children of cancer patients. Ellen says this was an unmet need for families.

"Patients want to know how this is going to affect the children. Will they have trouble in school cause I have cancer? We have child specialists who work with families. Young parents will call and say they need to tell their children what's going on. I don't think anybody intentionally overlooks children. I think knowing exactly what children need at a particular age, and how much information, and what is the right amount, is something the professionals can guide them. A three-year-old needs a different set of facts than a thirteen-year-old. So our experts are able to sort that out.

"There are certain people who touch our heartstrings more than others, and for whatever reason, because they might remind us of somebody in our family, or somebody we are close to. For me, when I see a young man who is losing his wife and he's got children to raise. That's a particular weak spot for me.

"When I leave here, I don't think about the people I have interacted with. I have trained myself. I might think about the budget, or a program I an planning. I try not to think of the participants. It's called a decompression routine. It has a name. It's really separating home-life from work."

Ellen says cancers are being detected earlier than ever. There are better ways of diagnosing it. People are living longer, so there is a greater need to offer them services. She says twenty-five percent of the participants at The Gathering Place are men. Forty-five percent of the women in various programs have been diagnosed with breast cancer.

"I call myself the guardian of quality. My job is to make sure everything we do is of the highest quality. I want to make sure what we do is based on the needs of the people."

The Gathering Place has now opened a West Side location in Westlake. Many of the staff members in Beachwood have been on board since the very beginning.

"We all say we are doing our life's work and that we get more than we give. I kind of thought I was just going to retire from University Hospitals, and I have had this amazing opportunity to make this contribution. It's been extremely fulfilling for me and gratifying."

Ellen thinks it critical that the programs at The Gathering Place are offered free of charge.

"Cancer is costly. Even if people have the money, they don't have to worry. If they want to get a massage, the don't worry whether their insurance will pay for it or not. They can just come here. The cost is out of the equation."

The Gathering Place is now bringing its programs to the underserved. To people in inner-city neighborhoods. Ellen says for some people, emotional support during their cancer journey may be low on their priority list. They first have to be worried about food, shelter or their utility bills. Counselors go to churches or a cancer center and try to encourage people to use the services offered by The Gathering Place.

"Studies have shown, people have to hear about an organization like this, seven times before they come.

"This is a very hopeful place. People often think it's depressing here. They don't want to come to a support group because they will get depressed. But this is a place of hope. There's a lot of laughter and joy.

"People find hope cause when they are with other people who are going through the journey, when they see someone else doing well, coping well, it gives them hope that they too can cope.

"Managing the anxiety and the fear is probably the biggest struggle. Also maintaining their quality of life in the face of all of that is going on, the treatments, changes in appearance, the ability to function normally."

Ellen knows The Gathering Place is only serving a fraction of the people with cancer. The key is to be able to reach more people. In 2007, 3,500 people were served. There were 15,000 visits.

"Resilience, for some people, it's innate. They come with more resilience and coping strengths. When I assess someone, I always try to determine how they have coped with stresses in the past. Because people when they get cancer, they cope in the same way they have handled other things. If they have had difficulties in the past, or have gone through depression, we might anticipate those things would emerge with a cancer diagnosis."

The people who enter The Gathering Place forge strong bonds with others. They have a common problem and a common purpose.

"They are very connected with one and other. We just lost someone from one of the groups, so everyone rallied around, went to the funeral, and utilized the group time to talk about the feelings of sadness. We encourage people to continue their relationships when they are not at The Gathering Place."

The support groups serve cancer patients in many ways.

"You may have people just starting on the journey. In the same group, there could be people who are dying. The newer people are reassured they can handle this. They get an idea of what may be ahead. How they can cope. How they can deal with it. There's a lot of learning from each other."

Ellen Heyman says The Gathering Place has exceeded all of her expectations. She says it has been an amazing experience to watch it grow.

"I can't wait to get here. The gratification of the job outweighs the stressors. Helping people at this difficult time in their lives is a very intimate experience. So even though it's very sad, and can be overwhelming, it really isn't sad, because you feel so good about what you do.

"The staff gets together every other week to talk about the work, so that's kind of a built-in safety net. We work very well together so if somebody is down, or a death has particularly touched you, we immediately go to our peers and have a chance to talk about it.

"This is different than hospitals where the nurses and social workers are working so fast and so hard, that when they lose a patient, they don't have the opportunity to grieve that loss before they have to invest in the next patient."

Fred Elsner, class of '67

"Nothing has ever come easy. It's tenacity It's hard work. I guess I was just wired with a lot of pride. It's like the tortoise and the hare. I'm the tortoise and I'm going to keep plugging away and get there."

Fred Elsner had a rocky childhood. He had every reason to throw in the towel, to complain about the hand life dealt him. He didn't moan and complain. He pressed on. His family was unlike most others in Cleveland Heights.

"I think I was the only kid I know in our generation that their parents never owned a home. My dad was an alcoholic. He had these demons he couldn't control. He couldn't keep a job.

"My mom was a saint. She worked retail her whole life. She was the bread winner. Somehow, we were always dressed well, we had good food on the table. Looking back, I don't know how she did it."

Freddy, his older sister, and younger brother never knew what to expect when their father Marvin Elsner came home at the end of a day.

"My dad was never physically abusive, but verbally abusive. He'd come home and start yelling at Huntley and Brinkley or whoever the newscaster was on TV. He'd be callin' them a dumb son of a bitch. It got loud and verbal. It really took a toll on my sister and my brother.

"I turned out to be the little protector, and it made me stronger. I protected my mom, my sister, my brother. He had bottles stashed in the house. We used to find them. I didn't feel sorry for myself."

Eleanor Elsner stayed with her husband for the sake of the children. She would leave their half of that duplex on Glenmont Road and walk to the bus stop on Mayfield Road. She would ride the 7 bus downtown. She sold women's clothing at Winkleman's and at Casual Corner. She never made it into management. She would be a saleslady all of her life. Her husband's life and health were spinning out of control. He stood five feet, six inches tall yet his weight ballooned to four hundred pounds. Right when Freddy's brother Richard was graduating Heights High, Eleanor decided to take the step she had dreamed about.

"She was going to leave my dad. She was old school. She had stayed with him for the sake of the kids, for the family. She thought she did the right thing. The realization she was going to leave him, had sunk in, and our roles reversed. I became the father, and he was the son. He was crying to me, 'I can't make it, I can't do it.'"

Freddy was home for the summer from Ohio University. He did his best to console his father.

"You'll be fine. People like you. You'll be fine. I came home from work one day. I knew he was home. His car was in the driveway. I was calling. No answer. I go upstairs and found him dead. He was stone-cold blue, laying on the bed. He has a vile of pills next to him. He killed himself. My mother felt guilty."

Freddy's life had already suffered a major setback just a couple of months earlier. It was early spring. He was out partying with his best buddies at Ohio U. Max Weiss was his life-long friend. They had gone through school together from kindergarten on. Freddy and Max were the shortest guys in the class and year after year, wound up seated next to each other near the front of the class.

At Ohio University, they had become friends with David Tishman. He was from New York City. The family business was Tishman Construction. The builder of skyscrapers around the world.

"Tishman was going to be our ticket. We were going to work for him in New York when we graduated from OU. Dave was the nicest guy. He just wanted to prove himself to his dad. His dad was always so busy he never had time for him."

Dave Tishman didn't have to scrimp for money like Freddy had to. Dave drove around campus in a shiny Pontiac GTO. That night in March of 1970, Freddy, Max and Dave had gone to a bar in Athens and were listening to a group called the Stained Glass Band. Max and Dave and another friend Paul Dohlberg were going to leave, but Freddy decided to stay behind. They were going to come back for Freddy, but they never showed up.

"About five in the morning, I got a call from the Ohio State Patrol. They explained there was a bad car accident. I said what happened to Max? They said he got killed. So did Dave. Paul survived. Dave was driving. Max was sitting in the back seat behind him. It was a narrow, two-lane, back road. This girl, whose boyfriend had broken up with her, she was bawling her eyes out, she crossed the center line and comes up on this hill and hit my friends' car head-on. Max's head hit the roof of the car and he broke his neck."

The loss of Max, coupled with the loss of his father, were two tragedies in a short period of time. Freddy graduated and married his high school sweetheart.

"We knew when we got married we probably shouldn't have done it. We knew deep down, it was pretty much done. We were afraid to back out of it, because the wedding was such a big deal to her parents."

Freddy's marriage would last two and a half years. He and his wife had settled in San Diego, California. He started working for a chain of hardware and home improvement stores called Handyman. Freddy was just twenty-five. He would contend with yet another setback.

"I seemed to be perfectly healthy and strong. I was diagnosed with testicular cancer. At that time, testicular cancer was ninety percent of the time fatal. They told my mom I had six months to live. I knew it wasn't good. They sliced me open like a watermelon. Seven hundred stitches to sew me up. They cut right through the stomach muscles.

Now they move the stomach muscles. I was connected to a an IV and given very strong doses of chemicals for six weeks."

Freddy made a full recovery. He stayed with Handyman for thirteen years and then took a job with Price Club. He worked his way up to be a store manager and a buyer. After his company was taken over by Costco, Freddy had an opportunity to move to Seattle. He took over the store that was the original store in the Costco chain.

In the late '90s, when Costco moved into the Midwest, Freddy came along. He ran a store for three years in Detroit and then got a promotion to run the Costco in the Lincoln Park neighborhood in Chicago. It would be the first Costco within the city limits. He loved the vitality of Chicago, but always wanted to move back home to Cleveland. He got that chance in 2006, when there was an opening for a manager at the Mayfield Heights Costco.

"I wanted to come back to be around family and friends. I like what I do. It's fun. It's neat to be with a company that's so well-loved and respected by people. You treat people with respect, and you usually get it back. It's just common sense. It's not rocket science.

"Costco is great to work for. It's a quality house, quality company. It believes in taking care of its employees. and its members. It gives back to the community. Quality merchandise and great value."

Freddy Elsner is in charge of 175 employees at the Mayfield Heights Costco. He is an upbeat, positive person. His smile is broad and sincere. He is even-tempered, but admits on occasion, his role can be challenging.

"People want to push. People want to take advantage. People always want something from you. You give, and it's never enough. My employees are getting great benefits and great security, but it's like anything, after a while, people don't appreciate it. They say they are working too hard, not enough money. You just get used to things."

Freddy says it's important to keep a balance. He says he always tries to make his work day fun, but it's never easy. There are challenges.

"Workers want time off, you can't always give them time off. You are the bad guy. It never seems to matter how much you help them. The good you do. They resent you for it."

A boss has to be a boss. Is it difficult for such a good-natured fellow to be the heavy?

"The older I get, no. I'm getting more and more irritable in my old age. You always want to be the good guy. You realize you can't be. It's a business. It's not personal. It's a big business I'm running. It feels like a family, and we are to a degree. We have to do what's right for the business, as well as what's right for the employees."

Freddy says Costco does a lot to keep its employees happy.

"Costco isn't like Home Depot, Wal-Mart, or even Target that turn ya' and burn ya'."

Freddy is single and in a sense, is married to his job at Costco. It is common for him to be in the store ten to eleven hours a day. He admits it is physically demanding and oftentimes stressful.

"You are making twenty decisions a day. Fortunately, I make more good decisions than bad."

He says his uncle was a strong role model for him. Mike Meshenberg owned a floor covering business. Freddy worked for him during his high school and college years.

"He taught me how to work. How to keep my head down and keep going. I learned work ethics from him."

Freddy's other uncle, Bob Elsner ran the Heights Dog and Cat Hospital. He was also supportive and a strong influence. His uncles were father-figures for Freddy. They provided guidance. Fred's father did not.

"I didn't realize at the time, what a dysfunctional family I had. We never took a vacation. We didn't have the money.

"I'm the shortest guy you'll know. I'm the baldest guy you'll know. But it's been a good run. I'm blessed now. I've got my health."

Bonnie Pollock Morris, Class of '68

Bonnie Pollock Morris says when she goes to pick up her four-year-old granddaughter from pre-school, many parents presume she is picking up her daughter. The aging process has sidestepped Bonnie. Forty years after graduating from Heights, she could pass for a woman in her late thirties. She appears to be just a pound or two heavier than her high school days.

One could jump to the conclusion Bonnie has led a carefree life. In many ways she has been blessed, but at age fifty-two, Bonnie suffered a setback that upended her life and caught her off guard.

When Bonnie finished the ninth grade at Wiley Junior High, she was looking forward to entering Heights High that fall. One night that summer, she and a couple of girlfriends were dropped off at the roller skating rink at Golden Gate in Mayfield Heights. Bonnie had striking good looks. You can't blame David Morris for picking her out of the crowd.

"I was roller skating. He was roller skating with some kids, and we just, well I flirted maybe a little bit."

A storybook romance was off and running. As it turned out, Bonnie and David were both living in University Heights. Their homes were not too far away from each other's.

"His father had a 1946 Cushman scooter. He used to ride it over on the sidewalk if he didn't have a car."

David was a member of the last mid-term classes at Heights High. He was roughly a year and a half older than Bonnie. He would be graduating in January of 1967.

Bonnie remembers the date of that first encounter at the roller rink. It was August 8, 1965. They started going steady immediately. David would be the only guy she dated.

"We used to see each other in school. We used to go out all the time. When he finished at Heights, he went to Kent. By that time, I was driving, so I used to drive to Kent every weekend, or he would come home every weekend to see me."

Bonnie was only eighteen when David proposed. She says she would have married him right then, but David's parents urged them to wait a while longer. It was December of 1970 when they got married. Bonnie was twenty years old. They had already been dating five years.

"We moved into the Clarkwood/Granada Apartments in Warrensville Heights. I think our rent was $130 a month, so we could afford that. He was working in security at the May Company at Cedar-Center. I was working in a doctor's office. I did that until our son was born in 1973. We moved to Georgetown in Lyndhurst. We didn't get a house until 1977 when my daughter Brooke was born."

David would go on to own a security company. After a time, he branched out by also working as a private investigator.

"It was kind of like what you would see on TV. If somebody is getting a divorce and wanted their husband or their wife followed. If he was going out at night, he would say, 'I have to go follow this person.' It was boring. You would sit in the car and would watch someone. Everybody thought it was so adventurous. It's boring. He carried a gun. He had a permit to carry a gun. Eventually he got away from the security part of the business. He would locate people. Help adopted people find their parents."

Bonnie says David was a good husband and a good father. One day in 1985, she nearly lost him.

"He had a heart attack when he was thirty-five. A massive heart attack. He had it in the doctor's office. He died right there, but they brought him back."

Bonnie said he had gone to the doctor that day because he wasn't feeling well. David thought he had a bad case of indigestion.

"They told me to get down to the hospital. They didn't think he was going to make it. When someone that young has such a massive heart attack, they usually die."

Jason was eleven. Brooke was only seven.

"They were little. It was really hard. In the beginning, you do what you are told to do by the doctors. They say eat a special diet, quit smoking, exercise. Don't eat fatty foods.

"So of course he followed what he was supposed to do, but then he went back to smoking, ate whatever he wanted to. The only thing he did was exercise. He also had a family history of heart disease. Family history is a big thing.

"I knew he was in denial, to the day he died, I think he was in denial that he ever had a heart attack. That's the type of person he was."

Bonnie and David tried to get their lives back on track. She ran the front desk at a psychologist's office. David stayed active.

"He always had a horse. He loved horses. My kids loved to ride horses. He taught them how to ride."

David even started to smoke cigars.

"He lived on the edge. He lived for today and didn't care about tomorrow."

David would live for seventeen more years of tomorrows. In 2002, he went to the hospital to visit his ailing father. He arrived home about the same time Bonnie arrived home after she finished work.

"The heart attack when he died, I was there. He just died, he was fine and then all of a sudden, that's what happens when you had a massive heart attack. He was almost fifty-four years old."

Their daughter Brooke had moved to Chicago by then.

"She got on a Southwest flight and was crying from the time we told her, and she cried all the way on the flight. It was awful. My daughter has a hard time even now with Father's Day, his birthday, certain family things. It's really hard for her. My daughter got married without her father there. She had her two sons have their bris without her father there."

Bonnie didn't have enough money to pay for David's funeral. Bart Bookatz from Berkowitz-Kumin was gracious enough to let her make payments over the next year or so to pay for the funeral.

"I was left with nothing. I have a lot of anger toward David for that. The life insurance was barely anything. David had always said to me, 'Don't worry, you'll be taken care of.' I didn't know what I was going to do. I really didn't. I had to move from where I was living. David's father wound up in a nursing home, so while he was there, I moved into his house for a year.

"You get so lonely. Some of my girlfriends say it's so nice when their husband goes away for a few days. They can do whatever they want. It's different when you are by yourself all the time. The loneliness is hard. At least I had my job, my kids and my grandchildren."

Bonnie's life had been intertwined with David's for thirty-seven years. Suddenly she was on her own and unprepared for the financial challenges.

"That's why I think it is very important all women should sit down with their husbands and talk about the future. Be honest with each other and know where everything is. Have a will. They should know exactly what there is."

On the one hand, Bonnie advocates this business-like, hands-on approach, yet at the same time, the loss of David also drives home the lesson that couples should also be spontaneous.

"Do the things you want to do, and don't think about it. You are living for today. You don't know what tomorrow is going to bring. Who knows if you are going to be there tomorrow. At our age, if you want to go on a trip, you should go on a trip, because you don't know a month from now if you are going to be able to do it, if you will be alive.

"I never really went through a depression, but I would wake up in the morning and my routine was always the same. Going to work, coming home at night to be by myself. The weekends were the worst cause I'd spend the whole weekend by myself.

"We had friends, a certain group of friends. When you are by yourself, it kind of like changes a lot. I would feel when my son would have his in-laws over, I would come by myself. Even though people are nice to you, you still feel that loneliness because you don't have your husband."

Bonnie jumps at the chance to take care of her grandchildren. There are two in Cleveland and two in Chicago.

"One of the reasons I babysit so much is it keeps me young. It keeps me needed."

Did she help her children Jason and Brooke through the loss of David?

"I would say my children guided me a lot more than I guided them. That's the kind of kids they are.

"I was angry. I was angry that he died on me. I'm still angry today that he died on me. I don't want my kids to be left with no parent. I want to take care of myself. I don't want to die. As we get older we have to be careful. Breast cancer, colon cancer. All that stuff is scary."

Sharon Weissman Roszia, class of '59

"I felt I wasn't pretty enough. I wasn't sharp enough. I just wasn't enough and I never felt enough."

Those who know Sharon Roszia, and know of her accomplishments, would be stunned to hear she ever had feelings of inadequacy. But growing up in Cleveland Heights, she remembers feeling like somewhat of an outcast in her extended family.

Her father Leonard suffered from polio. That put plenty of pressure on her immediate family as well.

"I felt I had to be the older child, the social worker and the one who held things together. Heights High gave me a sense of belonging that was very deep. I wasn't feeling it so much in the family."

Sharon lives in Southern California, but spends most of her time on the road. She is an international authority on adoption. She is a scholar-in-residence for a facility called Kinship Center. They develop courses for social workers and counselors who deal with adoption issues.

"People will ask me if I'm adopted, and I'll say no. I'm not adopted, but I know what it feels like to be different. I have been sensitive to what it feels like to lose connection and not feel like you belong."

Sharon was inspired by a history teacher at Roxboro Junior High and she set her goals on becoming a history teacher as well. But when she got into college, the education courses proved to be a disappointment. She hated them. She steered her life toward social work.

"What drove me was my father's illness and some of the losses I experienced. I know what it is like to lose a parent, to feel like you don't belong. I often felt like an outsider. I think that has driven me to have a compassion for the infertile families I work with, for the kids who have lost their first families, and for the birth mothers who have lost their children."

Sharon was a trailblazer in regards to opening adoption records that had been sealed by law. There was a reform movement in the '70s. Adopted children thought they were entitled to find out who their birth parents were. There were tremendous changes in the '80s as records were opened.

To carry matters a step further, Sharon played a pivotal role in coordinating open adoptions. From the outset, birth parents would know where their child was being placed. Adoptive parents would know who the birth parents are. Lines of communication would remain open.

"It makes adoption about addition, not subtraction. You don't have to lose your family connection in order to gain permanency in a family that can give you stability. If there are relatives who are unable to parent you, mom is too young, dad is still in school, mom or dad has been abusive, it shouldn't cost that child all their history and the information that might be helpful to them in the future."

Sharon says an open adoption provides ongoing information. In the end, the adopted child is better served and that should be a priority.

"Adoptive parents say their job is easier because they know more about the child and his or her family. They can call up and ask about family health history, or ask if there have been signs of learning disabilities. Find out if there are allergies to medications, or anesthetics.

"Medically it has been helpful. It has helped emotionally. As the child grows into adulthood they have less mystery. Children would grow up and not have enough information, or the information they had was old. It wasn't useful."

Sharon says open adoptions are the healthiest adoptions taking place today. Closed adoptions were often difficult for children.

"It's kind of the day to day stuff that wears them down. You don't look into the world and see mirrors. Adoptees grow up in families where they don't have anybody they can look at and say that person is just like me. They miss that incredible mirroring that is so important to our self-esteem and to our psychological development. Often children of color who were adopted, don't see anyone of color staring back at them and they begin to wonder where they came from. There's a constant reminder, I'm not like the people I love. I'm not like the parents who love me."

Kindergarten students are usually asked to bring in a baby picture of themselves to put on the wall. Many adopted children don't have baby pictures. When they are older, students may have to work on a family tree in school. People going to doctors are asked to write down their family medical history. Many adoptees just don't know.

"When I was growing up, I had no conscious memory of knowing anyone who was adopted. There was more secrecy around it back then. People weren't talking about it so openly.

"Other kids can be cruel. They would ask, 'Don't you want to know who your real parents are? Why didn't your real parents want you?'"

Sharon's company provides instruction to licensed professionals, social workers, psychologists and child welfare workers. Insights are shared on how to move children from one family to another, how to work with birth families, how to prepare adoptive families, and how to find the right therapist, if one is needed.

"I love it. This is my forty-seventh year. I am absolutely dedicated to this field. It's always exciting. It's always changing. No two families are the same. I feel very needed and very appreciated. I'm very gratified. I love the people I get to meet. I have friends all over the United States, Canada, Australia, New Zealand and Great Britain. I get to go to the weddings of the children I placed years before."

Celebrities like Madonna and Angelina Jolie have drawn attention to the idea of going overseas to adopt children. Sharon says that works for some people, but it has its drawbacks.

"Most of the people think international adoptions will be easier. That they won't have to deal with the issues of birth family and they won't have to deal with the risk the children will be returned to the birth family. They see it as less of a risk, less of a bother.

"Once they get into it, they realize the costs are phenomenal. Not knowing your child's history is very problematic in terms of health and learning disabilities. It's painful for the children, growing up not knowing anything about their birth parents.

"Children coming from South America have a little bit more information and they seem to have been cared for a bit more. Kids from Asian countries are coming with an awful lot of problems.

"People are tending to look at foreign adoptions a little less positively now. More foreign countries are finding ways to keep their children at home. They are only sending out the children who have the highest needs. There are now fewer children coming out of China, Russia, Ukraine and Southeast Asia."

Adoptive parents could wind up paying as much as $30,000 to get a child. They have to pay an agency to do a home study for them in their locale, there has to be an agency or a sponsor in the country where the child is coming from. Someone has to do all the legal work from the other side. Some countries require people to stay there for a week to a month while the paperwork is being completed."

Serving adoptees and their families takes a certain skill set.

"Adoptive families have different and additional stressors that often bring them to mental health professionals. They need specialized skills to address those particular family needs. Families can go in with a great crisis. Adoptees may think of committing suicide. A birth mother who relinquishes a child, might have years and years of deep depression. Often times these people are not treated with the skills we know are available. Folks treating them don't realize the specialized factors that exist in the adoption community."

The social workers and psychologists are more accustomed to seeing women.

"Typically, it's the mother who has voluntarily given up her child, or may have lost her children to the courts because of abuse or neglect. It's the adoptive mother who has issues about infertility, and it's frequently the female adoptee who struggles the most with the lack of information about their own history.

"Our culture is not very welcoming to men who are struggling with these kinds of issues. Almost all adoption agencies and child welfare department are staffed by females. It is usually not comfortable for birth fathers to come in and get the support they deserve."

Sharon says it's normally a female adoptee who is compelled to track down her birth parents. Men are not encouraged to process their feelings about a lost history.

Sharon's history at Heights High was solid.

"I loved it. I have nothing but happy memories. I felt included and popular. I felt at home with my friends."

And she has dedicated her life to making displaced children also feel at home in their new homes.

Barry Bernzweig, class of '68

"I'm a fabric care specialist. That's the way I have to look at it."

Some might look at what Barry Bernzweig does, and surmise he merely peddles wire hangers. He views his job as something more complex than that. He is a cleaning consultant. A friend to dozens of dry cleaners. A one-man support system for business owners who face a growing number of challenges.

His territory seems to expand every week. He now covers all of northeastern Ohio and a section of western Pennsylvania. He provides all sorts of supplies to dry cleaners. Besides the hangers, he deals in plastic laundry bags, packaging and cleaning chemicals.

"Dry cleaning has suffered quite a bit. There is still a need for professional dry cleaners. We are selling to many foreign-born people now. It has changed the whole industry. I think they bought too many stores, too quickly and they are now closing many of the stores, because they can't stay in business. The fabric care is needed, but not in every little mom and pop store, one after another. There are too many stores on every corner.

"An individual buys one store and then another, and opens one right across the street from another, and cuts his prices. I think we are seeing a weeding out of that. It's happening across the country."

The dry cleaning industry was already challenged, even before this wave of over-saturation.

"Casual clothing is what did it. People don't dress up. My belief is you should dress for the job you want, not the one you have. In today's world, everything is casual. Nobody dresses up when they go out. There was a certain pride. People in the '40s, '50s, in the '60s and even in the early-'70s. It's changing because they don't have that pride now. They don't want to dress up. It has hurt the industry."

Barry says he is now trying to encourage those on his route to push their customers to bring in their casual clothes. Khakis, casual sweaters and polo shirts. He says if you have paid big money for a good quality shirt, you want to take good care of it.

"You can't just throw those clothes into the washer. They don't last."

Bernzweig Supply was started in 1935 by Barry's father, Sam.

"It actually started out of his car. He was driving around in a big car. He did that for a long time. He had actually been a driver for one of his competitors. Then he started his own business. He sold zippers and cleaning supplies. He started buying hangers from the Cleaner's Hanger Company. They helped him get going. He eventually opened a store on W. 25th Street."

Sam Bernzweig had a big year in 1935. Not only did he launch his business, but he married his childhood sweetheart, Mary. Sam was twenty years old. Barry says his father was known for his honesty and integrity.

"When he told his customers he was going to do something, he did it. He would always go out of his way. If somebody wanted one zipper, he would deliver one zipper. He took care of his customers and he raised me up the same way. Every customer was the most important person."

Back in Sam's day, the Bernzweig Supply delivery trucks would go as far east as Ashtabula and as far west as Lorain. They didn't venture too far south of the Cleveland city limits. In recent years, Barry has been forced to broaden his territory in order to maintain his volume.

"We now go into Pennsylvania and soon will expand to Pittsburgh. We go to Vermilion, Sandusky and Huron. We go to Canton, Wadsworth, Rittman, New Philadelphia and Millersburg.

"I started helping my dad, probably at age nine or ten. I was a jumper on the trucks. I worked summers and vacations. I would hitchhike to work when I got a little older. My parents would give me fifty cents to take the Rapid, and I would hitchhike so I could save the fifty cents."

Barry's older brother Mel has been in the family business all of his life.

"He had a special permit to drive our trucks when he was thirteen. He never had much of a social life as a kid. He worked all the time."

Like his brother Mel, Barry was destined to work in the business. He entertained other dreams for a while.

"When I was twenty years old, I wanted to be a cartoonist, but I never really tried. I don't think I was artistically talented enough to really make a good living at it."

Barry says his years at Heights High helped prepare him to be a businessman. He took part in the work-study program.

"I worked at the Mr. Junior clothing store. I made a dollar an hour. I thought I was rich. I met a lot of girls at Mr. Junior, because they came in to buy Levi's. Girls would buy boy's Levi's back then. They thought they fit better. It was my job to measure them. I was very happy.

"The work-study program taught me work ethics. Heights High was a wonderful experience. I loved it. I had a lot of nice friends and good teachers. You could really learn there. You could have fun, but you could learn too."

Over the years, Mel became Mr. Inside and Barry was Mr. Outside. Mel ran the day to day operations, and Barry would travel from store to store, taking orders from dry cleaners. He maintained a basic approach.

"I work on the level that we are equals. If you walk in like you are a lowly salesman, you walk out as a lowly salesman. The person at the front counter, you don't know, she could be the next owner or next manager. I treat every person with respect. If there are ten people who run the counter, you should get to know all those ten people, because those are your people.

"They are all working hard to make a living, and they are to be respected. I imagine a lot of salespeople think they are better, which is wrong. They are the same as everybody else. Nobody is higher or lower.

"The guy who sweeps the floor, that's the guy you want to know. The guy who sweeps the floor could be the key to getting you in the door. You just don't know. So why be disrespectful in any way to that person. That person could be the person that says, 'I like that salesman. He makes it a lot easier because his driver puts things away nice, or he treats me nice.' Everybody is equal. Everybody is the same."

Barry forges friendships with his customers over the years. He is committed to taking care of their needs. He always tries to connect with them, one way or another.

"People are just people, As much as people are strictly business, they still want to talk about their family. I was told don't go into places and tell them about your family, when in fact, that's exactly what they want to know. They want to know about you, your home, what you did last weekend, your ups, your downs. That's the person they are going to buy from, that's the person they like as a friend."

Some salesman will do just about anything to close a sale. Barry says he doesn't carry a bag of tricks with him.

"I don't play tricks. The main close is just to be a nice person. Being honest with the people. You are going to sell your goods. People don't like a wise-ass. They like a nice guy. I have never raised my voice to a customer. If they want to yell at me, feel free to. I don't care, because when they are done yelling, then we are going to talk.

"I never lose my temper in a customer's store. It's their store. I'm on their property. I have to be respectful at all times, no matter what kind of day they are having."

Barry says his longtime customers become part of his extended family. He attends their children's weddings. He pays his respects at family funerals.

"I like people. When the customers are really tough, that's what

I specialize in. That's what I look for. If they are very tough, why are they tough? They are just dads and moms, brothers and sisters. You can always find something about that person that is nice. Some customers only care about the price, so after you get them a good price, then you work on the social part of it."

Barry says he hasn't taken a full week off since 1996. He has six children and much of his income has gone toward tuition bills.

His father died shortly after he left the business in 1999. Barry says his brother Mel has been a perfect partner. He says Mel is completely honest. He always does what is best for the two of them. The partnership always comes first.

Barry and Mel were not so lucky when it came to employees. In 1995, Federal authorities had to be called in to investigate a bookkeeper for the company. A man who had worked for Bernzweig Supply for decades, was pocketing money. He allegedly skimmed cash for many years before his scheme was discovered.

"He was there when I was a young kid, so I looked up to him like he was another brother. When you are a kid, you had your heroes. He was one of the people I really looked up to. Eventually, I realized he was just a bad man. We changed the locks on the doors, and he was gone.

"He only cared about himself. He didn't care about his wife. He didn't care about his children. All that mattered was himself. After he went to prison, his wife died. His wonderful son died of Lou Gehrig's disease. He was left with nothing. I don't even know if he is still alive."

Barry doesn't know how long the man was siphoning all the money. He might have been honest for twenty years. Maybe he never was. Mel discovered the discrepancies. He pursued the criminal charges. Federal investigators got involved because his actions involved a bank.

"What he did was cruel to my parents, and I think I have learned enough in life to say, when someone is like that, you can cut them out of your life the next day. You have to be cruel. You have no choice. They have done the damage. We are just fine now, and he's not.

"It was very painful for me. I actually walked him out to his car the last day. I brought a couple of his sport jackets out. He said none of this is true. I said I hope it isn't for your sake. He said, 'I'll be back here on Monday, everything will be fine.'

"When he left, I knew nothing was fine. I knew what was going to happen. I knew he was lying. There are some people who will lie, and it doesn't matter who they will hurt. It hurt, but so what. You move on. You have no choice. His car was taken away from him. His home was taken away."

Barry and Mel made a business decision. From that point on they would be the only ones at Bernzweig Supply to ever touch the money.

"The learning experience is that strangers can do this to you."

Barry says his wife Jill provided tremendous emotional support after the scam was uncovered. He said she was understanding when he would have to work seven days a week to help clean up the financial mess at the company.

The business has changed dramatically since Barry's father got things underway. More and more of Barry's suppliers are from overseas.

"There is just one hanger company left in America. I haven't bought foreign plastic bags yet, but I'm sure that is probably coming. I got a call from Vietnam today. At trade shows, many of my meetings are with Korean distributors. People manufacturing in South Korea or Vietnam. I am having dinner meetings with people who don't speak one word of English. We have interpreters."

Barry is grateful he has satellite radio in his car. He drives 35,000 miles a year calling on customers and taking their orders.

"I get up at five in the morning. I go to Erie, Meadville, Greenville, North East, Lake City and Clarion, Pennsylvania."

Barry says if he fails to land an order, he doesn't dwell on it, he just moves on. If his father could see what is going on with the business now?

"He'd probably say we were too big now. He'd be proud, but probably wouldn't want us to be such a big company. But these days, it's grow, or die."

Through the setbacks, all the changes, and the increasing challenges.

"I'm happy. I'm happy I wake up. I'm happy I have the friends that I have. I am happy I have a great family."

Janice Davis, class of '66

"Before Cedar-Center closed, people came from all over the country. One woman came from Texas. She heard we were closing. She came to take pictures of the store before it closed. It's the truth. It's unbelievable. It makes you feel good. I'm telling you. It really does."

Janice Davis has grown up with Davis Bakery. The family business was started in 1939. A single store on Taylor Road. Her father Carl was only twenty years old when he joined forces with his older brothers Ben and Julius.

"When I was thirteen, my father used to take me down to our plant on Euclid Avenue and I used to stand all night long, putting cherries on cookies from eleven at night to six or seven in the morning, in our busy season when I was on vacation. And then we would stop and have breakfast on the way home."

Those one-on-one moments with her father were rare. Janice was a percussionist with the Heights High marching band and the orchestra.

"He didn't attend one concert in all the years I played at Wiley and at Heights. All of the Davis men were married to the business. It was difficult. In a sense, I really didn't know my father until I started working for his company. That was how he made his living. That was how he led his life."

She says her mother Shirley was forced to do double duty when it came to raising Janice and her younger brother Joel.

"She was a mother and a father. She did absolutely everything because my father was so busy at work. As we were growing up, we would only see my dad once a week. We would get up and go to school and my dad would be sleeping. We'd go to bed at night and he wouldn't get home until eleven or twelve at night. He worked six days a week all of his life.

"The Davis men will always tell you the reason they were so successful is because of their wives. The three Davis women, Ruth, Evelyn, and Shirley all got along very well. They kept the Davis Brothers on their toes."

Janice went to work full-time at Davis just a few months after she graduated from Heights. She has stayed at it for forty-one years. As the years went on, she gained more and more authority and became the only Davis woman to be in management.

"I brought more softness and compassion to my employees, being a little gentler, and understanding the situations my employees could have. Sometimes they can speak with a woman easier than a man about certain situations. The men were always good-hearted and understanding, but I had maybe, a softer touch."

For many of the employees, the job at Davis bakery was their first in a new land.

"We had many, many survivors of the Holocaust working for us. Many Europeans, Russians, Lebanese. We had them all. We were always willing to give people a chance. There were so many people that came to work for us that hardly knew the language. Most of the time, the customers were very understanding.

"It was hard for them to go to a new country and you don't

understand the language. It was a pleasure to see them grow with their language. A lot of them, once they learned the language, they quit and went on to better jobs."

Of the many Holocaust survivors who worked at Davis over the years, few cared to discuss their years of terror.

"I never brought it up, out of respect for their feelings. I didn't want to open up bad wounds for them. I think they were very, very special people. I could never imagine going through what they went through. Coming to the United States and starting a new life. A lot of them had lost all of their families. I just had a lot of respect for them."

There was a lot of respect in the business world for the Davis brothers. That one bakery in Cleveland Heights was only a start. At one point, the chain grew to thirty-nine locations. In the early '60s, Davis bought out Smayda Bakeries and Lakewood Bakeries. They took over the large Smayda plant on Euclid Avenue which was near the Windermere Rapid station.

At its peak, the company had 450 employees. It had a bakery counter inside the Kresge's store downtown, just inside the Euclid Avenue entrance. Davis had a second counter just inside the E. 4th St. entrance as well. You could hardly miss them at Southland. There was a free-standing store, one inside Uncle Bill's and another inside Sears. Davis Bakery became one of the first tenants in Beachwood Place.

Janice's brother Joel is in charge of keeping all the Davis Bakery recipes. She says they are treated as top-secret documents.

"If you ask a baker for a recipe, he will never give you the right recipe, because it's his recipe. Ask him for it, and then three months later ask him for the same recipe, it won't be the same. So you have to take what they give you and try to figure out what it really is. Bakers will go to the grave never giving a recipe, ever."

Janice fondly remembers the mob scenes at the Cedar-Center store just before the Jewish holidays.

"In a two-day period, we would sell over 4,000 challahs."

She knows diet-conscious customers often try to stay away from sweets and carbs.

"Eventually they all come back. Everyone of our sandwiches we make, they will come with a pickle and a cookie. Very rarely will you hear a person say, 'Don't give me the cookie.'"

The Davis empire began shrinking once unionized supermarkets started opening up on Sundays and at night.

"Supermarkets were getting bigger with in-store bakeries and delis. It affected our business and we had to start closing down those little mama and papa stores we had. We were spread out kind of thin and had to start condensing. My brother and I felt if we got smaller, it would be a little easier to control.

"With most wives working outside the home now, they like to do that one-stop shopping. They want to go into a supermarket and get absolutely everything. All their deli, all their bakery, all their produce, and they are done.

"We have to give people a reason to come into Davis Bakery. What is that reason? A rye bread. Our rye bread is famous. Everybody loves our rye bread. We ship it all over the United States. People call from Texas, California, and Florida. 'Please ship me rye bread. Ship me Russian tea biscuits.' Our products, everything is made from scratch. We don't use any preservatives in our products. Our rye bread has no shortening, no sugar, no preservatives."

Davis Bakery now has one retail location. It's on Chagrin Boulevard in Woodmere. It also has a small outlet in front of its plant on Renaissance Parkway off of Emery Road.

"I look forward to Thanksgiving and Christmas when I see people that I see only once a year when they come home. They come into the bakery. They load up on the Russian tea biscuits and the coconut bars to take back with them. They tell me every time they come home they have to come to Davis.

"It makes me feel so proud. They come from a family that for forty or fifty years, these people come back and say, 'I used to shop at your Cedar-Center store. My mother or my grandmother would bring me on Sunday mornings. We would get lox and bagels.'

"People I don't even know, come up to me and tell me I want you to know I love your bakery. We have the best Russian tea biscuit dough. I have had Russian tea biscuits from many other bakeries, and none has the taste of ours. We have the best chocolate chip cookies. We have the best cream cheese pastry. We have the best coconut bars. A lot of people tell us Cleveland is one of the few places where they can get coconut bars."

After the first of the year, Janice heads down to Florida for three months and leaves the bakery in the capable hands of her brother. Her whole life has centered on the bakery business.

"As I look back on it, I wouldn't change a thing. I love my customers most of all. People I went to school with. Doctors, lawyers, kids that I hired to pack bags at Cedar-Center, they come in with their kids. It's very nice. I came right into this business out of high school and I'm not sorry.

"The relationship my father had with his brothers was always so special. The Davis brothers weren't three, they were one. We always tried to work as one, instead of pulling in opposite directions. You hear a lot of stories of businesses that broke up because this one wanted to do this, and that one wanted to do that. Working with family, it's so important to get along.

"An excellent name. Davis has always had a very, very good name in Cleveland as far as product, caring about our customers, and doing whatever we could for them."

At age eighty-nine, Janice's father Carl Davis still comes in once in a while to help out during the holidays.

"He's very proud. He would like to see Davis Bakery continue on."

Jim Barle, class of '87

"I would say that Forest Hill is probably one of the most diverse parts of Cleveland Heights. Rockefeller's purpose in building it was to exclude people. I probably would not have been able to live there because my mom was Italian."

Jim Barle is now the sole owner of the crown jewel of Forest Hill, the Heights Rockefeller building. It opened in 1931 at the corner of Mayfield and Lee and was intended to be a gateway to a massive planned community on what once was the summer estate of John D. Rockefeller. The building is a mix of retail shops, office space and fourteen apartment units.

Only eighty-one of the homes were built. They featured a stunning French Norman style. The intention was to have six hundred. But the

Great Depression stopped Forest Hill in it tracks. Decades would pass before the rest of the property was developed by home builders.

The Rockefeller Building featured Streich Pharmacy, Kroger, and the Jack Frost Beauty shop. Cleveland Trust had a bank on the second floor of the building. The old bank space is now rented for parties. It features classy oak woodwork, high ceilings with wooden beams, and impressive stone work.

"John D. Rockefeller Jr. had the building constructed. He had an office here. It was on the second floor and supposedly that's why the bank was on the second floor, because he didn't want to go to a different floor to do his banking."

Customers had to climb a long set of stairs to reach the bank from the front entrance.

"One of the antique dealers in the building tells the story of during a run on the bank during the Depression, the bank manager at the Cleveland Trust supposedly stood on one of the bank tables, stomping his feet, saying they were a stable bank and people could come and take money out when they wanted to. He tried to alleviate people's fears about the run on the bank. Who knows how true that is?"

To drive by this stately building now, you might assume it is owned by some real estate conglomerate, not by a young man whose previous real estate empire consisted of a single-family rental unit on Meadowbrook and an eight-suite apartment building on Lancashire. Jim Barle became the sole owner of the Rockefeller Building in 2004. He was thirty-four years old.

"My parents were a little nervous cause it was such a big thing. I think they knew I would be able to handle it. I remember my dad said he wishes when he was my age, he had the courage to do something like that. I said when you were my age you had five kids already and that took more courage than buying a piece of property. If I fell flat on my face, I don't have anyone else to worry about. It was just me."

Richard and Angela Barle would go on to have one more child and bring the total to six. The family lived on Pembrook Road in the Monticello area. Richard worked for many years as the custodian at Booth Memorial Hospital.

"I was in the eighth or ninth grade. My dad was really unhappy in his job. He told my mom he was going to quit and run his own business. He was going to be a plumber. My mom washed all of his work uniforms from the hospital and folded them up. They had two thousand dollars saved. He bought a van and put an ad in the *Sun Press*. He was in his early fifties.

"When I was growing up, my mother had a paper route. She delivered *The Plain Dealer* when I was in elementary school. She delivered it in that horrible winter of '77. She had the route for at least ten years. Thinking back now, I'm ashamed of this, but I remember being embarrassed that my mom delivered papers because the kids in the neighborhood would make fun of me. She did this so she could buy us Christmas presents. Now, I'm ashamed I was embarrassed, and I am proud of her. It was a walking route on Pembrook. She woke up every morning at five. She told me she used to drink fifteen cups of coffee a day when we were little kids."

Jim Barle got his start in the business world in that same neighborhood.

"In elementary school, I would walk around and cut grass for people. There was a woman on Rushleigh, which was one street over from Pembrook. Beth Leutenberg, she was a career Army woman. She was retired. I cut her grass from the time I was nine years old until the time she died in 2001. Every now and again, Beth would say, 'Ya know, I think I'm going to give you another dollar to mow the lawn.' Right before she died, I was getting eleven dollars to cut her grass. Some of the guys on the crew were saying, 'By the time you pay us, it's not really worth the time.' I said it doesn't matter. I've been doing her yard forever. Over the course of twenty years, the price probably went up about three dollars."

In those early days, the farthest Jim would venture was Penfield. That was three blocks away.

"I would walk there with my lawnmower and my Weedeater and a broom. I didn't have a blower. That's what I would do every Saturday morning. All through high school. All through college. I needed a job to pay for school."

Jim Barle played on the Heights High Hockey team for three years. The team was successful. It was a real brotherhood.

"We've known each other our whole lives. We had played together since we were eight or nine. In our junior year, we lost the state championship game. That was our first loss of the year. We finished the season 30-1. Our senior year, we won the state championship game. We were 29-2. We were a good team. We had a lot of good players, good coaches. We had a foreign exchange student from Finland. We played against guys who went on to the National Hockey League.

"At Heights, I wasn't the smartest student, but I worked hard. I think we had some of the best teachers. I thought Heights was a little more challenging than John Carroll was. I had some great professors at John Carroll, but students would come up to them when papers were due and ask if they could have one more week to write it. Whereas in high school, if you had a paper due, you handed it in, or you didn't get credit for it."

Jim had visions of becoming a journalist and landed a couple of internships.

"It just didn't do it for me. I told my parents I think I am going to see where my landscaping business goes. Then my accountant suggested that I buy a rental property for the tax advantages. I thought I would just try it out for a year or two, and one thing led to another."

Jim was only twenty-seven when he bought that apartment building on Lancashire.

"The best and worst part of business is the people you meet. You meet some great people. I've met the nicest people and then you meet some pistols. Some people are not very clean. That's a bad thing about rental properties. You'll go a month not hearing anything, and then you'll get calls from tenants four straight days. 'It's too cold, there's no water pressure.' You just find the balance. No matter how mean or how nice you are, there are always people who are going to try to take advantage, and there are some people that won't. You just have to recognize it."

Jim got to know John Barr who founded Nighttown in Cleveland Heights. Barr was the owner of the Rockefeller Building. They developed a friendship, and in 2001, Jim was invited to buy into the building.

"I bought in at 25 percent and I had ten years to buy him out. In 2004, I had a good opportunity with a private investor who was willing to hold the note. That's when I bought him out. I think he feels the building is in good hands."

Jim has held on to his original properties in Cleveland Heights.

"I get very attached to properties. I want the yards to look nice and the tenants to be happy. So it's hard for me to sell them."

Jim's father didn't launch his own business until later in life, but he always pushed the idea that being your own boss was the only way to go.

"He always stressed to me, start your own business, then you'll never have a such-and-such as a boss."

Running the Rockefeller Building has some special challenges.

"It's in very good shape, but it's not in great shape. Eventually we need to put a new flat roof on. We need to put new sidewalks in. The actual structure of the building is fantastic. Some of the stone has deteriorated over the years from salt and age. All of these things are going to be costly because you have to do it historically accurate because we are listed with the National Historic Register.

"People who grew up in Cleveland Heights, everyone has a story. 'Oh, I used to go to the Rockefeller Building. I used to go to the pharmacy. I used to bank there.' We have some retail tenants who have been here thirty years. The biggest thing when I show people the party room where the bank used to be, is 'I never knew this existed.' It has a real different kind of feel to it."

There used to a waiting list for the apartments. Now there are occasional vacancies. Most are one-bedroom units. They go for $675 a month. There are a couple of two-bedrooms. They rent for $1,500.

Jim has never let youth stand in his way. He tried his hand at barbering. It was picture day in his kindergarten class at Oxford Elementary. He and his pal Eric Silverman thought they should look their very best. Each grabbed a pair of scissors and gave each other a haircut. Jim has to chuckle every time he runs across that picture. His hair has an unusual slant.

But as far as buying properties at a young age.

"Ten or twelve years ago, when I owned something, I didn't want people to say, 'Oh he was too young to handle that. That's why it failed.' I didn't want to give people the satisfaction they thought I was too young to do something. Although there were moments when I thought I was really in over my head."

Jim is the caretaker of a local treasure. The building still adds a touch of class to Cleveland Heights.

"I care about what I do. If my name is attached to something, I want to do the best job I possibly can."

All of the class and elegance of the building endures. Yet legend has it, John D. Rockefeller's final request in 1937 was based on absolute simplicity.

"He specifically requested a very plain, I think six or seven dollar, pine casket. That's what he was buried in. The workbench where it was built is still in the basement. I saw a picture in an old Forest Hill flyer or newsletter. They had a picture of the man who built the casket for John D. Rockefeller and you could tell it's the same workbench. It's interesting to me he wanted a six dollar casket. He was the richest man in the world."

Dr. Donald Abrams, class of '68

"I've seen a heck of a lot of cancer patients who are nauseated, who have weight loss, who have pain, who have depression, and can't sleep. For them, there's one medicine that can take care of all of those problems. I do recommend cannabis to a lot of my cancer patients."

Donald Abrams is an oncologist at San Francisco General Hospital. Most of his patients there are poor, homeless, or both. He also has a practice at the Osher Center for Integrative Medicine at the University of California, San Francisco. His patient base there is not indigent. He says there's no reason anyone in his care, at either facility, shouldn't be a candidate to use medical marijuana.

"In this country, with marijuana being the number one cash crop, we are kind of losing quite a bit of revenue and taxation by letting it all stay underground and denying a patient a drug that's useful. It doesn't make a lot of sense to me. I don't think it's based on science. It's more just politics."

It was in the early '90s that Donald started fighting the government to allow him to use marijuana for his patients who were infected with HIV.

"It allowed me to be a pioneer in a new direction. I pushed and pushed and in 1997, the government gave me a million dollars and 1,400 marijuana cigarettes to study the interaction between cannabis and traditional drugs in patients with HIV. It was more of a safety study to make sure it was safe. We showed it was safe, and it may have even been beneficial to the patients who smoked marijuana, or who took it in pill form."

In 1999, Donald was involved in another study to see if marijuana did indeed provide medical benefits.

"Patients who had HIV and painful nerve damage actually benefited from smoking marijuana, compared to smoking placebo marijuana. The people who are anti-marijuana say there's no evidence it has any benefits. Our study was published in *Neurology*, and it showed there is a benefit."

Donald says some thought the actual smoking part of the treatment is not an ideal delivery system. So in the next study, they used a smokeless delivery system called the Volcano Vaporizer. That misting system offered less toxicity. He thinks that in some situations, patients who use medical marijuana in one form or another, may be able to take fewer pharmaceutical drugs, and that could reduce the severity of side-effects.

"I'm trying to establish that cannabis is useful medicine. It is only since 1942 that doctors in the United States have not been able to prescribe cannabis. I can safely say it has been in medicine for a lot longer than it hasn't been."

Donald Abrams earned his medical degree at Stanford. He remained in the Bay Area to continue his medical training at Kaiser Hospital in the late '70s.

"In my medical training we treated toxic shock syndrome and Legionnaire's Disease, both of which came out of nowhere. They were easily figured out and treated with anti-biotics. At the beginning, it was another one of those."

"It" was a mysterious illness. A large number of gay men were coming into the hospital. Unusual symptoms. Rapidly advancing illnesses. Donald was little more than ten years out of Heights High and found himself in the middle of a health care crisis.

"So being a gay man, and knowing what questions to ask, I found these patients had too many sexual partners, too many sexually transmitted diseases, and were doing too many recreational substances. So I told them, why don't you move out of the fast lane."

Getting out of the fast lane was a start, but this mysterious illness would not be figured out quickly by medical researchers.

"In 1979, I first became aware there was something amiss. I was an internal medicine resident, we began to see large numbers of gay men with swollen glands, swollen lymph nodes. The doctors kept sending me these men and said you figure out what they had. We did lymph node biopsies and found the glands didn't have lymphoma or cancer. The glands were just stimulated, or over-stimulated. Their immune system was cranked up.

"In 1981, they took me in to see a guy with pneumocystis pneumonia. I didn't know why I was seeing this patient. He was inhaling poppers, which is what some gay men were doing to relax sphincters and blood vessels. I told my team he had pneumocystis pneumonia because he's killed off the defenses he had in his lungs from inhaling these carcinogens. I didn't appreciate the magnitude of that particular patient, and it was two months later the Centers for Disease Control reported the outbreak of pneumocystis pneumonia in gay men.

"Some started developing cancer. It was a big mystery. Is it because they are sitting in tanning salons and have suppressed immune systems? Is it because they have hemorrhoids or fissures and are using steroids in their butts? Do they have internal parasites? We didn't know what it was."

Donald was seeing scores of his patients die from what came to be known as AIDS. In 1986, he developed a relationship with a man named Mark. Mark was diagnosed with AIDS. Donald stood by helplessly as Mark's life withered away.

"Treating AIDS and finding a cure became a mission."

Donald won numerous awards for his contributions to putting an end to the AIDS epidemic in the United States. He was one of the first doctors to recognize some of the manifestations of HIV disease, and credited with being one of the pioneers in AIDS care and research.

"Those diagnosed with the HIV virus take ATRIPLA. It's one pill once a day and I'll see you in four months. The earlier drug regimens were very complicated and onerous."

Donald has traveled to Africa three times as a visiting professor, an authority on AIDS. The problem there is by no means under control.

"When you go to Africa, it is sort of like coming back to San Francisco in 1981 or 1982. It's an incredibly devastating disease that impacts a huge percentage of the population, and whenever I go there, I walk away with a tremendous desire to help, or to do something in some way. But the infrastructure there just isn't the same as it is here. There are so many other variables aside from the virus itself.

"There are cultural things. There is a strong belief in traditional African medicine. The fear or distrust of Western medicine. What I have heard is, if people appear to be well, if they still feel well, they don't understand why they really need to take the medicine. There's a need for more education. The people who are HIV positive, the ones most likely to be spreading the virus, think they are doing well, they are not sick, why should they take a medicine. The enormity of the number of the people involved is staggering."

Donald's latest passion is integrative medicine. He did a fellowship with Dr. Andrew Weil at the University of Arizona.

"When I met him, I was struck by his humanness and his eloquence and his common sense. I became quite taken with his wisdom."

Donald was compelled to take a different direction. His work in AIDS had lost its challenge.

"At the time, the work was very urgent, it was very exciting in a bad way, and you really felt you were on the front lines and doing something very valuable by being involved in trying to get an understanding about what this disease was.

"So that was a real rush, if you will, at the beginning of my career, and then the disease, fortunately for those who live with the virus, has greatly decreased. People can now live a relatively normal life. HIV is being relegated to a position of a chronic illness. It lost a little bit of the excitement it had at the beginning of the epidemic."

So Donald's latest challenge is to encourage those with cancer to take a comprehensive approach to their illness.

"I've seen a lot of progress made in the treatment for cancer. I know cancer has to be treated with a conventional regimen, but we are also going to talk about nutrition, physical activity. Supplements, Chinese medicine, mind-body medicine, massage, spirituality, and all this stuff, and weave it into your program of conventional cancer care.

"Cancer patients are just not used to their oncologist telling them anything about nutrition, doing anything about supplements, talking to them about spirituality. I have established a Center for Integrative Oncology at Osher."

At San Francisco General, Donald is more of a traditional oncologist.

"People that are urban poor, without insurance. I treat them with chemotherapy and I refer them for radiation and surgery. For these patients, cancer is the least of their problems. Two-thirds of the patients I see, I'm not speaking English to those patients. I'm speaking through an interpreter in Chinese or Spanish. They don't know where their next meal is going to come from. I can't say to one of these patients they should be eating organic food, which is so much more expensive.

"But at Osher, I tell patients I am not treating the cancer. I'm healing a person with cancer. I'm serving as their integrative oncologist. What I tell them is that cancer is like a weed, and they are the garden, and my job is to keep their soil as inhospitable as possible for the weed to grow and spread."

Donald has gone from being an expert on AIDS, to an expert on the use of medical marijuana, to an authority on integrative medicine. He takes part in conferences all around the world. He has flown more than 100,000 miles a year, for the last fifteen years.

"At Heights High, our teachers were brilliant, and my classmates were stimulating. It was a very special place. I know I got some write-in votes for Homecoming Queen, but what can you do, I still loved it. It was a great experience.

"It was comfortable and it seemed we were good kids. There weren't a lot of hoodlums, not a lot of crime, or teenaged pregnancy. It was a pretty wholesome, mom and pop, *Leave it to Beaver* kind of place to be. It was also very forward-thinking with a lot of opportunities and options for people to do whatever was of interest to them."

At his recent fortieth class reunion Donald chatted with former classmate Dave Tanaka. As a Japanese American, Dave had been a definite minority at Heights High. Donald felt he was a minority as well. But another kind of minority.

"Probably then I knew I was different in that I was a gay man, but I hadn't expressed it. I told Tanaka at the reunion he was somebody who was outwardly different. I was inwardly different."

Donald put on quite a floorshow at his reunion. His wild gyrations on the dance floor would not give observers the impression he is a brilliant doctor who has won acclaim around the world.

"That has always been me. Scott Holden told me that night that I haven't changed at all from high school. For me, at the reunion, I was just regaining the essence of my spirit. It's still Donald. My mother told me that I never got any older than twenty-two. Just my body aged. My mother told me that, and she's right."

Julie Hamos, class of '67

"Barack Obama was nowhere. A guy with a funny name, nobody had ever heard of him outside his own district. He did some nice work in Springfield, but we never assumed anyone would know him for that."

January 2009 was a month of contrasts for Julie Hamos. Her work as a kingmaker paid handsome dividends. Her early support of a fellow legislator in Illinois was a first step on a journey that culminated in his inauguration as President.

Shortly before the inauguration, Julie played a much different role. She was, in a sense, a high executioner. She was among the members of the Illinois House who took part in the investigative committee that set the wheels in motion for the ouster of Illinois Governor Rod Blagojevich.

"It does make our job a lot harder. We've got to straighten it out.

This is the second governor in a row that's corrupt. The last governor, George Ryan is serving time in a federal penitentiary."

Julie represents the 18th District in the Illinois House of Representatives. It covers the north side of Chicago and then heads up the Lake Michigan shoreline encompassing the wealthy North Shore suburbs like Wilmette, Winnetka, Kenilworth and Highland Park.

Barack Obama was serving as a state senator. He had his sights set on the United States Senate. He turned to Julie to get his campaign jumpstarted.

"I told Barack, he came to me cause he needed me to open some doors in the white, more progressive communities of Illinois. That was his strategic outlook to move ahead. I said we are still in a legislative session, people tell me I shouldn't jump into this so quickly. Let me think about it, but you know what Barack, I'm going to watch you, and let me see how you do this session."

Barack Obama was tackling a controversial issue at the time. A lot of attention had been focused on a number of high-profile murder cases. Cases that had been overturned because the convicted killer had eventually been proven innocent. There was a call to have video cameras rolling whenever confessions were being made to police. It was intended to provide an added safeguard of a suspect's rights. To wipe out any doubts about the circumstances surrounding a confession.

"Barack is the guy who got it done. He rolled up his sleeves. It was a very big problem we were having with innocent people on death row being coerced into confessions by police. Nobody wanted to touch it with a ten-foot pole. It was very controversial. Police and prosecutors hated the bill. Barack, although he was already running for U.S. Senate, he decided to roll up his sleeves and take that on."

Julie was watching this young lawmaker and she liked what she was seeing.

"He sat down with the groups. Brought everybody to the table. He used all of his skills. Negotiated that agreement. The reason we have that law in Illinois today is because of Barack Obama.

"The next day, I said, you know, it doesn't get any better than this. If we had somebody who had the skills to negotiate good policies, and have the political courage to try, this is as good as it gets.

"He came to me to endorse him very early on, a full year before he was actually in a Democratic primary. It turned out to be a big election. Seven Democrats were running for an open seat. So politicians like me, had to pick a horse. Many people stayed out of that because it's hard to pick a horse."

Julie Hamos decided to go ahead and endorse Barack Obama. She was one of the first Illinois legislators to commit to him. She invited him up to her part of the world.

"I spent the entire summer and fall with him. Every week, we had different house parties. We introduced him to a whole part of the world that fell in love with him and gave him a lot of money. I have actually been very close to him since the beginning of his career. He was my soul mate. In the legislature, we agreed on many issues. We worked together on many issues."

Flash forward to the night of the Presidential election in 2008.

"By that time, he belonged to everybody. At first, he was just my guy that nobody had ever heard of, and I had to beg people to come to living rooms. Even after he gave his speech at the Democratic National Convention, by that point, he belonged to everybody. It's hard to have a piece of Barack anymore.

"He did invite me to the inauguration to meet with him and a small group of thirty people. That was nice he remembered the early people who signed on. All of Illinois feels he's our favorite son. There are no words to describe how excited we are."

Julie Hamos is no stranger to excitement. In her early years, she was exposed to plenty of it. She was an eyewitness to history in the making. She was born in Budapest, Hungary in 1949. Her parents were Agnes and Gary Hertz. Julie says three of her grandparents died in Nazi death camps. Even after the war, anti-Semitism still thrived in her homeland. Julie was three years old when her parents decided to change their last name from Hertz to Hamos. They didn't abandon their Jewish religion, but thought it was best to abandon their Jewish-sounding last name.

Julie, her younger brother James, her parents and grandmother Bella Fisher, all lived in a small apartment in downtown Budapest.

"I have snippets of flashbacks of walking along the Danube with my father, going to a child care center with my mother, taking a trolley with my father. Those kinds of little flashbacks, but what I really remember is the Hungarian Revolution.

"I was almost eight years old when the Revolution came. It was just outside of our window. We lived on one of Budapest's main streets and the tanks rolled down our street and I watched them killing people.

"My real strong memory is no one could leave their home. So our parents did not go to work. They had to stay in, and they had to figure out ways to entertain us. My mom spent hours and hours and hours doing cut-out dolls that we turned into villages. We had them standing in villages, on street corners and we created this whole fantasy world using pieces of paper and scissors and glue."

Julie says that home confinement lasted about two weeks. One day, her grandmother left the apartment, and when she came back, she made the announcement that she had made arrangements for Julie, James and their parents to flee Hungary.

"They had twenty-four hours to make their entire dream come true, which was always to leave Hungary and become Americans. They had no opportunity to make plans, to say goodbye to anyone. We walked out of Hungary the very next day.

"We took the train to the border. We stayed with this farmer family that my grandmother had given some money to. She had made arrangements. She had bribed somebody to take us in, give us our last supper, and then take us to the border, so we could walk five miles. I have memories of the gunfire, the searchlights.

"We were in danger. We were sneaking across the border in the middle of the night. It was a cold winter night. It was muddy. It wasn't an easy walk. There were cornstalks. My parents talked about how they lost their shoes. They were walking in bare feet. Their feet were all bloodied up from the cornstalks."

That walk to freedom was a life-changing experience in many ways.

"My parents taught us from that point forward, in our home, our family home, to be courageous. Seize the opportunity. Take risks. Don't be afraid. Don't hold back. Fight for your principles. That courage is so ingrained in me, that it makes me a very different kind of legislator. Being a leader on some issues, means ruffling a lot of feathers, taking on special interests, and not being afraid. Not being afraid to lose. I lose quite a bit, too."

The Hamos family walked those five miles into Austria. They

wound up in a displaced persons camp and stayed there for a short time. Luckily, they had a sponsor, so they were able to get out of that camp and complete their journey to America. Since Julie's parents both had brothers living in Cleveland, that's the destination they chose. Her grandmother remained in Hungary.

"She was a courageous woman. That's a theme that runs through my family's generations. She decided she would stay and they wouldn't harass her because she was an older woman. She tried to sell off some of our belongings and accumulated a little money. She thought she could get out a year later, and she was right. At that point, they weren't stopping older people from leaving Hungary."

The Hamos family found a place to live in East Cleveland.

"We had no money. Not a penny to our name."

Three years later, they were able to move to a house in Cleveland Heights on Superior Road across from Taylor Elementary.

"My mother was hired by a Jewish-owned company. At first, she spoke no English. They took her in. The owner was tinkering in the back room one day, and he invented Super-Glue. So my mom stayed with this company. And she became a corporate executive. She retired in 2008 at the age of seventy-nine. She was working every day of her life until seventy-nine."

Gary Hamos took on factory work for a couple of years, but was determined to follow through with his dream of becoming an accountant.

"The two of them would sit at the dining room table at night. My mom with the dictionary and my dad with his accounting books so he could study for his CPA. He was very successful as a CPA. Until the day he died, he had a very thick accent. He had a great, very loyal clientele. People believed in him. His accent was so thick, I'm surprised people even understood him. He was a very hard-working guy with a lot of integrity. He passed on to me a very strong value system of honesty and integrity."

At Heights High, Julie's first exposure to politics was a stint on Student Council. Government was not her main interest at that point. She was a talented artist. She was the artistic director for the prom her senior year. The theme of the evening was a Tale of Three Cities. It was

Julie's assignment to make the Heights High cafeteria and social room look like New York, Paris and London.

It was her passion for art that took her to Washington University in St. Louis.

"I started in fine arts. It was during the Vietnam war activism many of us went through. That's when I realized way back then in college, that I was more of an activist than an artist. When I switched out of the art school, I really found my home. I was an activist, but I really didn't know what to do with that.

"Someone caught me at the right time, the right day and said, 'Young lady, if you want to help communities, you'll go to law school.' Law school was not out there as an opportunity we ever thought about. I went to law school in Washington, D.C. and I discovered government and policy work. From my first minute on, as a young lawyer, I realized policy work was the world I was heading in to.

"Policy work is very fulfilling. It's an opportunity for me to look at a problem and to think about how to extrapolate that, and to have broader vision on how to solve it, and how to bring coalitions to work together to resolve it."

After getting her law degree at George Washington University, she worked on a subcommittee for the U.S. House Ways and Means Committee. Then it was off to Springfield, Illinois where Julie became an advocate for low-income families. She continued her involvement while working for State's Attorney Richard M. Daley. She served as an advocate for victims of domestic violence and sexual assault.

Julie was elected to the state legislature in 1998. She was a member of the impeachment committee that investigated Rod Blagojevich.

"As a young child, I along with my family, escaped from a totalitarian country and I am sensitive to the use of government power. I know firsthand that power can be used for worthy goals or misused or abused for evil purposes. We have solid evidence chronicling a tragic betrayal of public trust by our governor and justifying the cause for impeachment."

The shake-up in state government could have a direct impact on Julie's future. The current attorney general in Illinois may chose to run for governor. If so, Julie may run for attorney general.

"In Illinois there's a culture of corruption. We've got to figure out how to straighten that out. We have lots of ethics commissions put together right now. We are looking at laws and polices with a whole new brush because I think the public is demanding it."

The Illinois Legislature is facing mounting challenges at a time when revenue streams are drying up. People will have critical needs.

"We have to make sure there are safety nets in place. We are as broke as any state right now. We have to contend with the poorest of the poor, and the newly laid-off. The people who are already struggling are the ones who are going to feel the impact of the state budget, even more than the federal budget. Our state government really impacts a lot of people. We provide direct services across the board."

The economic realities are harsh, and Julie knows there are tough decisions to be made.

"We may need new revenues. That means we'd be asking the public for some new taxes. That would be hard to do. It's hard to do in the best of times, but now the idea of doing it when the economy is hurting people so much, and also at a time when people are thinking we can't manage things. I think it just triples the problems that we might have to get us out of this."

Julie doesn't shirk from her responsibilities. She thinks lawmakers have a mission.

"While I admire the work teachers do and doctors, nurses and social workers do, my work has an impact for hundreds of thousands of people in one broad stroke. That to me, is the exciting world of policy."

Julie Hamos is confident that Barack Obama is the right man to lead the nation now.

"I think this man has so much potential. He's really brilliant. He digs right in to make policy happen. He's never changed. That's the way he does business. He's going to learn everything there is to learn about the issues and use all of his skills to bring people around.

"My greatest hope is his perspectives on the world and how the world is resonating to him and changing America's image in the world. It's a real opportunity to be a real peacemaker, and to be a real world leader."

"He's bringing the best and the brightest on, so there's a confidence level that the government is being run by people who really care and really want to do him well. That's fantastic. It is so reassuring that when this country is going through this economic crisis, I have confidence people are there for the right reasons. He has the ability to attract people and draw that out of them."

Julie Hamos has gleaned something from her relationship with Barack Obama. As she ponders running for state-wide office, she is plugging into the Internet at cyber speed. She has launched a revamped Web site.

"For the last nine months, I have been looking at Barack's campaign and using that as a model and building a grassroots campaign. My Web site is using all the new, modern technology. We learned all of that from watching Barack's Presidential campaign."

Gary Stromberg, class of '68

No, this wasn't my date to the senior citizens prom. I was presenting the first Heights High Golden Card to the charming Luci Prescott. She was ninety-nine.

It must have been the very first assembly I attended at Cleveland Heights High. Student Council president Barry Gordon marched on to the stage in the auditorium to begin the proceedings with the Pledge of Allegiance.

Barry was an impressive guy. Definite leadership qualities. I wondered if two years later I would have the chance to be Student Council president. Later that school year, I was elected junior class president. The stage was set for a run at being Student Council president. In the spring of my junior year, I won the election. That fall, I would be president of the school.

That was bittersweet news. Sure, I was up to the challenge. I was eager to contribute what I could. The downside was, like Barry, I would have to preside over the school assemblies. Since the school had such a large enrollment, on days when assemblies were scheduled, we would actually have to hold two of them back to back. Half of the students would attend the first one. The remaining students would show up for the second one.

Walking out on stage in front of 1,600 people, not once, but twice, was a bit overwhelming. What if I tripped, what if my voice cracked, what if I froze up? I had the entire summer to worry about how I would do up on stage.

Our first assembly would be a pep rally to get the students fired up about the first football game. I would introduce the participants and then I would wrap things up with a fiery speech of my own. Could I go up there and just talk off the top of my head? Since this was the first assembly, I was a bit more nervous.

I decided to put my thoughts on paper. I had neatly typed a speech. I carried that page of paper with me as I walked on to stage and carefully placed it on the lectern. The assembly began. I introduced the cheerleaders first. Then I introduced a couple of the players.

Head football coach Frank Gibson was next. I had gotten to know him during my first two years at Heights. I would often interview him for *The Black and Gold* and *The Sun Press*. Coach Gibson was a good leader and a nice enough fellow. He didn't come across as a guy who could think on his feet.

That fact was driven home during the first assembly. I introduced Coach Gibson and stepped to the wings of the stage to listen to his speech. I don't know if he got nervous, or had a mild panic attack. But as he began his speech, I couldn't help but notice it had a familiar ring to it. A couple of sentences in to it, I realized Frank was actually reading my speech that I had left on the lectern.

He wrapped it up and stepped off stage. He passed by me and I headed back on stage with a lump in my throat. What should I do? Should I try to make something up? I settled in behind the microphone and saw 1,600 sets of eyes glaring at me.

I hesitated for a brief second or two, and then mapped out a plan of action.

"Yes, as Coach Gibson just said."

That's right. I read my speech again. Sure, it was a calculated risk, but I figured I could at least deliver it with more enthusiasm than the coach did.

As time went by, I became more comfortable with my role as Student Council president. I have to admit, I felt pretty important when I would be handed mail that was addressed to President of Student Council. It was invariably from a company that was hoping we would choose to sell their products for a fundraiser. Companies that peddled candy, pennants, or even Heights High license plates.(Yes, I fell for that one.)

Those license plates were as wide as a normal license plate, but only half as tall. The idea was, you were supposed to bolt them on to the bottom of your normal license plate. It was a great way to show your school spirit. Sadly, if you ever had to back out of a driveway, that symbol of Heights High pride would wind up scratched at best, smashed at worst.

The entire Student Council sold about one hundred Heights High license plates. I was actually able to sell ten of them myself. It either showed my skills as a salesman, or reflected my desire to save face for having chosen the plates as a fundraising project. Those Heights High license plates held up just fine if you tacked them up on a bulletin board or wedged them in to a spot on your dashboard.

But getting back to the concept of me receiving mail addressed to President. I guess that started going to my head. One day, I came home and started flipping through the mail. I spotted a letter that I thought was addressed to me. Gee, how did a fundraising company get my home address. I ripped open the letter and realized it had absolutely nothing to do with official Heights High business. I took a closer look at the envelope. Turns out it wasn't addressed to President, but to Resident. Oh well.

Hoping to bounce back from the Heights High license plate fiasco, I did bring the Turtles to the school for a concert. I was proud of that accomplishment. As I spelled out in my first book, *Aren't You That News Man?*, that turned out to be a great strategic move since my guidance counselor Mary Graham wrote in my letter of recommendation to Northwestern that I had brought the BEATLES to Heights. Wow.

Well, by arranging the Turtles concert, I got to know Walter

Maskey. He was the associate producer of the *Upbeat* show on Channel 5. Walter invited me and a posse of Heights students to a taping of the show. Don Webster, the host of the show actually interviewed me. I remember I was bragging that Heights High had two swimming pools. One for the boys, and one for the girls.

It was strange that I would talk about the pools at Heights. I was never a very good swimmer. I had been told that in order to graduate, you had to swim a lap of the pool. I probably spent many a restless night as a child in my bedroom worrying about that requirement. Would I have to repeat twelfth grade, five or six times until I finally was able to do a lap?

As luck would have it, just before my tenth grade year, I developed a large plantar wart on the bottom of my left foot. It was very painful. If you happen to step on something right at the point of the wart, it felt like a nail was being driven through your foot.

I went to podiatrist Charles Cavolo. He said he would have to treat it by applying a small amount of a chemical once a week. The bothersome wart would eventually disappear. My part of the deal was to promise not to get my left foot wet.

This scenario was unfolding at the time I was assigned to swimming class. I got a note from Dr. Cavolo and presented it to my swimming teacher Robert Khoenle. Khoenle seemed to me to be a rather gruff guy who enjoyed being on a power trip. He wasn't thrilled when I told him my plantar wart would prevent me from joining in on all the brand new fun in the pool that semester.

During the course of my interviews for this book, one universal theme emerged. The boys from my era kept bringing up the fact that they couldn't believe we had to swim naked. They said they have told their children about this barbaric situation, and their kids were stunned we had to splash around with nothing on but a grin. Fourth period you are sitting next to Robert Zelwin in history class, and ten minutes later you are both buck naked in a swimming pool.

There were concerns that swimming class participants could contract some sort of deadly foot disease. Perhaps athlete's foot, corns, callouses, or God-forbid a plantar wart. So the procedure was, you would go to the locker room, take off all of your clothes, take a quick shower and then head towards the pool. But first, you had to walk through this trench of water. It apparently had all sorts of anti-bacterial chemicals in it. Even three or four steps through this six-inch-deep pit, would miraculously prevent all sorts of medical maladies.

Well getting back to the lovely and charming Robert Khoenle. When I presented my doctor's note to him, I presumed he was going to tell me that I should report to the grandstand area above the swimming pool during class. That way, I could actually make some use of my time while the other boys were swimming. I could study, or even get my algebra homework done.

Khoenle was not that progressive. He determined that I would have to come out to poolside and spend the session seated on the bench where members of the swim team would sit during swim meets. Those swimmers had an advantage. Not only were they wearing swimsuits, but they had the luxury of wrapping a towel around their waist while on the bench. It was fashioned out of some sort of tile and did tend to get rather cold.

Khoenle said I would have to sit on that cold, cold bench for roughly thirty minutes. I would have to be naked like the rest of the boys. You know, the normal boys who were not coming up with some lame excuse not to take part in swim class.

I thought I had Khoenle on one point. I reminded him that according to my doctor's orders, I was unable to get my left foot wet. That of course was the reason I was not in the pool to begin with. How in the world could I walk through the shower area, make my way through that trough of chemicals without getting my tootsie wet.

Khoenle, who as teacher, earned the right to keep his clothes on for the class, was not going to budge. He made it clear I would have to sit on that bench, and if I had to wear a shoe on one foot, so be it.

Picture this. I would take all of my clothes off, but leave on the sock on my left foot. I would then slip back into my left dress shoe. I would hop through the shower area on my left foot and then hop through the chemical trench. Keep in mind I was naked while I was doing this act of acrobatics. If the bottom of the trench happened to be slimy, I could have fallen. That would not only set back my treatment for my plantar wart, but could have led to a concussion as well.

And also realize, once I emerged onto the pool deck I had to hop to the bench and sit on that tile. Fortunately, all of this paid off. I did recover from the plantar wart and was able to go on with the rest of my life. I eventually took swimming and somehow managed to swim that required lap. Perhaps it was because I had gotten into great shape by doing all of that hopping.

I was hopping mad in the fall of 1967. I had just started my run as Student Council president and one of the first things I did was take a look at the books. Not the algebra books or the biology books, but the financial ones. I realized that the Student Council had to scramble to earn money through various fundraisers. Where did all of the money go? Well the biggest expense was paying to charter a number of buses to carry members of the Heights High marching band to away football games.

The figures have faded over the years, but I recall this was an expense of six hundred dollars per game. If there were five games, you are talking about a tidy sum of three thousand dollars of hard-earned money. I am not saying the marching band should not have represented the school at away games. I have fond memories of the announcer saying, "And what would a half-time show be without a tribute to….fill in the blank. A tribute to Walt Disney, Elvis Presley, whatever.

But being a somewhat logical young man, the thought crossed my mind, perhaps the athletic department should come up with the money for the buses. How about the Band Boosters? Or even have the members of the band knocking on doors, selling bars of the World's Finest Chocolate so they could travel to Parma or Garfield Heights.

I don't know how many years the Student Council had been forking over the cold cash for band buses, but I thought it might take a bit of the pressure off the council if someone else picked up the tab.

So one day, I happened to be cutting through the auditorium and ran into Kaarlo Mackey. He was the school's director of instrumental music. He was highly respected and I had always thought he had been at the school for decades. Actually he had only assumed that role five years earlier, after he had held a similar position at Conneaut High School. I knew his brother was Wayne Mack, a fixture on Cleveland radio stations for many years.

I introduced myself and I told him I was president of the Student Council. I explained that I had come up with this idea that the band should take on the financial responsibility of transporting itself to the various away football games.

Mr. Mackey's complexion suddenly turned beet red. He took one of his hands and thrust it deep into one of his pants pockets. I was beginning to wonder if he was reaching for a gun. He pulled out a handful of change, fumbled around while his hands trembled, and finally located a penny. He held it up in front of my face and in a booming voice challenged my suggestion.

"Not one penny. Not one penny. It's bad enough we have to stomp around in all of that mud and slop on football fields. We are certainly not going to have to raise the money to pay for that privilege."

Mackey spun around and stormed off. I was stunned. After all, I was only making a suggestion. Apparently he was more in tune with his role as director of the highly-respected Cleveland Heights High Orchestra, and saw the role of the marching band as a more pedestrian entity.

Sadly, that angry confrontation took place during the final days of Kaarlo Mackey's life. The account in *The Plain Dealer* said he was driving to Conneaut one night. His car veered off the highway and he was killed.

I got my start in journalism in tenth grade. I was assigned to cover the swim team. The following year, I was supposed to be assistant sports editor. Stanley Dub was a year ahead of me and had climbed his way up the food chain to be sports editor. At the start of that school year, Amanda Nunamaker, the adviser to *The Black and Gold* called me aside. She told me I was going to be sports editor. That was a position normally reserved for a senior, not a junior.

"What about Stanley Dub?"

"Don't you worry about Stanley Dub."

I had no idea what went on between Mrs. Nunamaker and Stanley Dub. It must have been something intense for her to boot him off of the newspaper staff.

About ten years later, I moved back to Cleveland and became a reporter for Channel 8 news.

Some twenty years after that, I ran into one of my former classmates Jean Rosenthal. She told me she had recently got divorced from Stanley Dub. Apparently over the years, Stanley blamed me somehow from his ouster from the newspaper staff. I had nothing to do with it. I still don't even know why it happened.

Jean said, "Any time we were watching the news on Channel 8 and you came on, Stanley would immediately change the channel."

So, the actions of Amanda Nunamaker back in 1966 would have an ongoing impact on television ratings for decades to come.

During my senior year, when I arranged for the Turtles to perform at Heights High, I had contacted WKYC radio. The station had switched to a rock music format and we worked out a deal where their disk jockeys could come out to the school and introduce the band that night. For their end of the bargain, they would plug the upcoming concert every time they played a Turtles record.

I was driving home one Friday night, I had the station on, and they played a Turtles record. There was no mention of the concert, so when I got home, I picked up the phone and called WKYC. The fellow who answered the phone that night was very polite and understanding.

We got involved in a conversation and he told me his name was Dave Louie. He was a senior at Lakewood High and had just been accepted to the Medill School of Journalism at Northwestern University. I told Dave that was a huge coincidence since I had just been accepted to Medill as well.

Dave and I have been friends now for more than forty years. After our freshman year at Northwestern, he served as an intern for the summer at Channel 5 in Cleveland. He encouraged me to apply for the internship the following year. It was actually a paid internship. I seem to recall the pay was about $1.25 per hour.

During spring break that year, I went to Channel 5 and met with news director Garry Ritchie. He had me go to the back parking lot and be filmed for an audition for the internship. He then took me back in to be introduced to station general manager Ed Cervenak. I had a feeling this was going to be my big break. A summer at Channel 5 would provide valuable experience, and look great on a resume.

I went back to Northwestern and waited to hear from Garry Ritchie. Weeks went by. He eventually let me know they had lost the film of my audition. He mentioned they had a sister station in Detroit. Perhaps I could travel from Chicago to do another audition. I thought this was all a little strange. If you are just starting out, why should you have to audition anyway?

I called him a couple of weeks later, and he said since the FCC had just banned cigarette commercials, TV stations were fearing a horrible drop-off in advertising revenue. Because of that, the station would be unable to hire a summer intern.

I should have offered at that point to serve as an intern on a volunteer basis. Scripps-Howard would not have to dip into the special operating fund to come up with fifty dollars a week for me. I was disappointed, and for the second summer in a row, I went back to picking up dirty laundry for the Independent Towel Supply Company.

But my news career was not over. When the school year resumed, I landed a part-time job with WGN TV and radio in Chicago. That was a great opportunity. While I was there, I entered a national news writing contest sponsored by the Radio Television News Directors Association. I was thrilled when I found out I won a one thousand dollar fellowship and I would be invited to the organization's convention in Boston.

The fellowship was awarded at a luncheon and I gave an acceptance speech in front of all of the bigwigs in the business.

Later that day, I went to a reception held in a hospitality suite sponsored by the ABC Television Network.

A middle-aged woman came up to me and said, "I heard your speech at the luncheon today. It was absolutely marvelous. You are quite an impressive young man. I must have my husband meet you. Stay right here. I'll get him."

So I stood there wondering who this woman was. Was her husband Av Westin, a vice president of ABC news? Was she married to anchorman Harry Reasoner? Who could this mystery man be?

Well, in what has to be one of the most awkward moments in the history of television, she drags over her husband. It was Ed Cervenak from Channel 5. The man who put the kabosh on my summer internship. His wife introduced us and gushed all over about how I was the greatest young journalist ever.

I reminded Ed we had met little more than a year earlier when I was interested in that internship. He may have squirmed a little. For me, it was pretty entertaining. He may have thought of punching me out at that moment, but I think he was afraid to mess with me since I was in such great shape from hauling all of those bags of dirty laundry.

The Cleveland Heights Library on Lee Road has a priceless collection of old yearbooks from Heights High. The Caldrons date back to the '20s. Each is a reflection of the style and tastes of that particular era, but I did notice something unusual. The outside company hired to take many of the pictures for the yearbooks, had a certain pattern. The yearbooks would differ from year to year, but if you graduated in 1968, like I did, and happened to pick up, let's say for example a 1963 yearbook, you would notice the photographer posed students in much the same way. I guess the idea was no one is going to sit there and look at a bunch of old yearbooks and realize there was sort of a template used to feature basically, the same photos but with different students.

I did find it unusual to flip through the section that featured pictures of teachers. You could see them much younger than when you had them in class, or much older, long after you had graduated. I felt somewhat uneasy seeing those pictures of teachers. Sure, I realized getting a teaching gig at Heights High was somewhat of a plum assignment. Some teachers spent twenty or thirty years on the staff there. But somehow you kind of pigeonhole your teachers as being there only for the three years you were there. What do you mean Mr. Coneglio was at Heights five years before I enrolled? Or why in the world did Mr. Klimek stay at Heights after I graduated?

It seems we had a perception that these were OUR teachers. They belonged to us. It was hard to give them up and picture they were working with other students. Even if those students were our own older brothers or younger sisters.

Besides spending all of my childhood worrying about the requirement to swim a lap of the Heights pool in order graduate, I had another ongoing fear. Rumor had it, you had to dissect a frog of some sort in biology class. I didn't mean to be a wimp about this requirement, but I must admit it was enough to make me steer clear of taking biology. I couldn't picture myself tearing into some unfortunate frog whose life came to an end solely so it could be the featured attraction in seventh-period biology.

This was a bad strategic move on my part. I was always pretty good at memorizing things like what are the components of a cotton plant.

I bet I would have earned an A in biology, but the squeamish side of me, forced me to take on a different option to fulfill my science requirement.

What a horrible decision that turned out to be. I was not made for chemistry. I struggled in it. I found the concepts and the math hard to grasp. Dr. Florence Arday told me she would have to give me a D for the first grading period. She assured me that the first grading period does not get recorded on your college transcript, so I still had a chance to bring it up to a C for the semester grade.

I turned to fellow student Gary Meckler for some much needed tutoring. I remember there was something I was supposed to learn called the Heisenberg Uncertainty Principle. I jokingly asked Gary if the Heisenberg Uncertainty Principle had anything to do with Ed Gally, assistant principal. Ed Gally was the school's assistant principal at the time. It became a running joke, as was my performance in chemistry. My fear of slicing into a frog, nearly cost me my opportunity to go to Northwestern.

Had I developed a modicum of courage, I no doubt would have taken biology with Larry Bauer. My sister Karin had been in his class a couple of years earlier. He thought very highly of her and we became friends. He was never one of my teachers, yet decades later, he nominated me to be in the Heights High Distinguished Alumni Hall of Fame.

Larry Bauer led a double life. He taught biology at Heights and did a good job of it. But his real passion in life was writing letters to the editor. It didn't matter if it was a newspaper or a magazine, Larry would drop them a letter. He had an opinion and a comment on just about everything. If it moved or breathed, Larry would write about it. If it didn't move or breathe, Larry would still write about it. It seemed a day wouldn't go by without Larry having something published somewhere. He made *Time* magazine. He was in *People*. He got more ink in *The Plain Dealer* and *The Press* than many of their reporters.

I once did a story for Channel 8 about Larry and his proclivity for sounding off. His house sat on the top of Belvoir Hill. It was a small bungalow. He lived a simple life. His only television was a black and white tabletop model that was perhaps thirty years old. The picture was fuzzy, but Larry's viewpoints were not.

Most of his letters began with the word kudos. Kudos is a singular noun that means honor, glory or acclaim. So a typical letter to the editor would begin with "Kudos to Mayor Stokes," or "Kudos to the Cleveland city council," or "Kudos to Rocky Colavito."

I don't know if Larry was aware that General Mills came out with a granola bar in the '80s called Kudos. If he was aware of that product, he would have no doubt written a letter to *The Plain Dealer* saying, "Kudos to General Mills for making Kudos."

As I bring this book to a close, I think it is only fitting that I wrap it up by using the writing style immortalized by Larry Bauer over the decades.

Kudos to the teachers and students from Cleveland Heights High. Your combined efforts made it a special place of learning. Lives were shaped in that building. Young people began chasing their dreams in those classrooms. The world was made a better place. Well done. Hats off to you!

Photo Courtesy The Cleveland Heights High Alumni Foundation

About the Author

Gary Stromberg is also the author of *Aren't You That News Man?* That book chronicled his thirty year career as a reporter at WJW TV in Cleveland, and also shared memories of his childhood years in Cleveland Heights. The author may be contacted on Facebook.